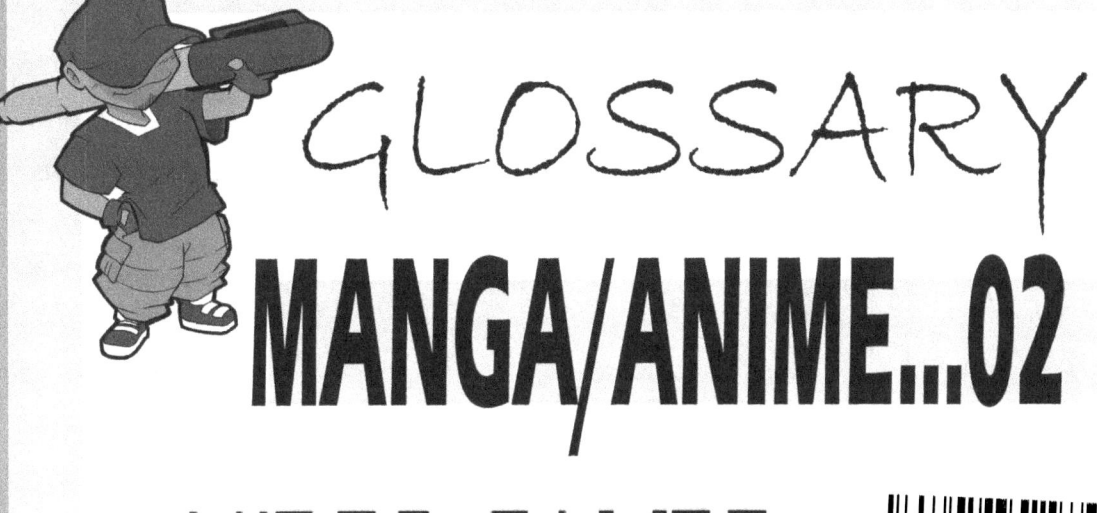

# GLOSSARY

I0475194

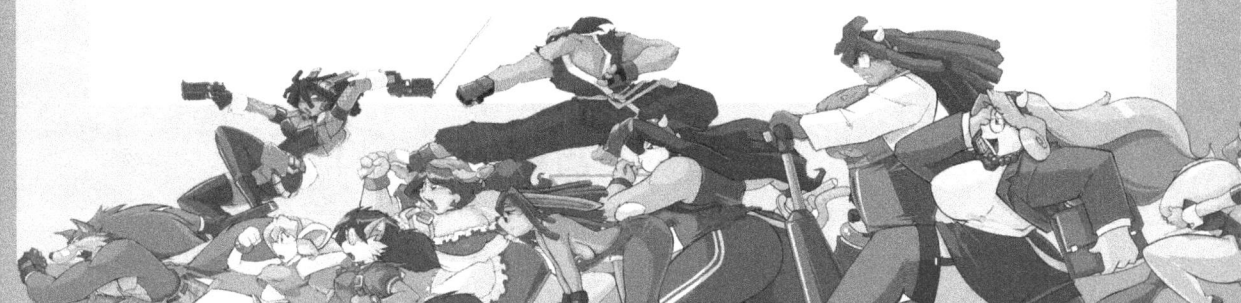

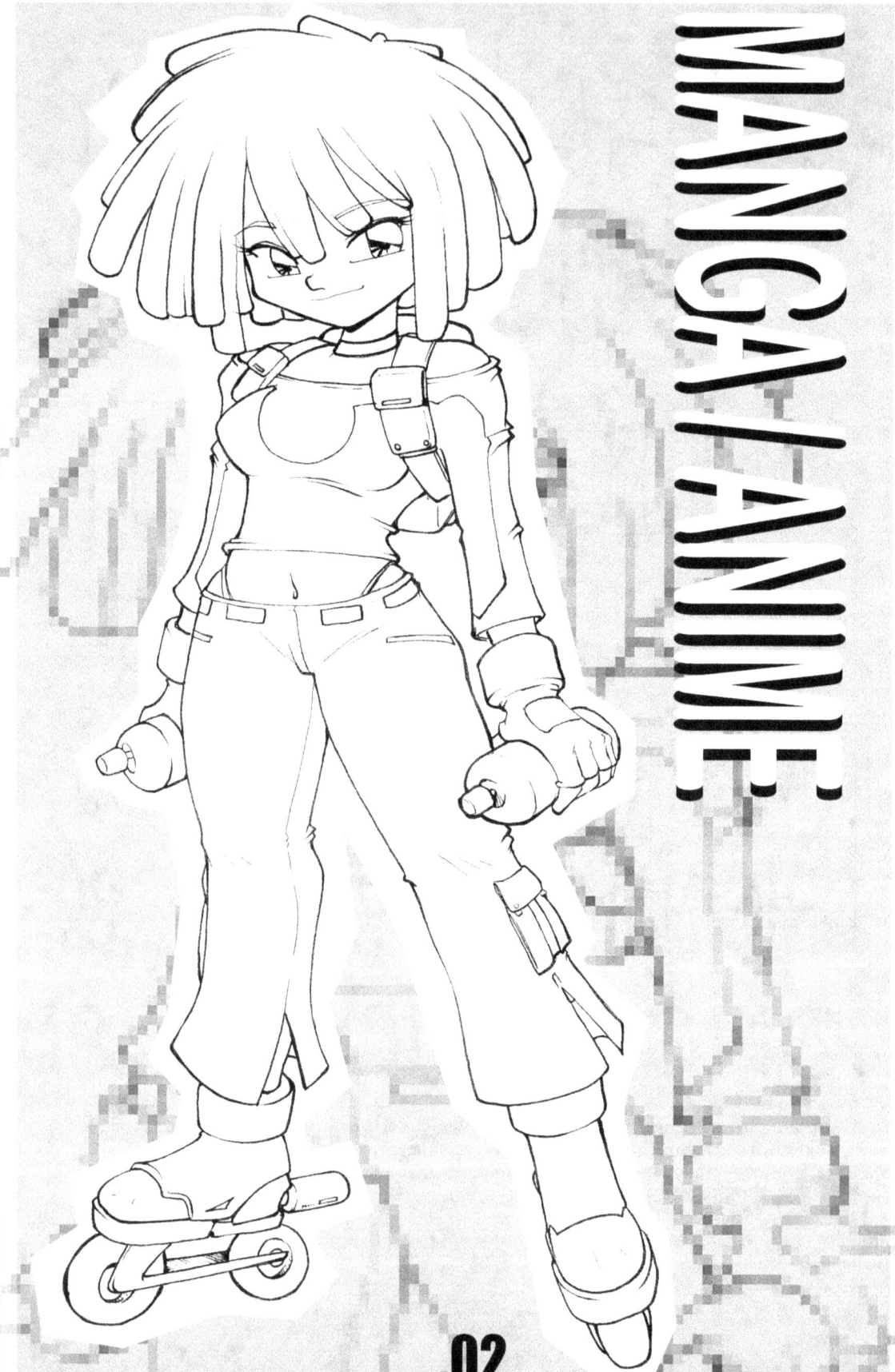

MANGA/ANIME

.02

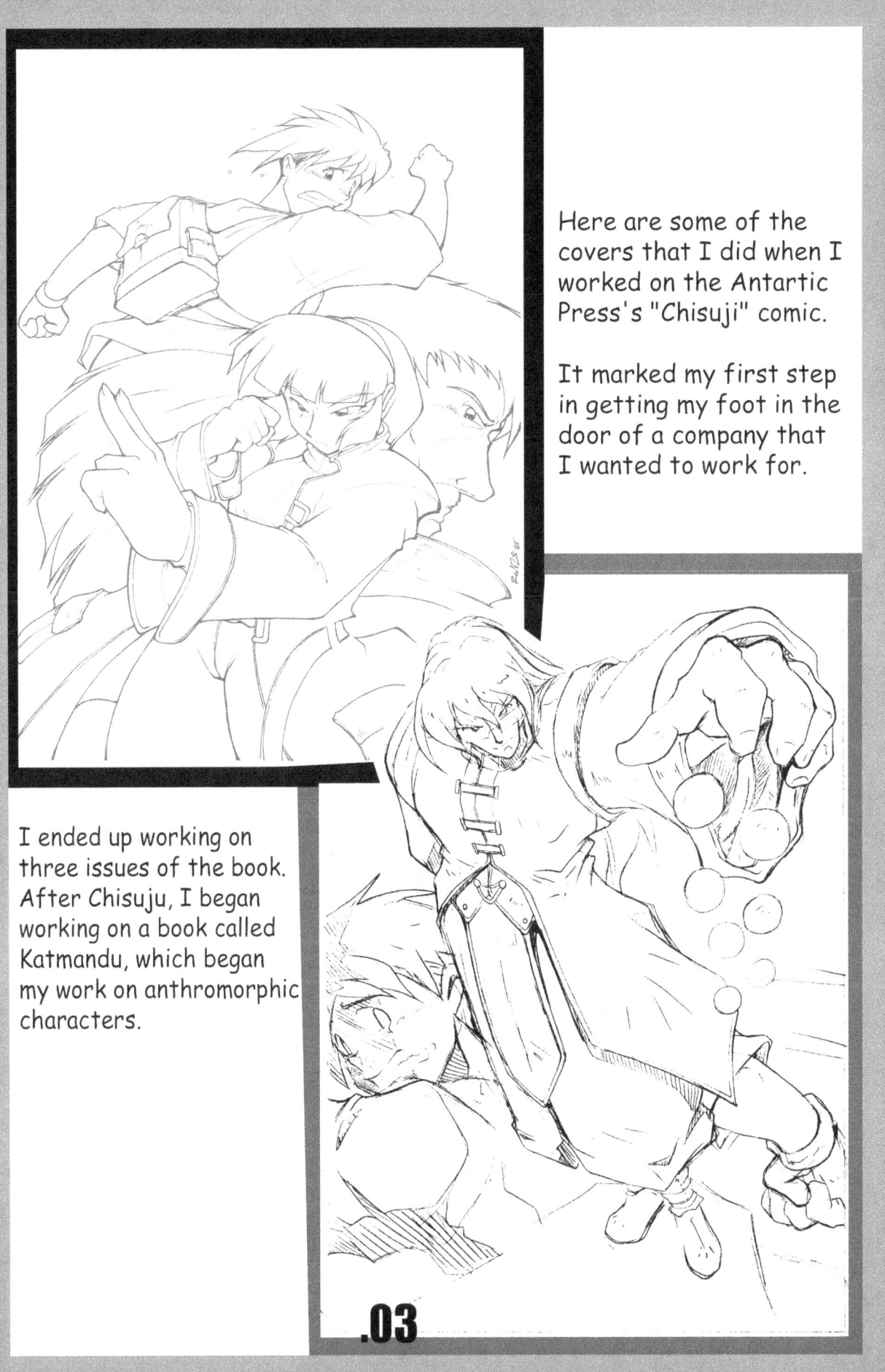

Here are some of the covers that I did when I worked on the Antartic Press's "Chisuji" comic.

It marked my first step in getting my foot in the door of a company that I wanted to work for.

I ended up working on three issues of the book. After Chisuju, I began working on a book called Katmandu, which began my work on anthromorphic characters.

.03

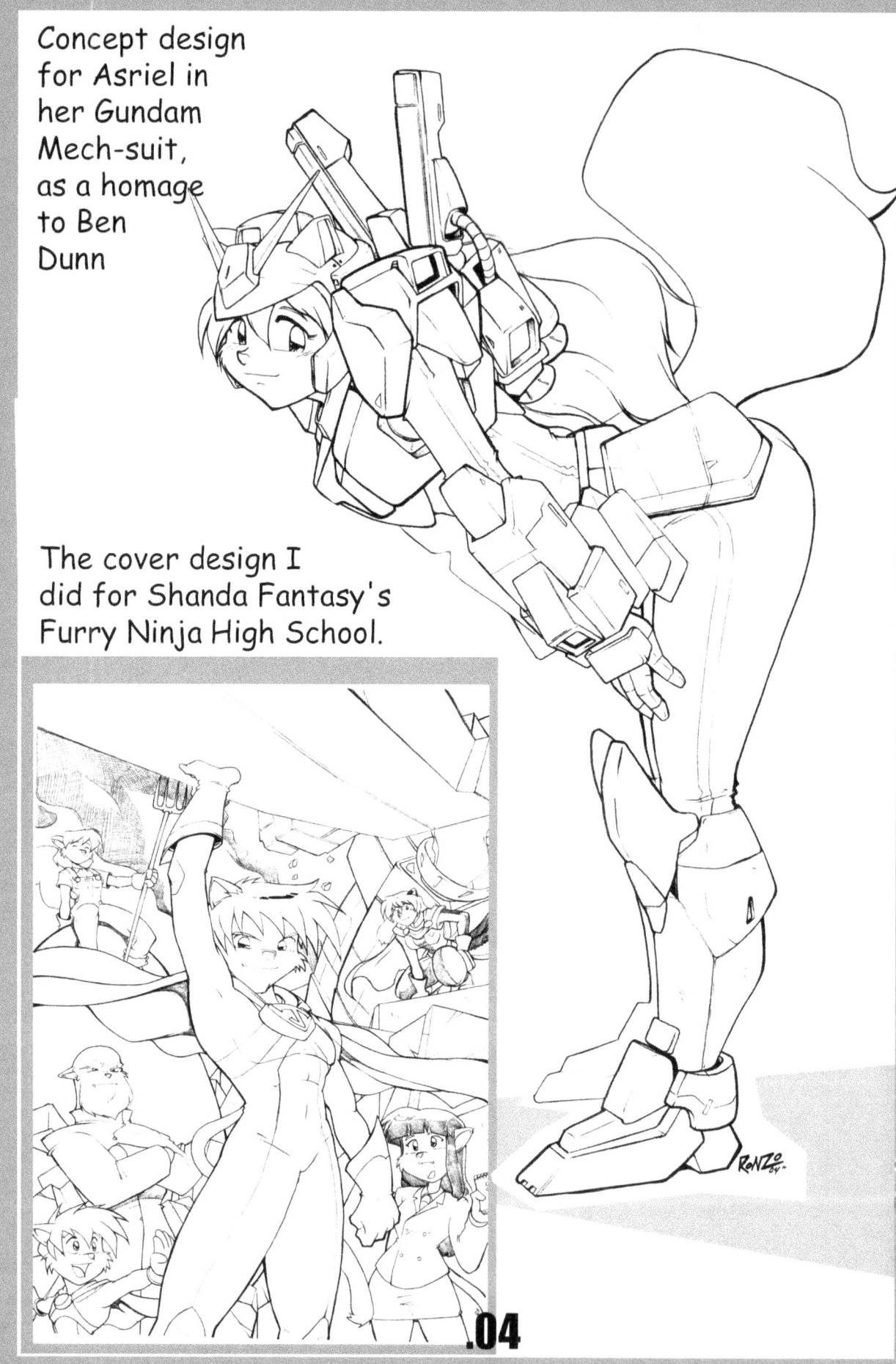

Concept design for Asriel in her Gundam Mech-suit, as a homage to Ben Dunn

The cover design I did for Shanda Fantasy's Furry Ninja High School.

.04

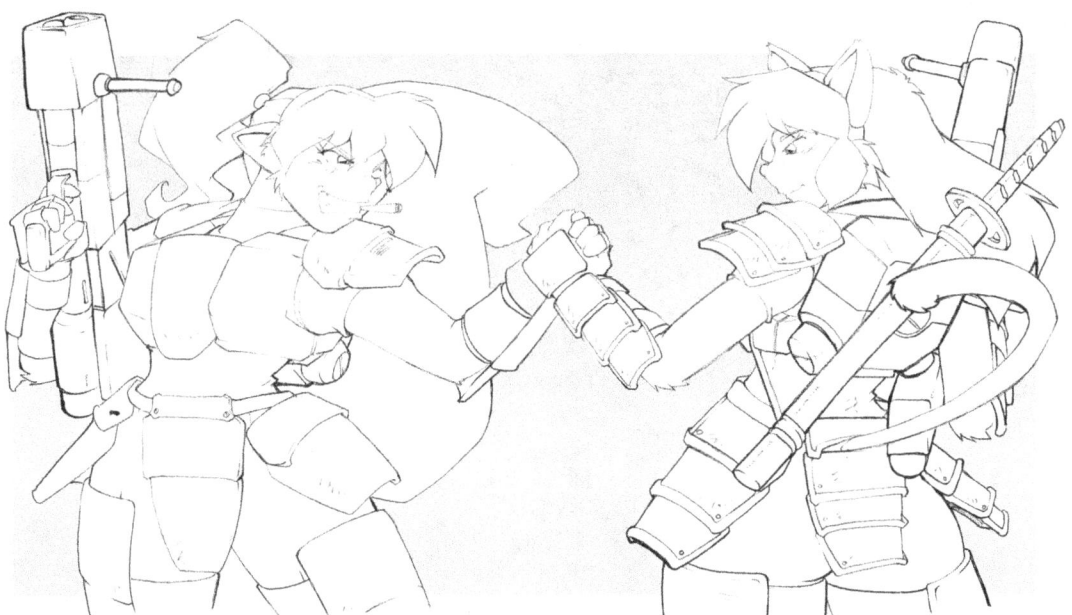

Both Ichi and Asreal dressed like the team from the game Neo Contra. This was to be an extra pic at the back of the Furry Ninja High School Comic that I worked on. Out of all of the pics that I did , this one was not used.

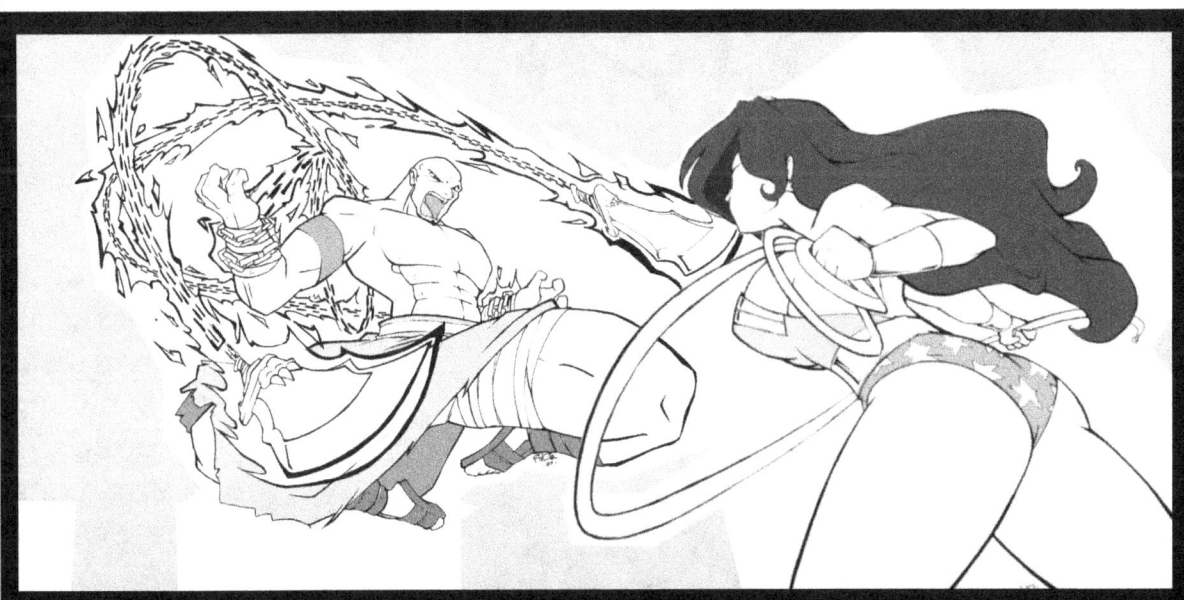

This pic was originally in color, but the colors came out so bad that I used a gray saturation on it and if came out like this.

I wonder who would win between a Spartan and an Amazon.

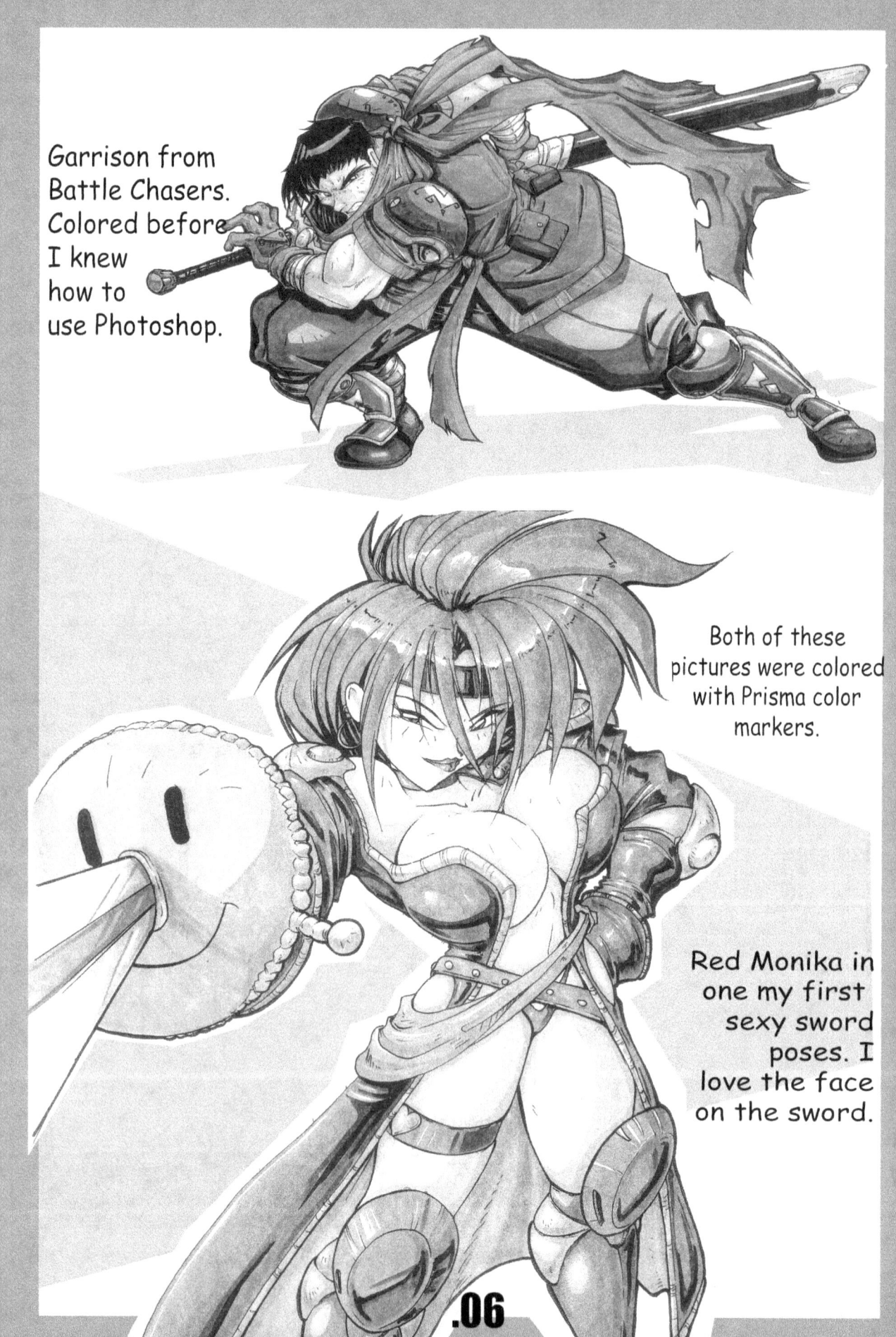

Garrison from Battle Chasers. Colored before I knew how to use Photoshop.

Both of these pictures were colored with Prisma color markers.

Red Monika in one my first sexy sword poses. I love the face on the sword.

.06

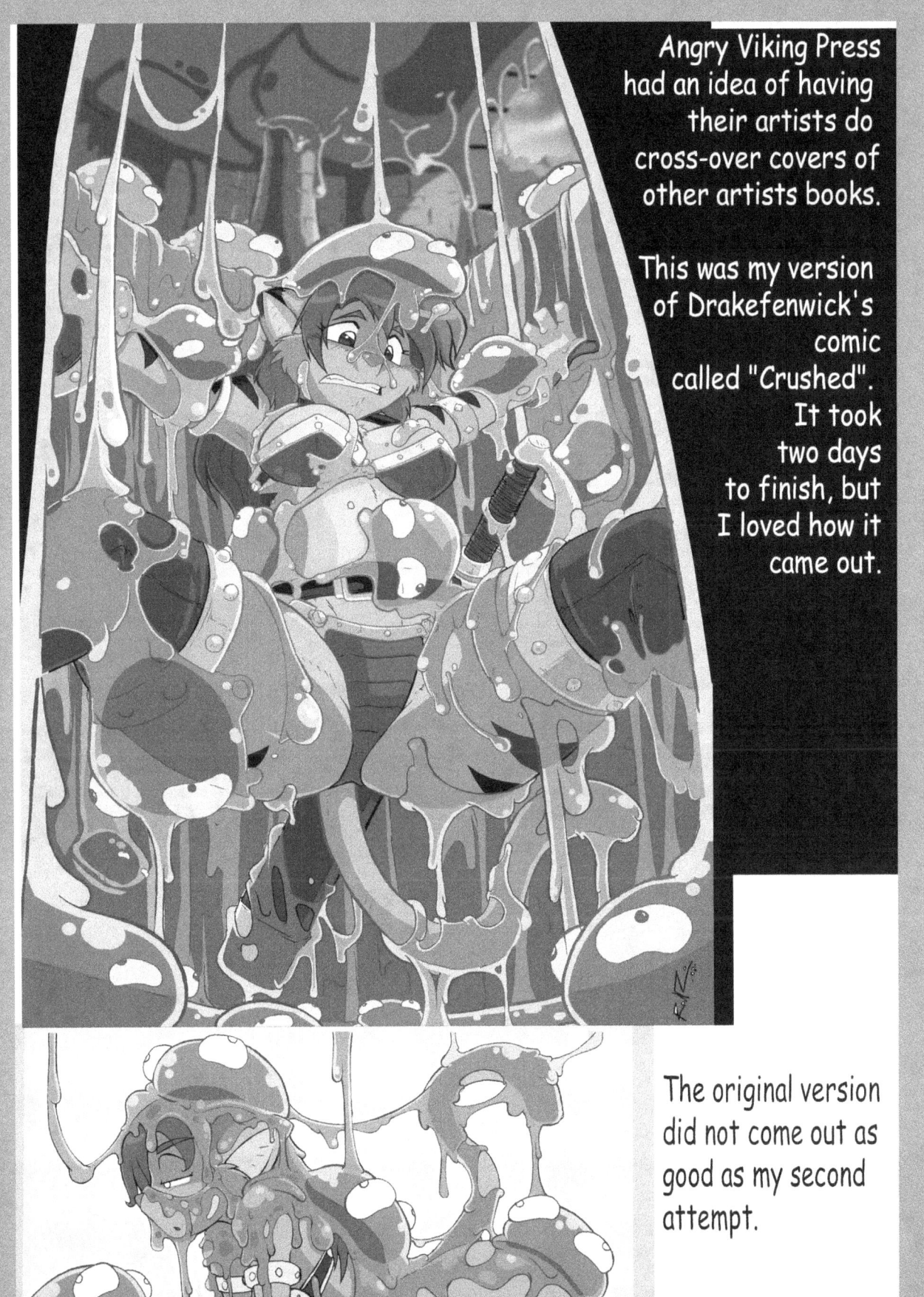

Angry Viking Press had an idea of having their artists do cross-over covers of other artists books.

This was my version of Drakefenwick's comic called "Crushed". It took two days to finish, but I loved how it came out.

The original version did not come out as good as my second attempt.

The next four pages are some of the the first works that I did for Shanda. It was for a book called "The Extinctioners" By Shawntae Howard. Me and various other artist contributed to the book.

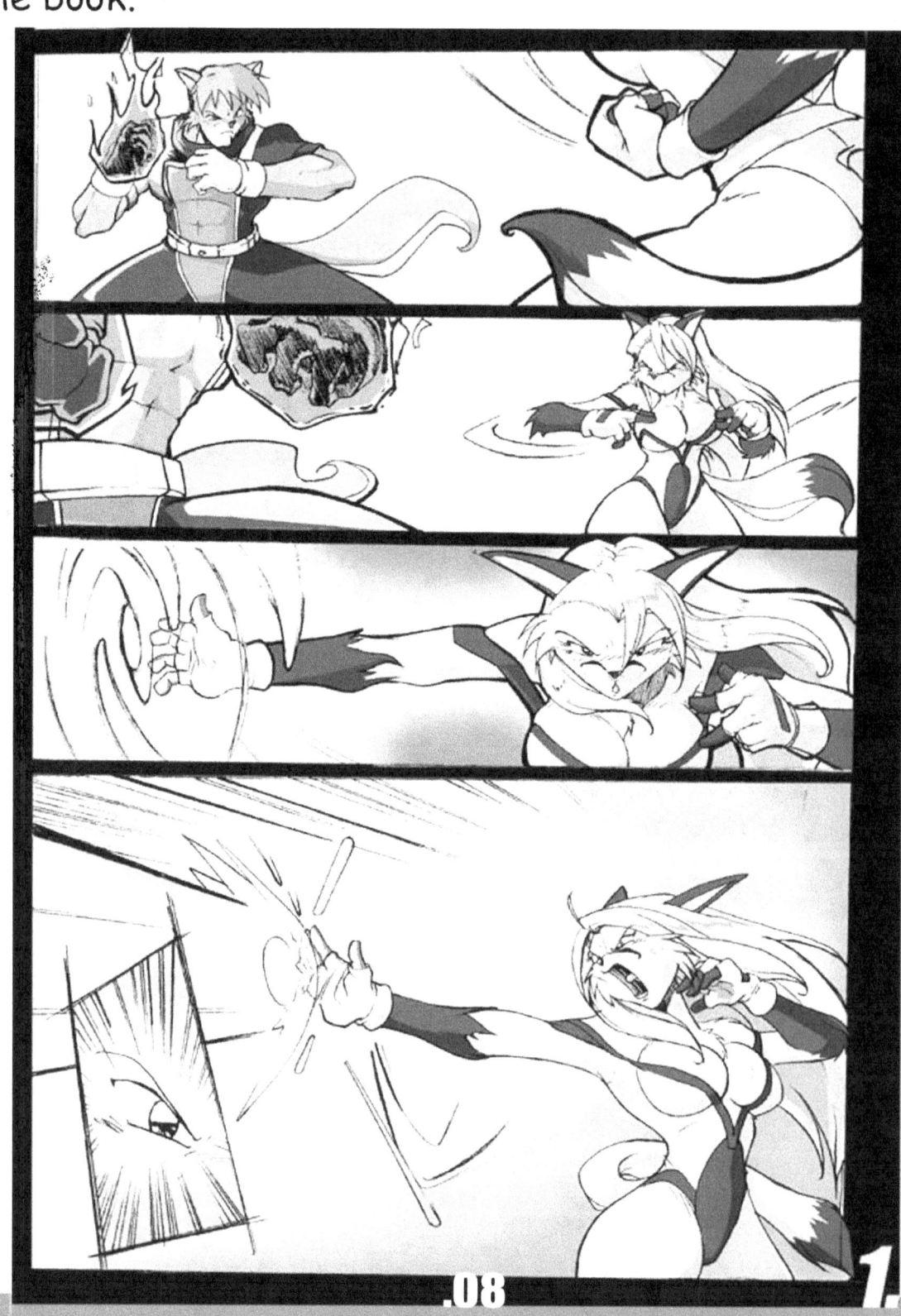

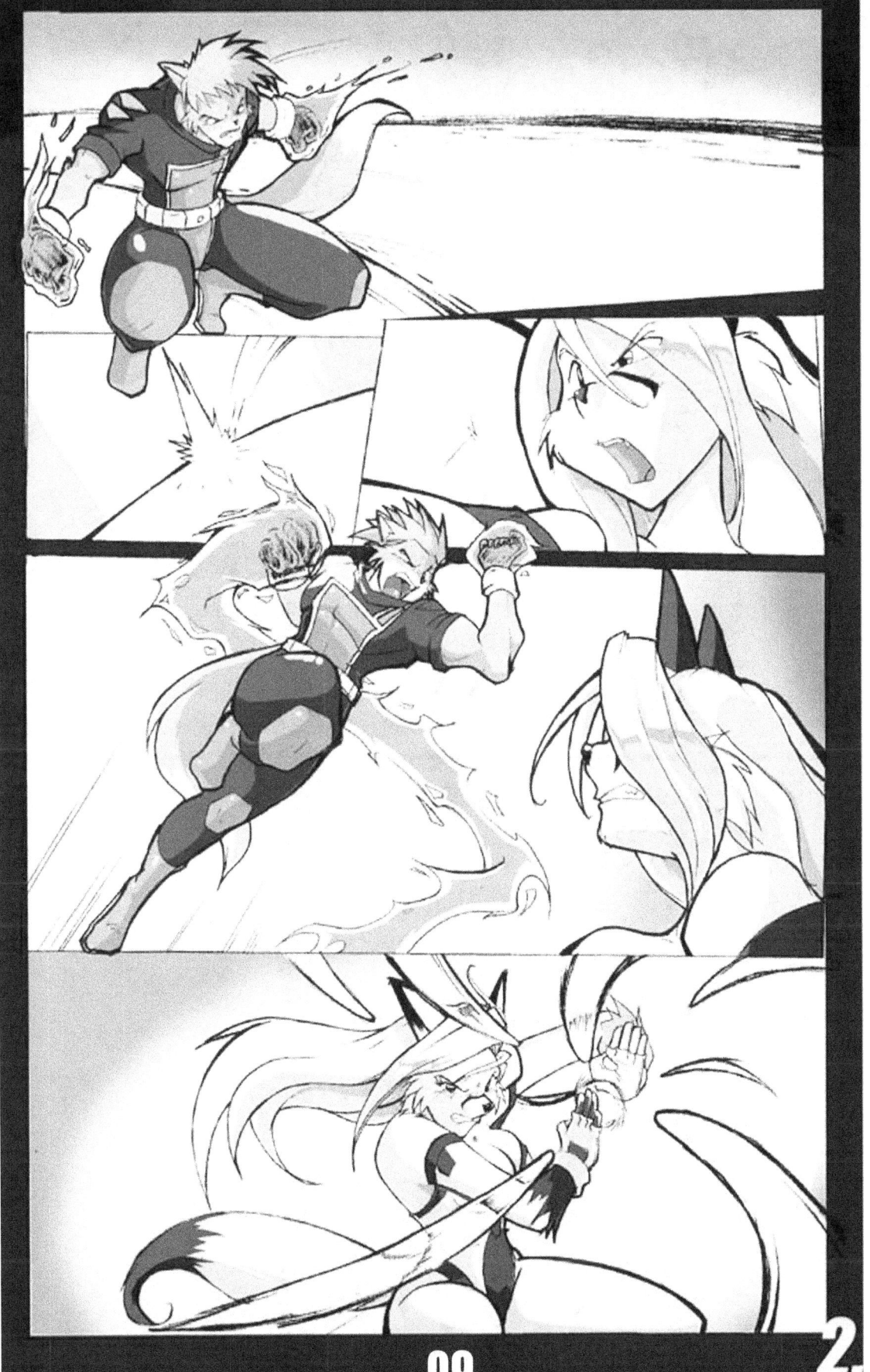

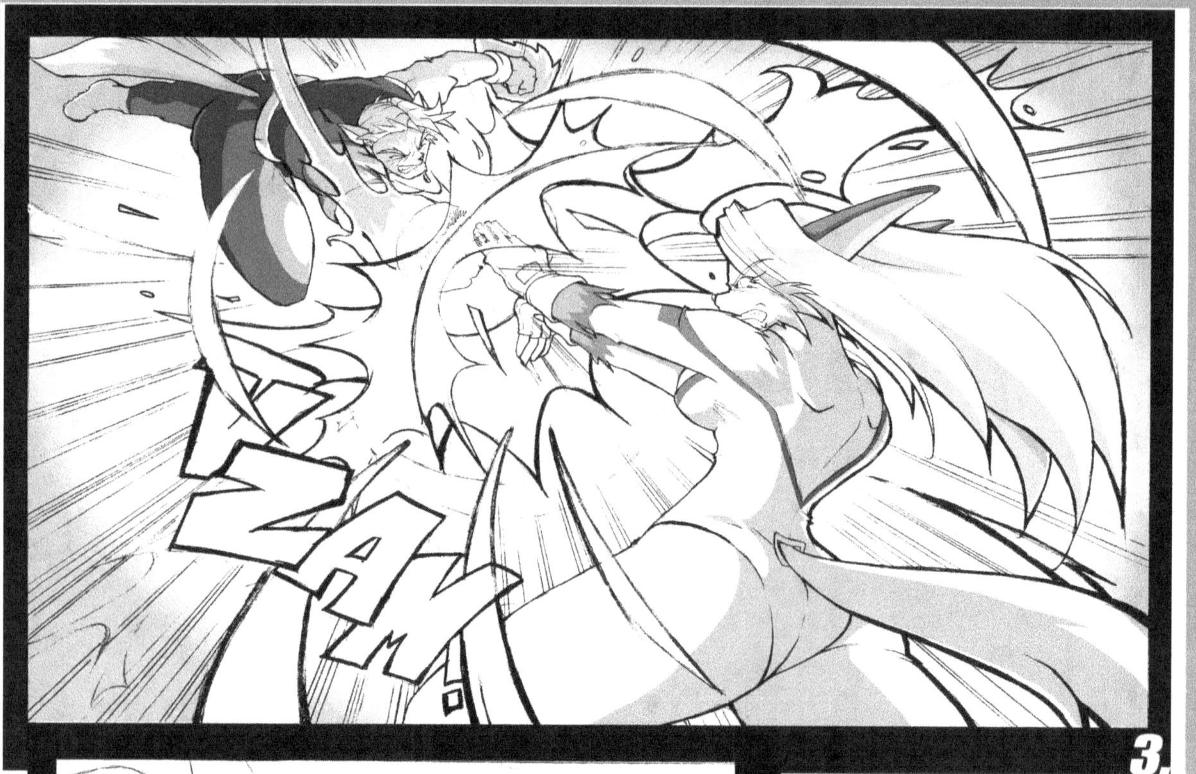

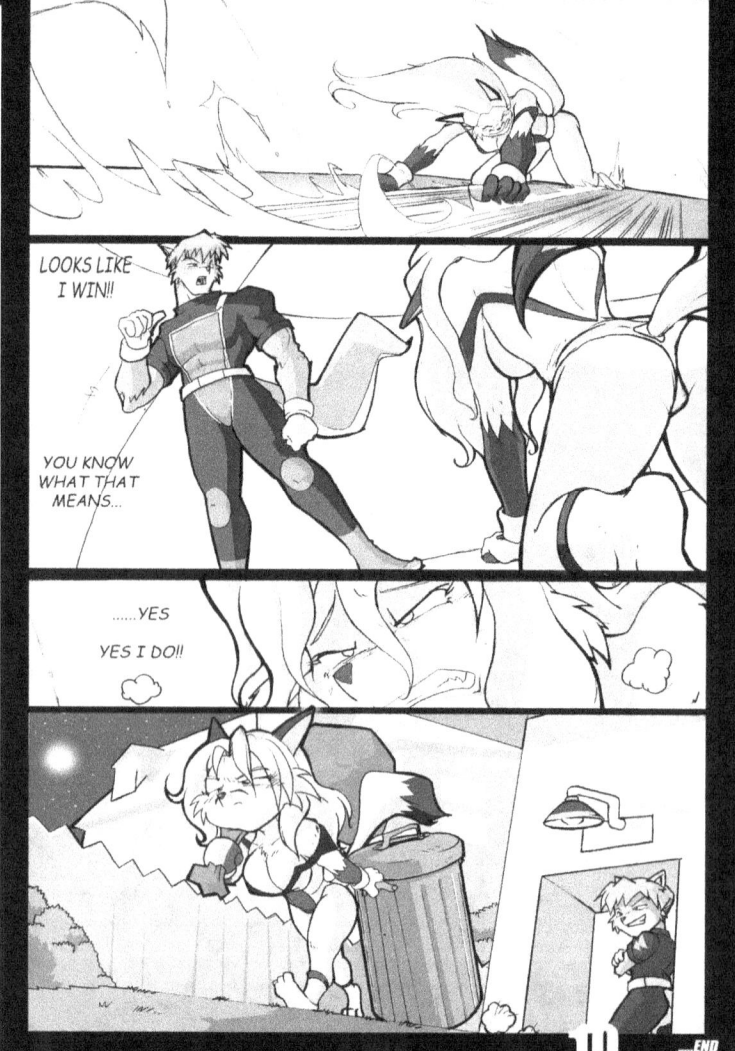

LOOKS LIKE I WIN!!

YOU KNOW WHAT THAT MEANS...

......YES

YES I DO!!

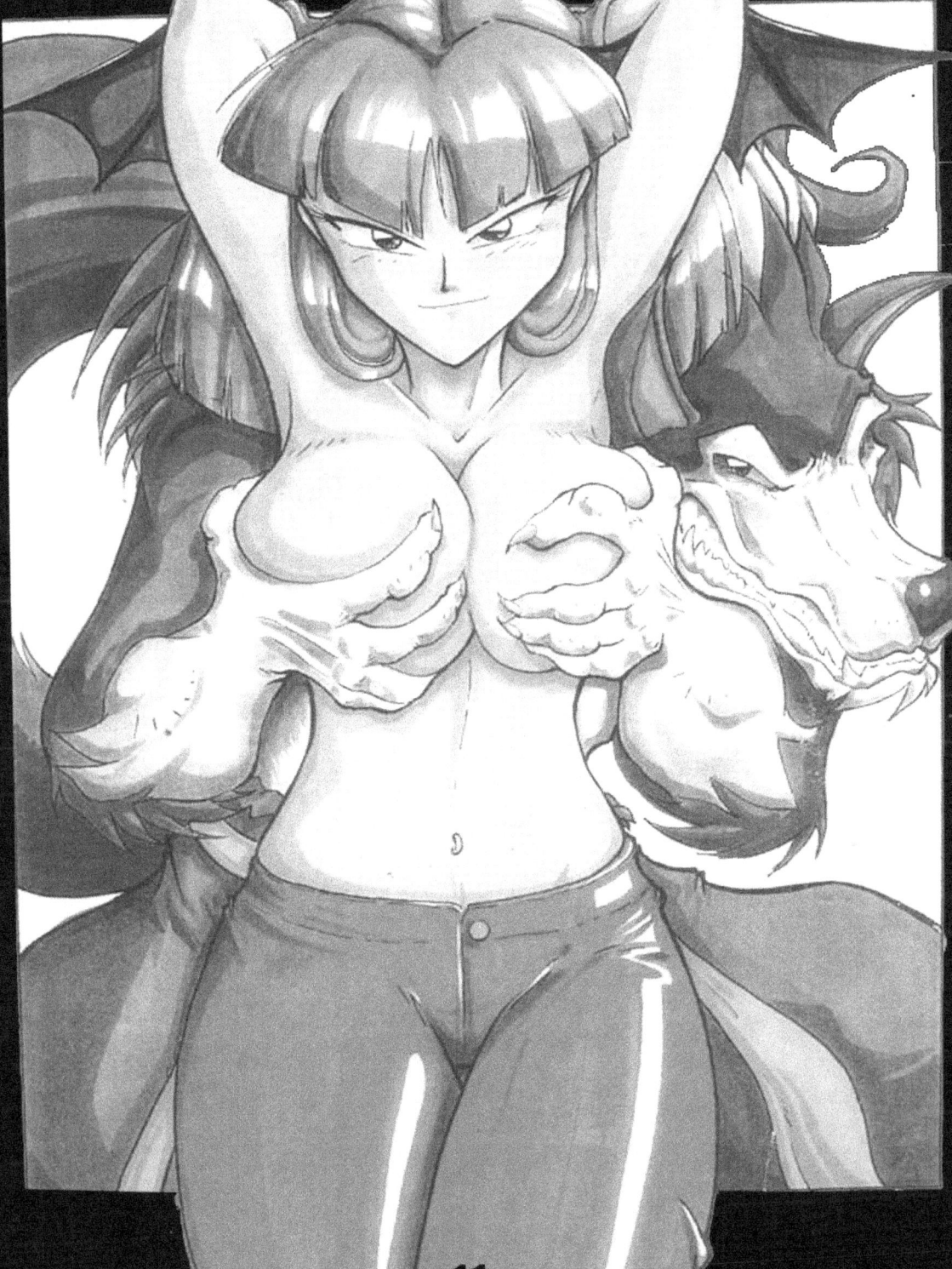

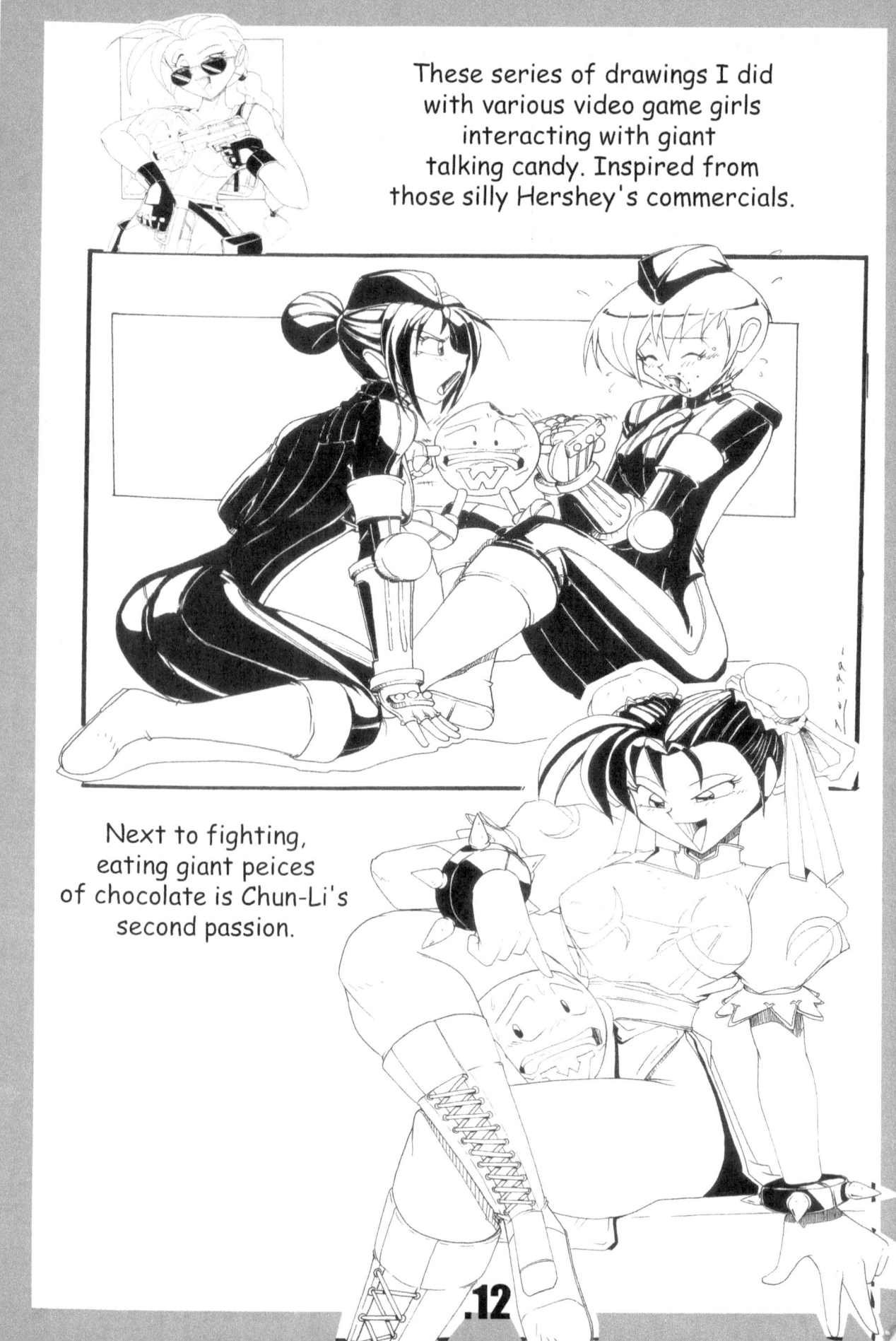

These series of drawings I did with various video game girls interacting with giant talking candy. Inspired from those silly Hershey's commercials.

Next to fighting, eating giant peices of chocolate is Chun-Li's second passion.

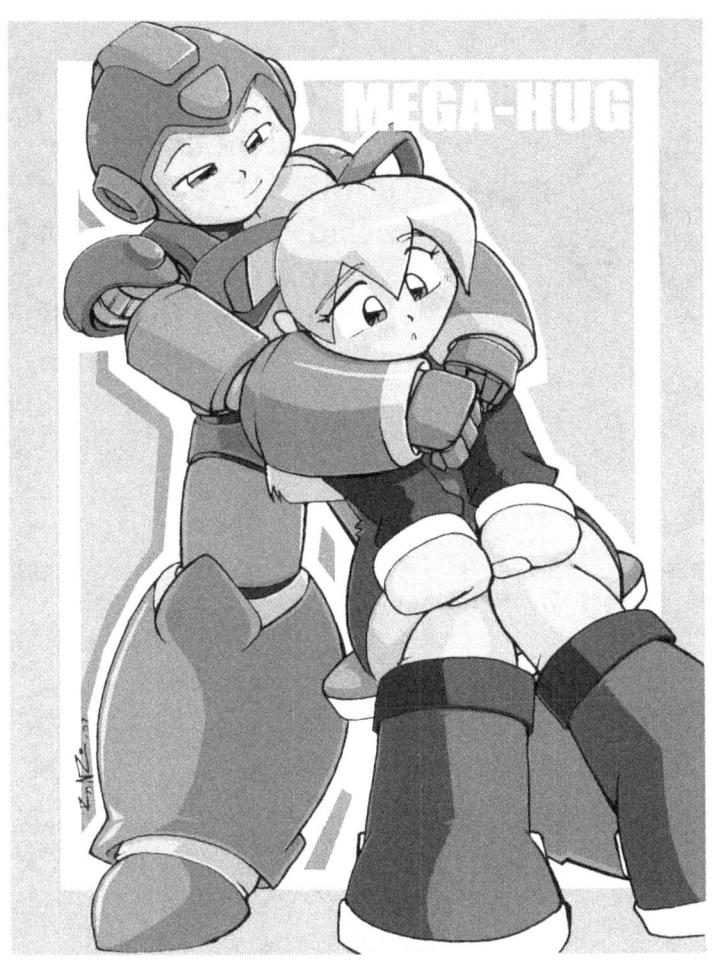

MEGA-HUG

A series of pics that I did for a guy that had a big thing for Megaman. I like to make him more Mechanical looking, by adding the gears in his detailed spots that make him look more robotic.

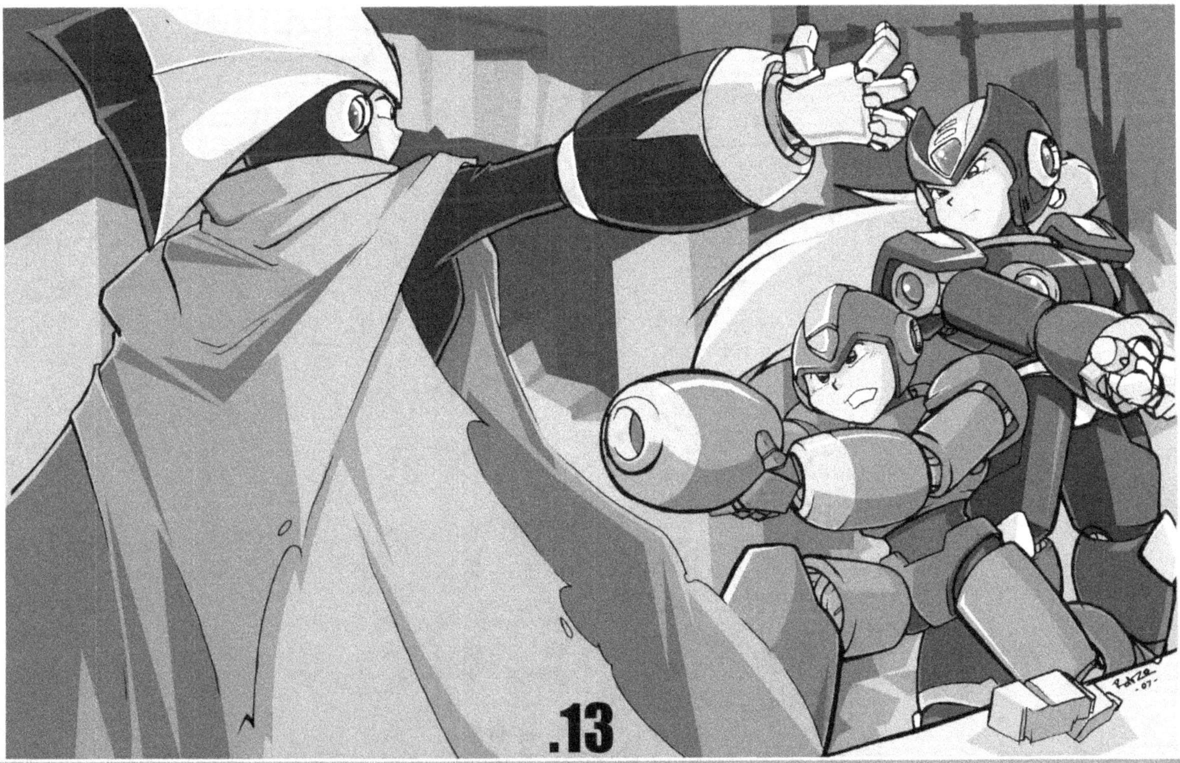

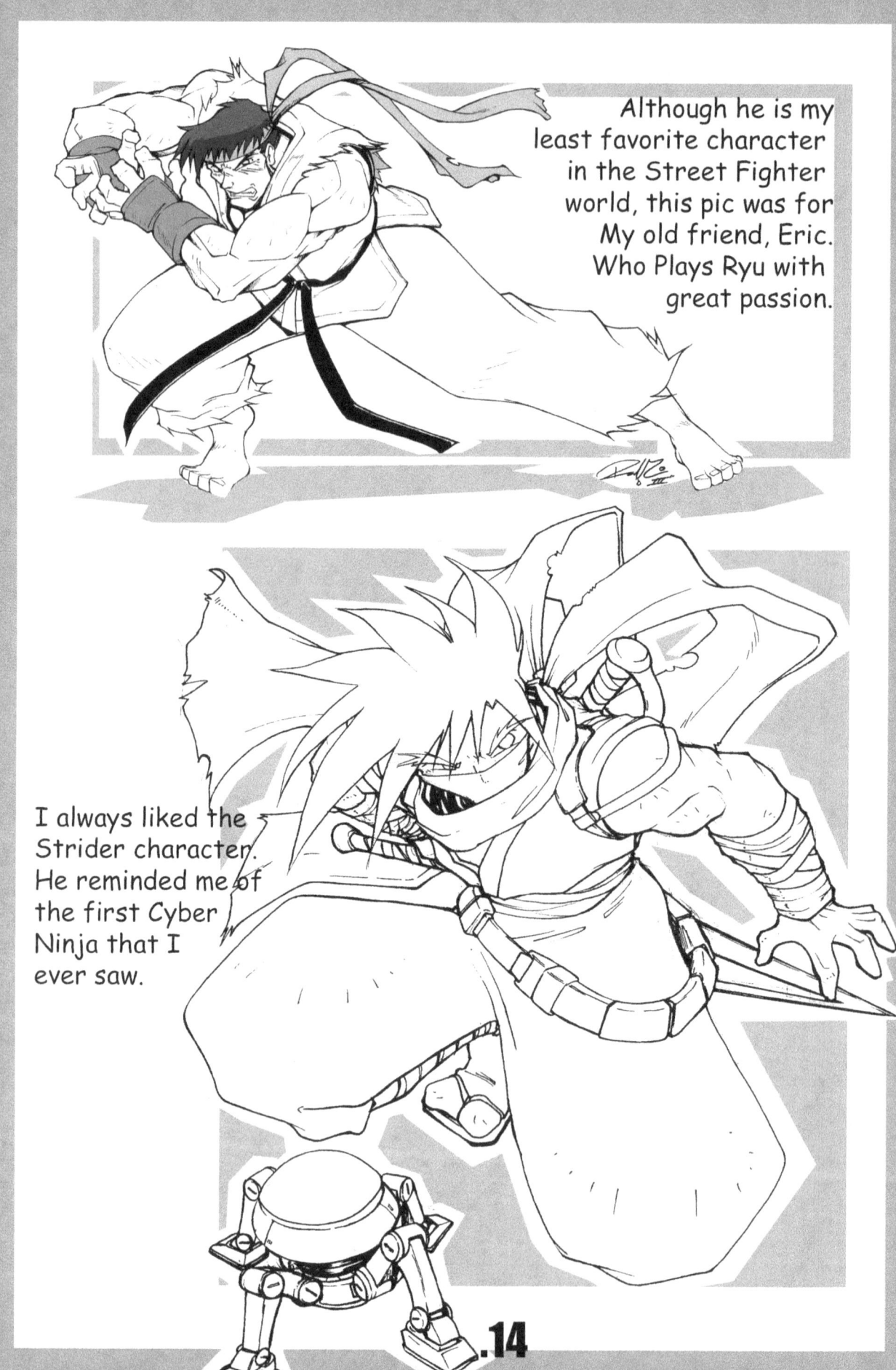

Although he is my least favorite character in the Street Fighter world, this pic was for My old friend, Eric. Who Plays Ryu with great passion.

I always liked the Strider character. He reminded me of the first Cyber Ninja that I ever saw.

.14

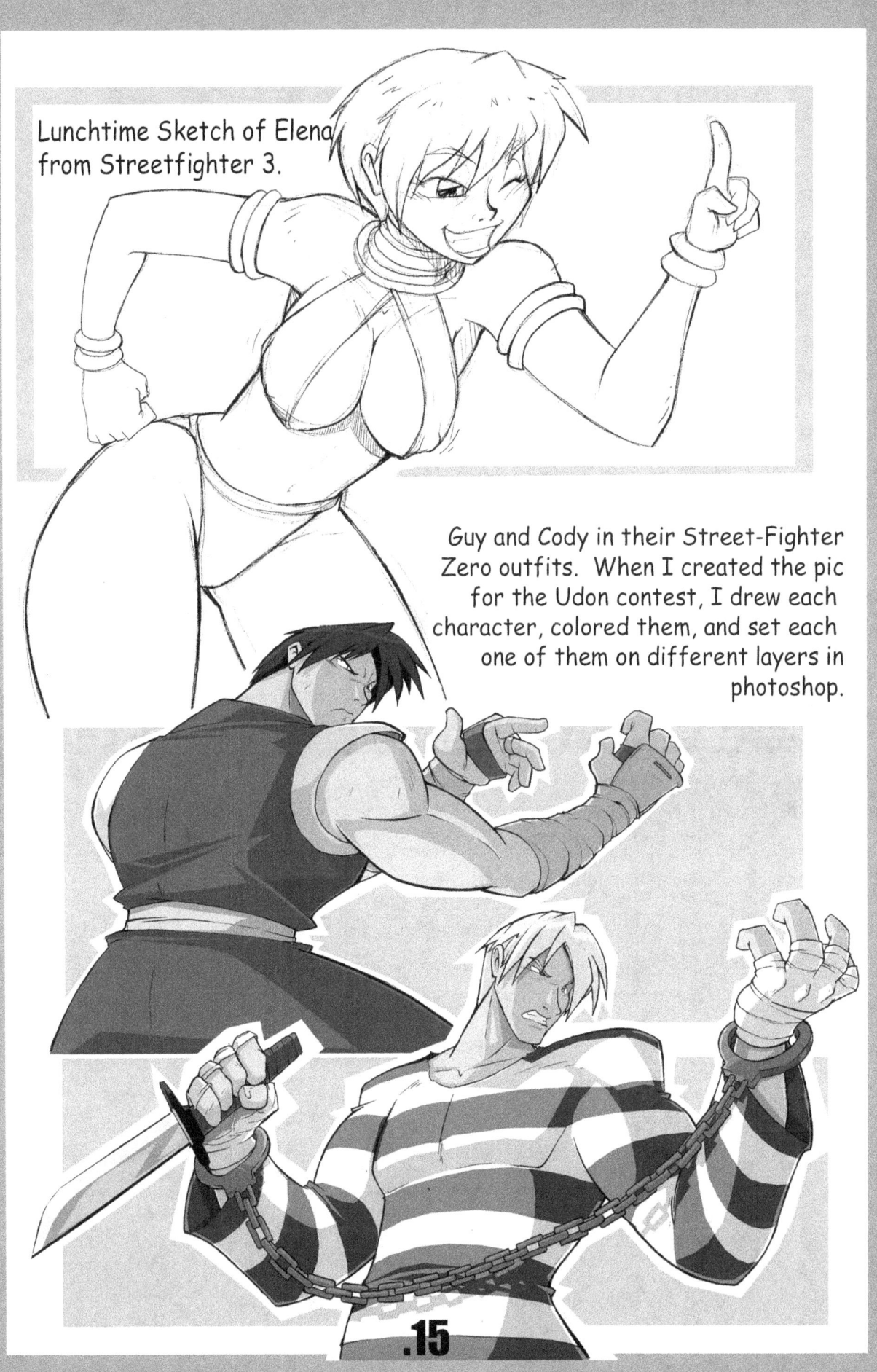

Lunchtime Sketch of Elena from Streetfighter 3.

Guy and Cody in their Street-Fighter Zero outfits. When I created the pic for the Udon contest, I drew each character, colored them, and set each one of them on different layers in photoshop.

.15

# FINAL FIGHT

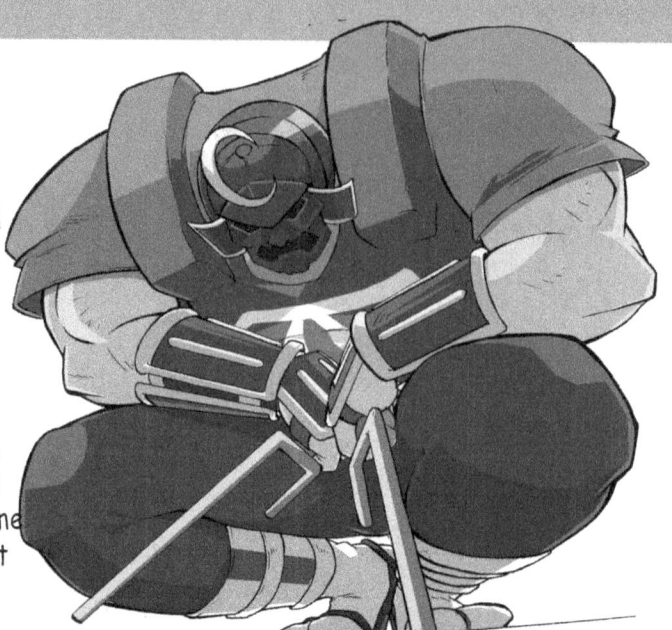

Udon comics had a Street Fighter art contest. I had an idea to create a picture with all of the characters that were originally in the Final Fight series. Unfortunatly, I did not make the cut to get into the book, but I liked how it came out. If Udon comes out with another art contest, I will give it another shot.

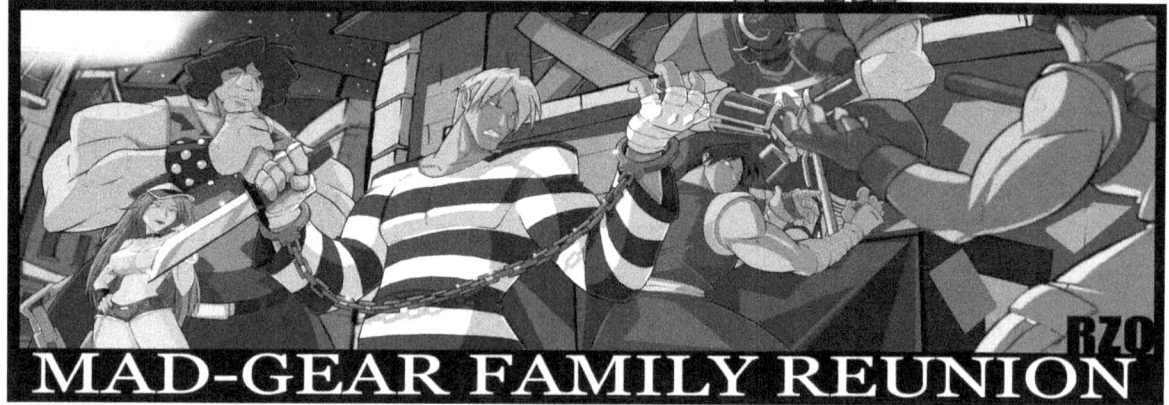

RZO

## MAD-GEAR FAMILY REUNION

Hugo and Poison, friends to the end.

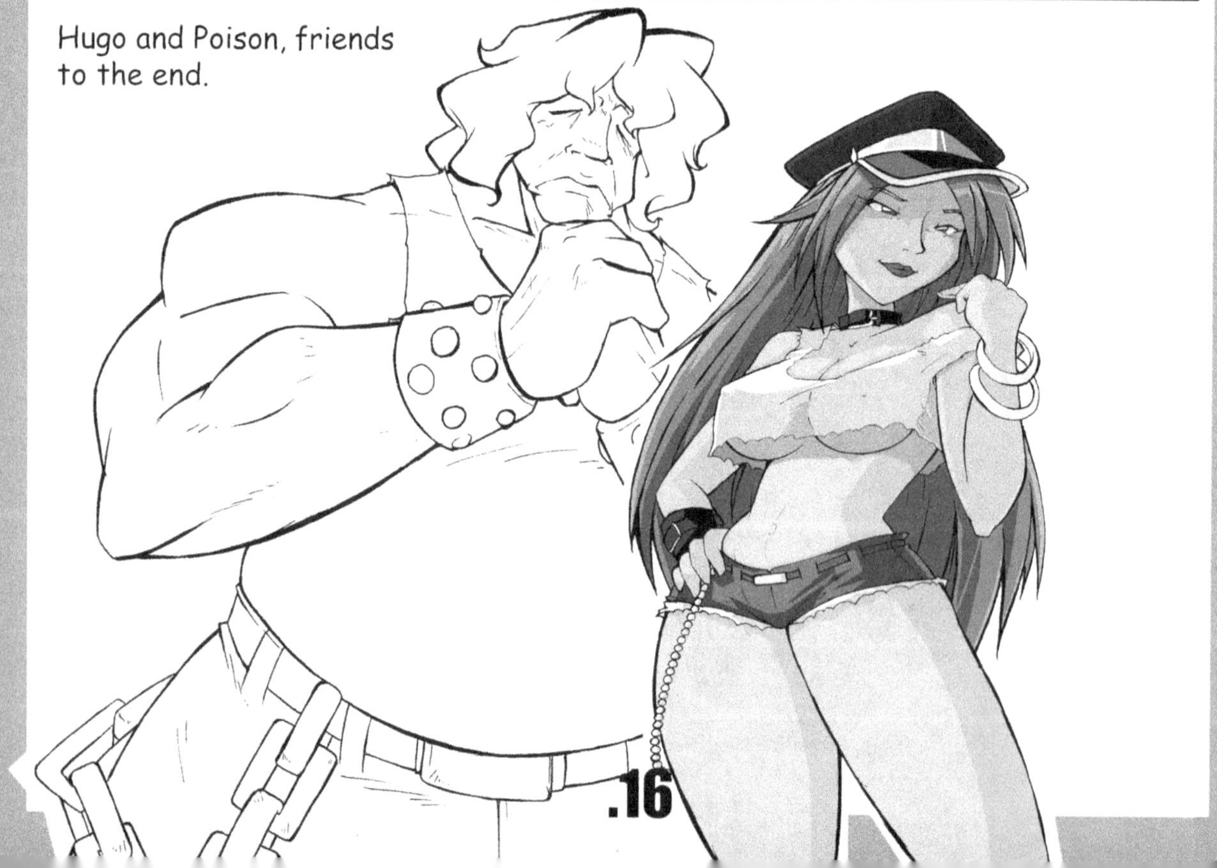

# GUITAR HERO

When Guitar Hero first came out, I was an instant fan, and stopped me from ever doing silly air-guitaring.

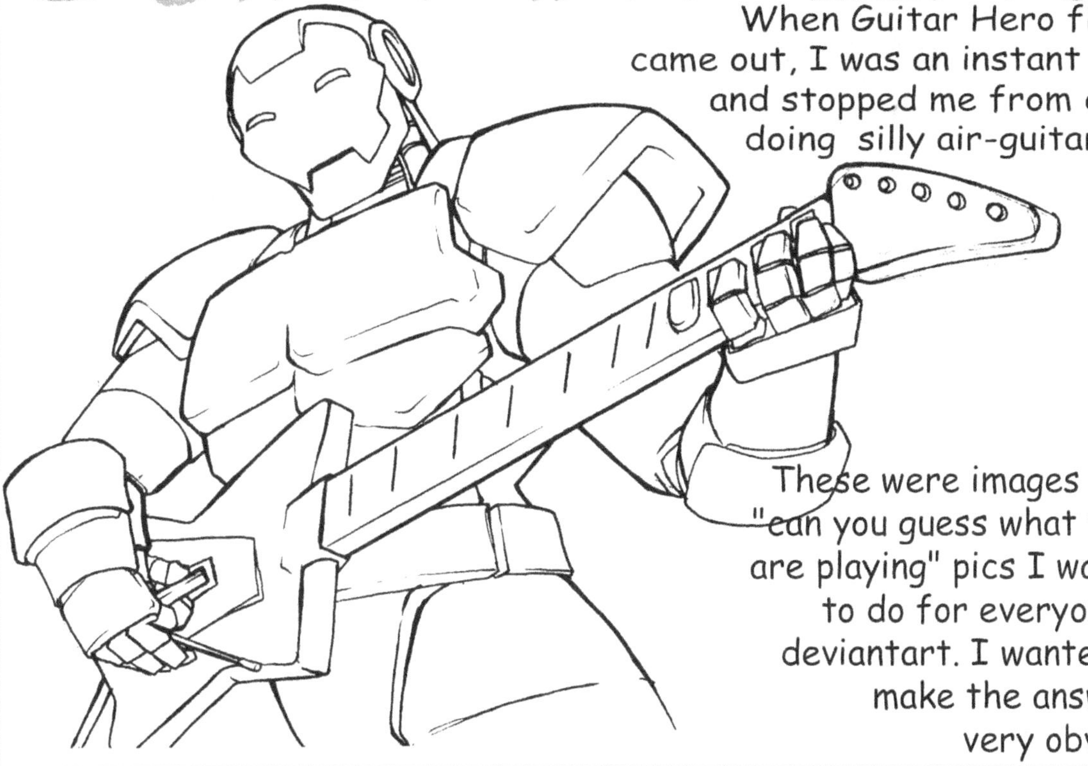

These were images for a "can you guess what they are playing" pics I wanted to do for everyone on deviantart. I wanted to make the answers very obvious.

Buckethead playing Guitar Hero. I bet he would be good at it.

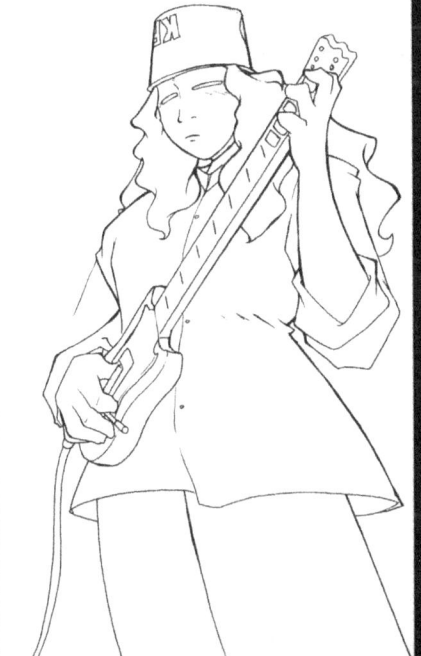

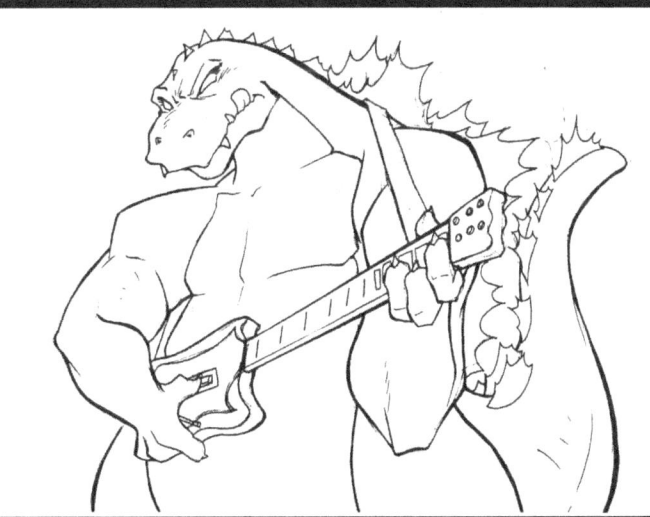

Godzilla playing Guitar Hero. Take a wild guess what song he would be playing.

# FINAL-FANTASY

This in how I believe the Kingdom Hearts game Should have ended.

..THAT'S RIGHT KIDS...MINE'S REAL ..AND I GOT MINE FOR FREE!!

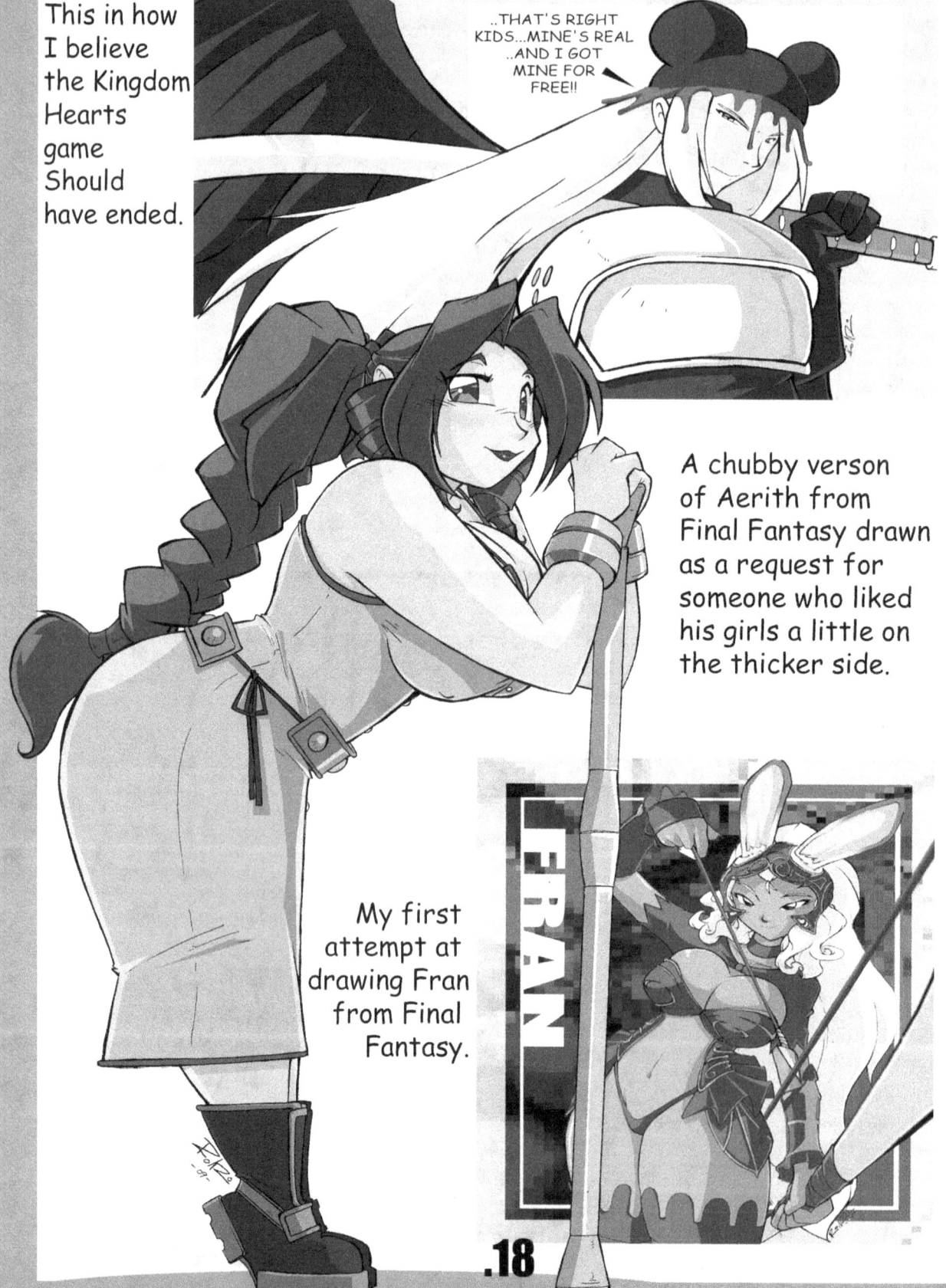

A chubby verson of Aerith from Final Fantasy drawn as a request for someone who liked his girls a little on the thicker side.

My first attempt at drawing Fran from Final Fantasy.

FRAN

# FATAL FURY

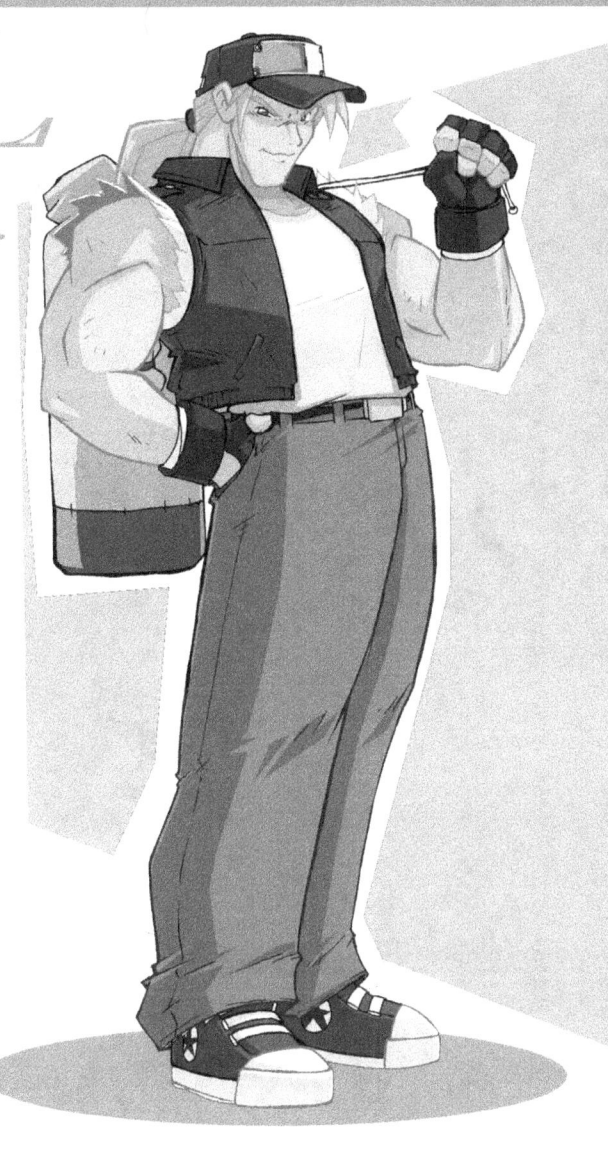

Of all of the characters from the SNK series Terry Bogard is by far my favorite. Unfortunately, I do not have that much art of him. I guess I spent too much time playing his games than drawing him.

This picture consist of all of the characters from Team Korea. This one took a while because each character was drawn indivisually.

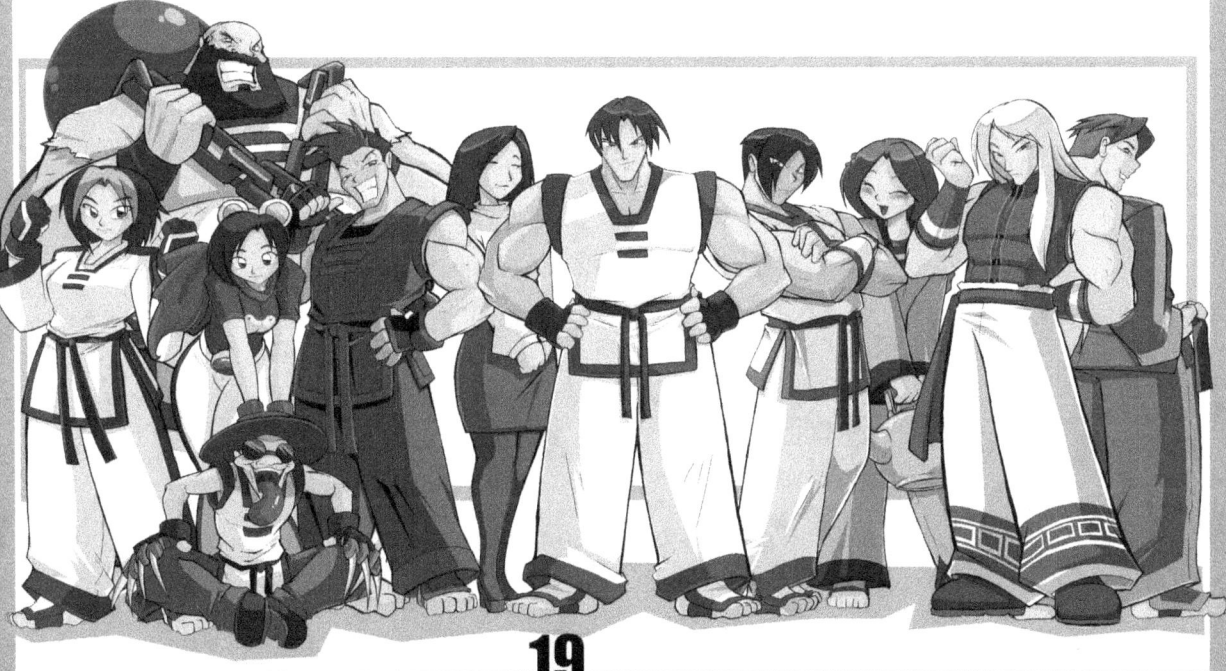

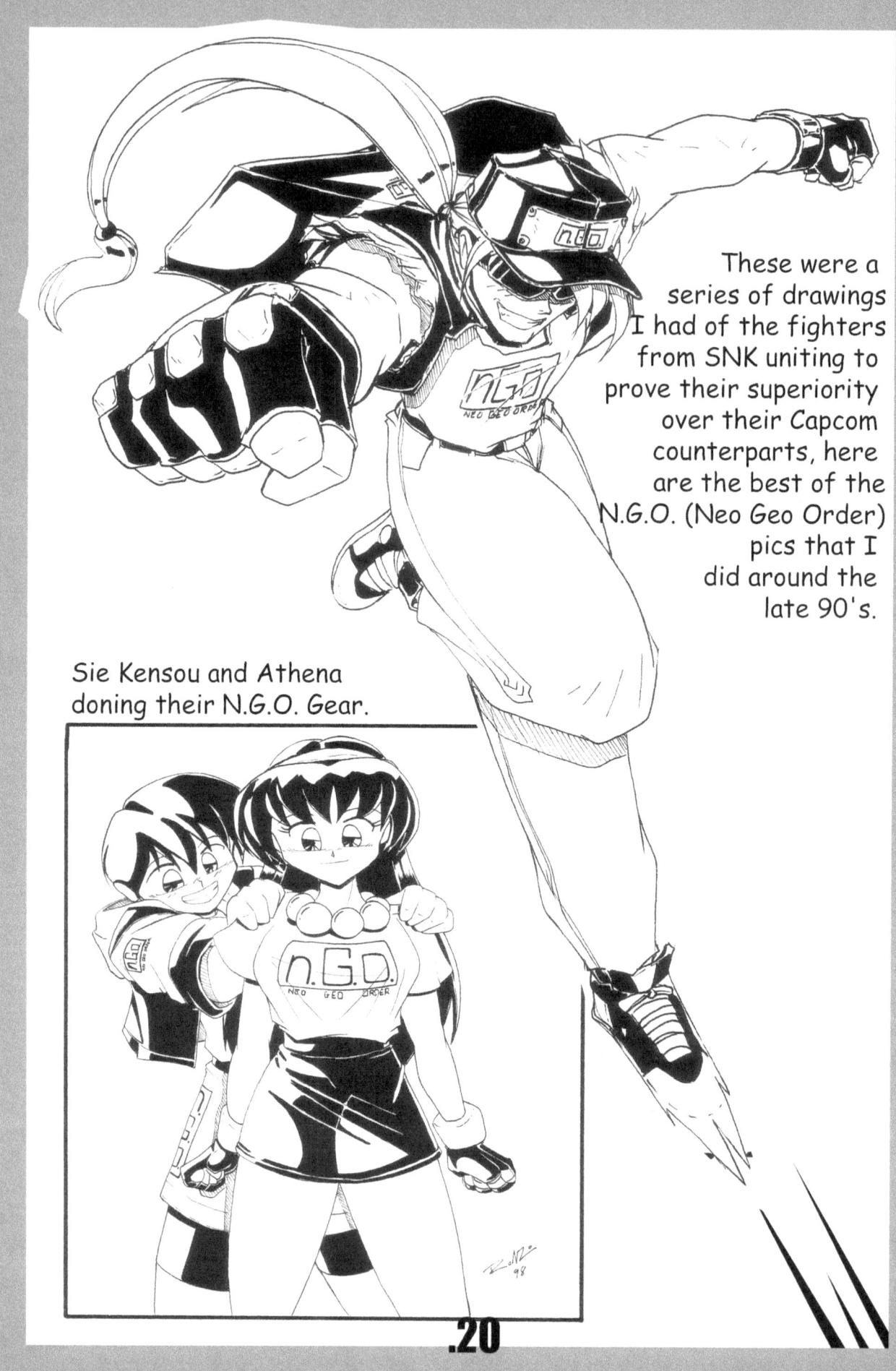

These were a series of drawings I had of the fighters from SNK uniting to prove their superiority over their Capcom counterparts, here are the best of the N.G.O. (Neo Geo Order) pics that I did around the late 90's.

Sie Kensou and Athena doning their N.G.O. Gear.

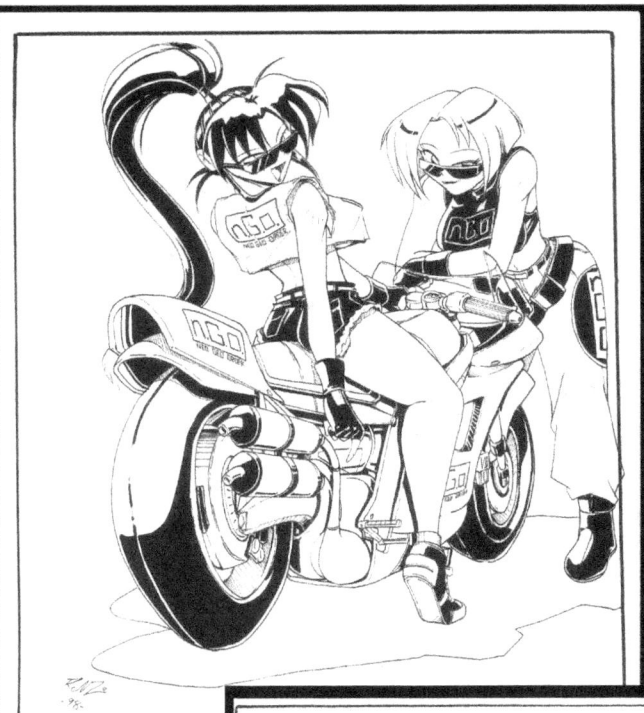

N.G.O. Mai Shiranui and Blue Mary posing on a bike. That is always sexy.

Another streetfighter falls to the might of the N.G.O.

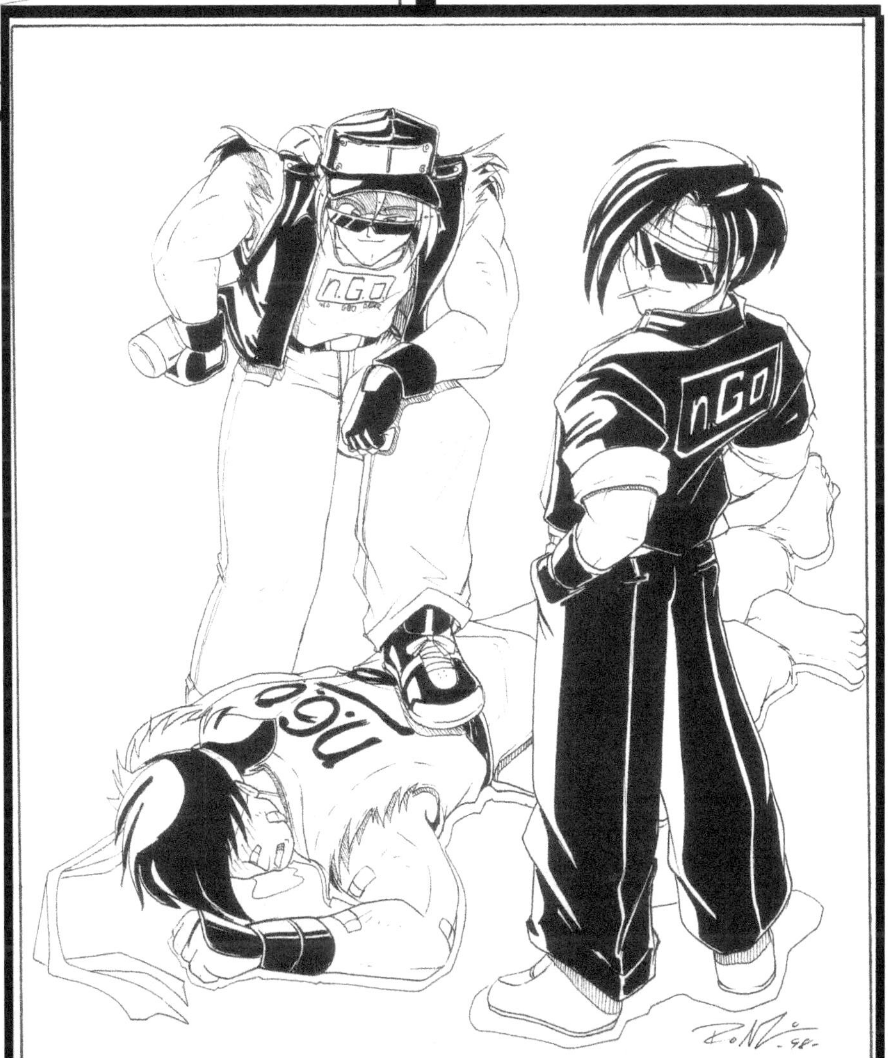

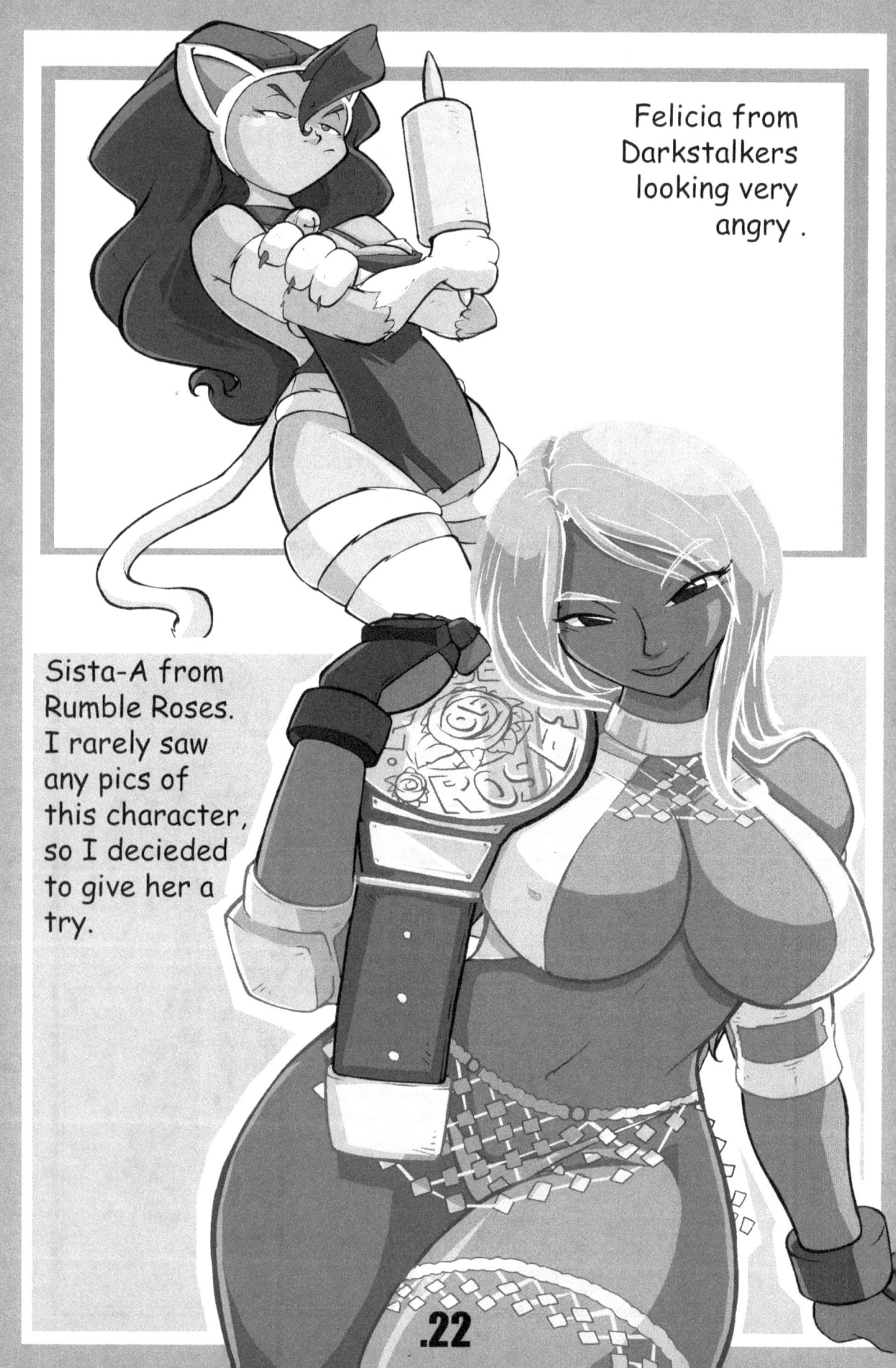

Felicia from Darkstalkers looking very angry .

Sista-A from Rumble Roses. I rarely saw any pics of this character, so I decieded to give her a try.

.22

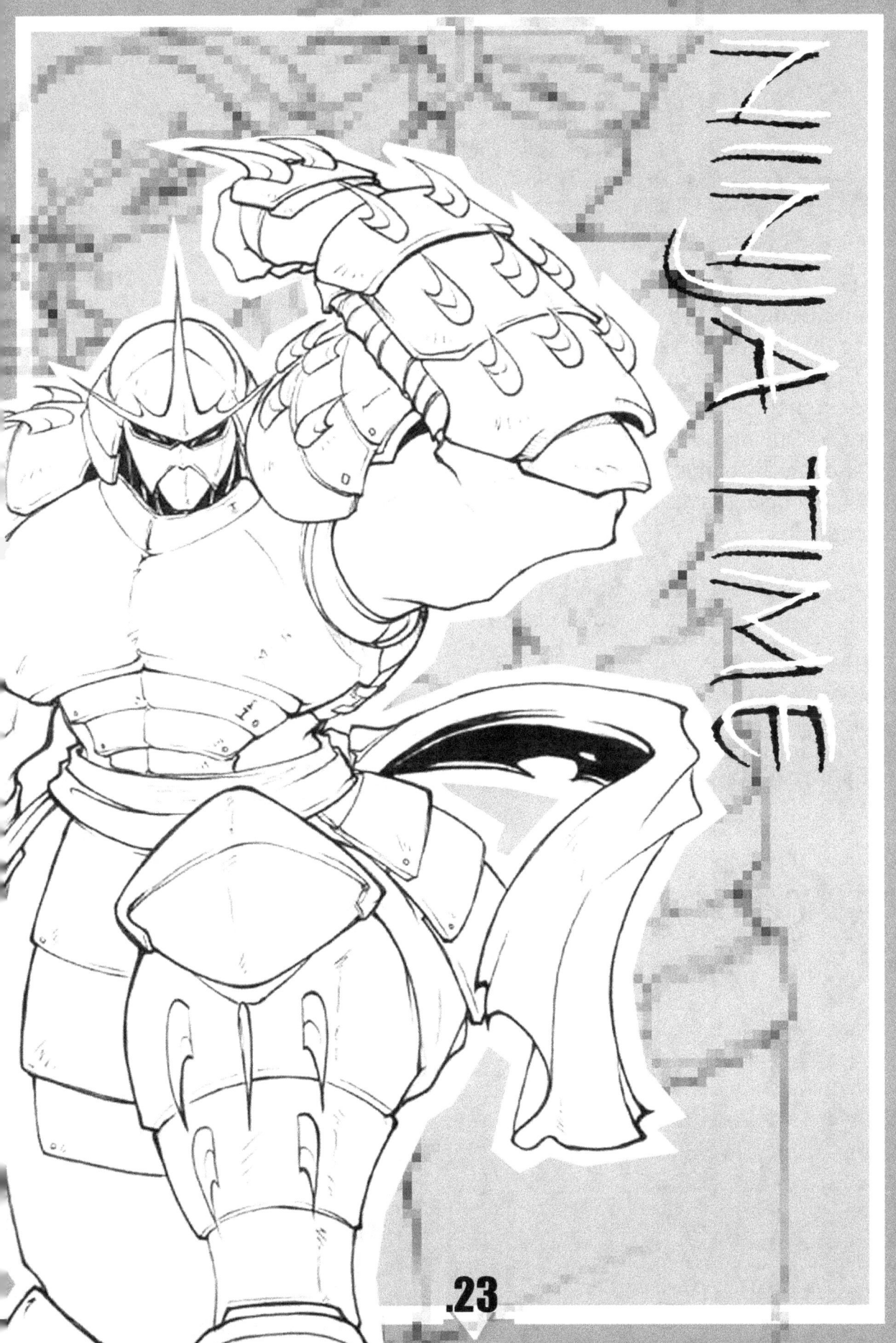

NINJA TIME

.23

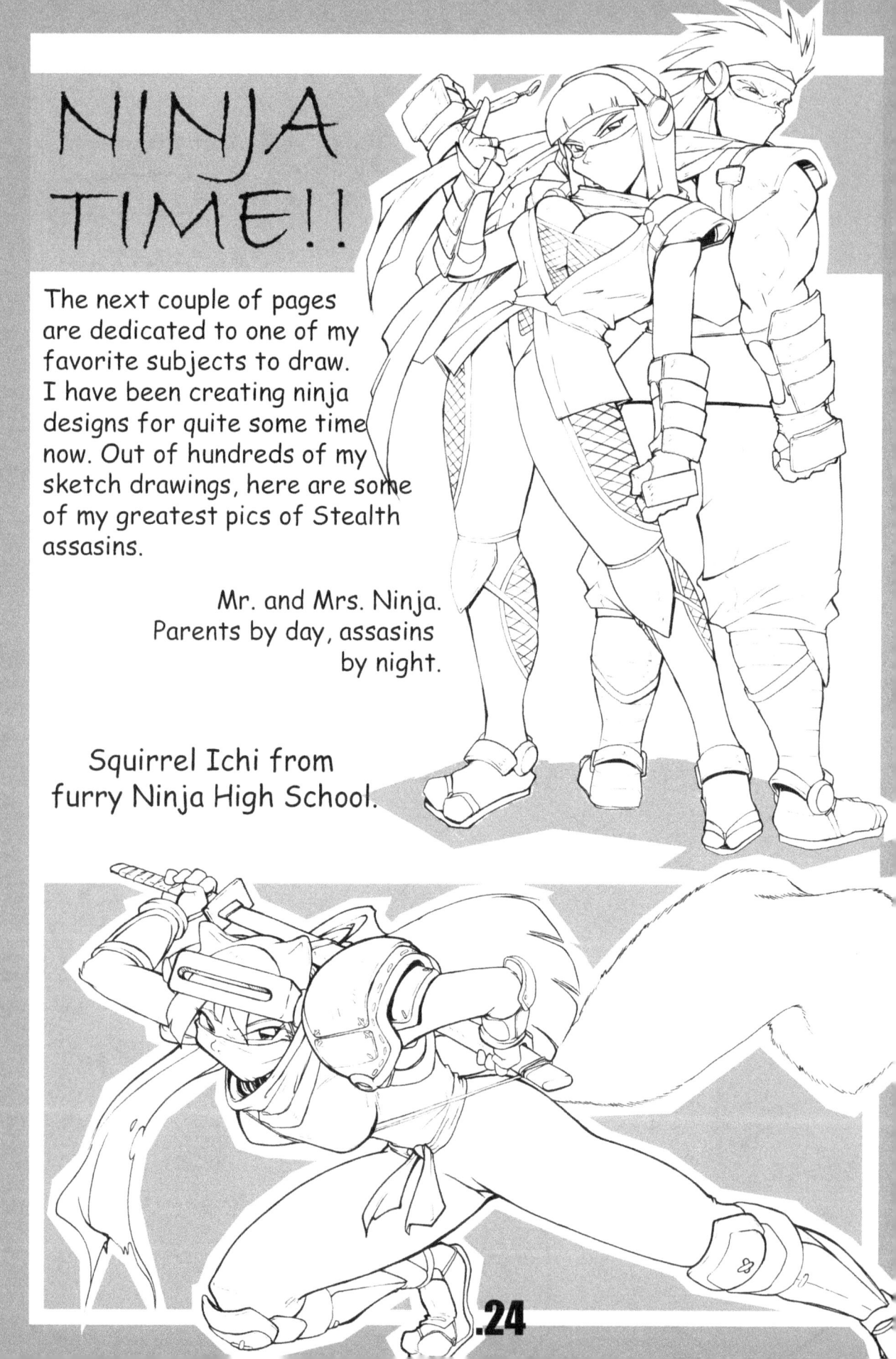

# NINJA TIME!!

The next couple of pages are dedicated to one of my favorite subjects to draw. I have been creating ninja designs for quite some time now. Out of hundreds of my sketch drawings, here are some of my greatest pics of Stealth assasins.

Mr. and Mrs. Ninja. Parents by day, assasins by night.

Squirrel Ichi from furry Ninja High School.

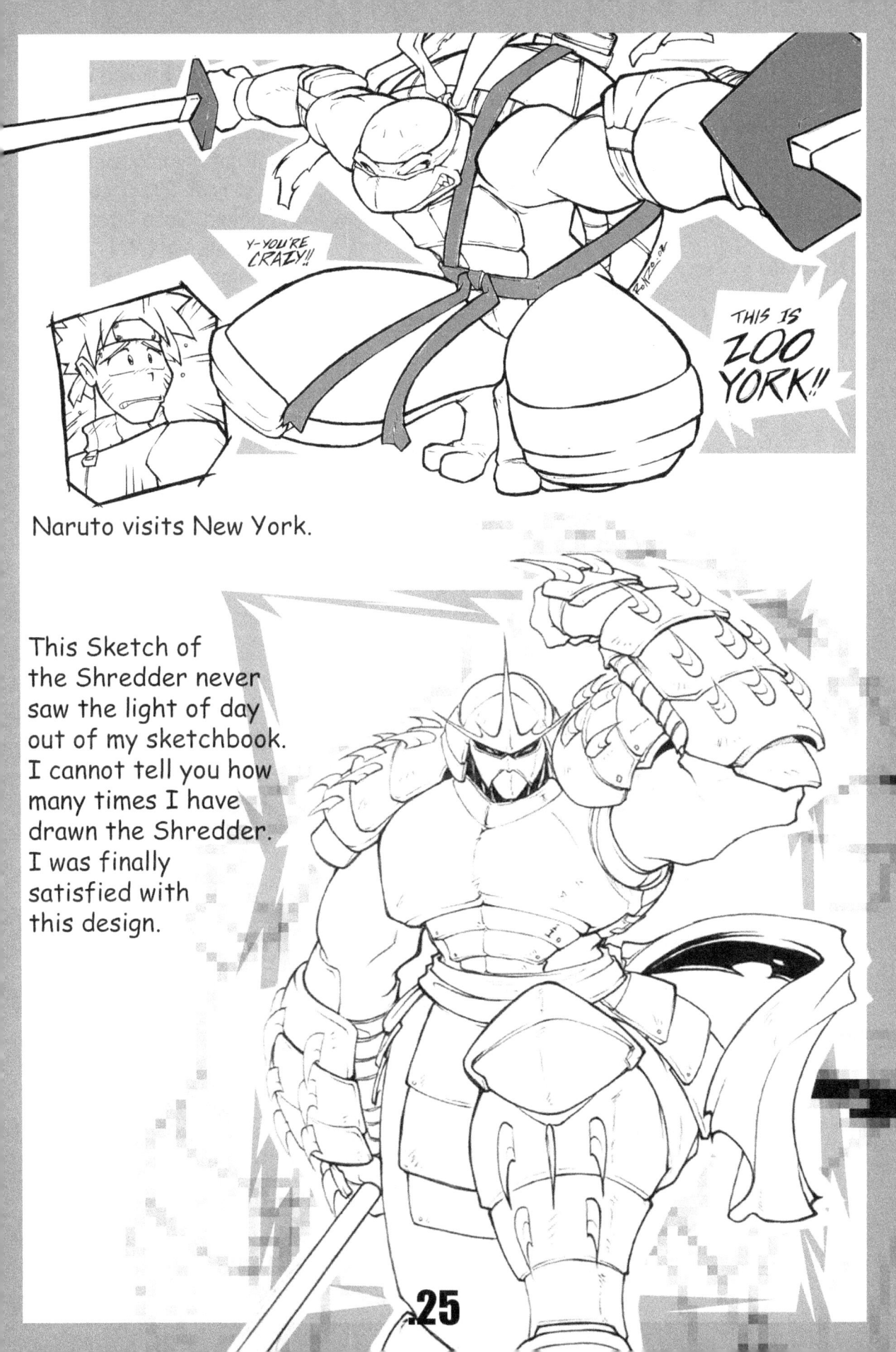

Y-YOU'RE CRAZY!!

THIS IS ZOO YORK!!

Naruto visits New York.

This Sketch of the Shredder never saw the light of day out of my sketchbook. I cannot tell you how many times I have drawn the Shredder. I was finally satisfied with this design.

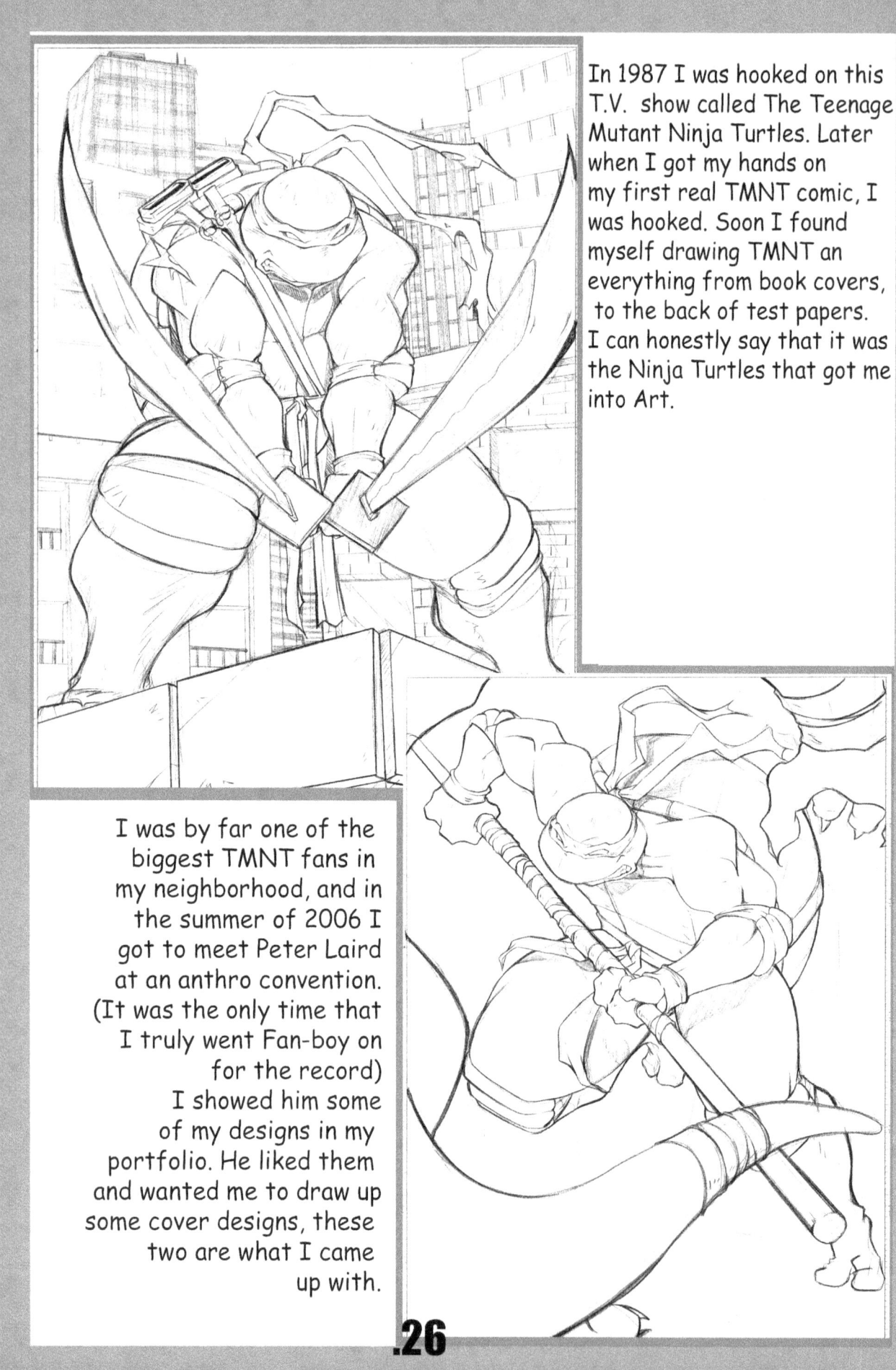

In 1987 I was hooked on this T.V. show called The Teenage Mutant Ninja Turtles. Later when I got my hands on my first real TMNT comic, I was hooked. Soon I found myself drawing TMNT an everything from book covers, to the back of test papers. I can honestly say that it was the Ninja Turtles that got me into Art.

I was by far one of the biggest TMNT fans in my neighborhood, and in the summer of 2006 I got to meet Peter Laird at an anthro convention. (It was the only time that I truly went Fan-boy on for the record) I showed him some of my designs in my portfolio. He liked them and wanted me to draw up some cover designs, these two are what I came up with.

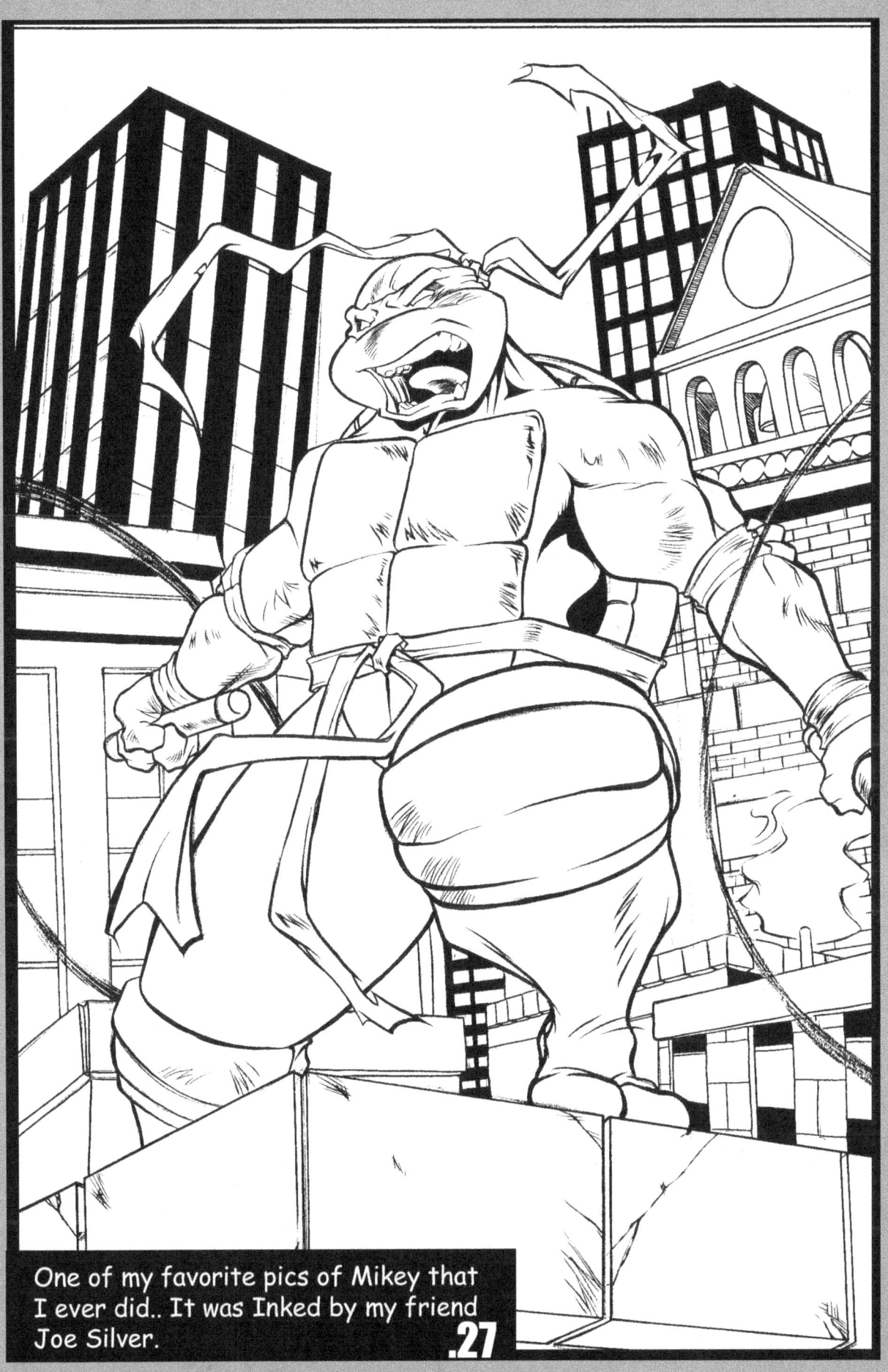

One of my favorite pics of Mikey that I ever did.. It was Inked by my friend Joe Silver.

.27

Leonardo pic used for and action card collection idea that I had planned.

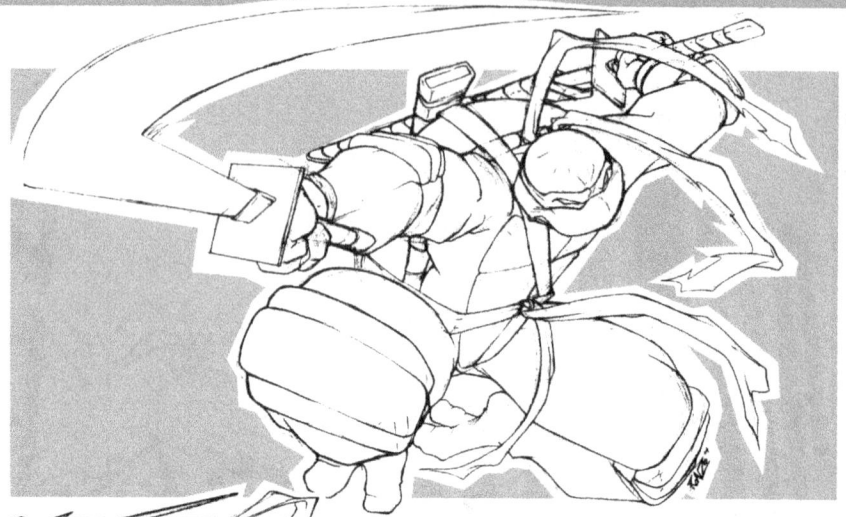

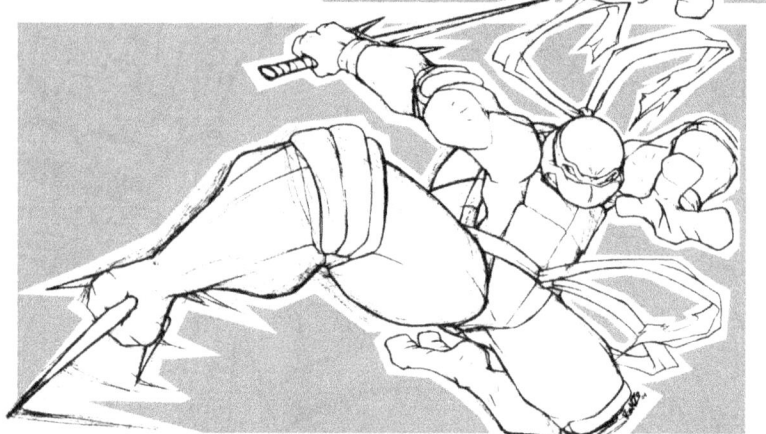

Although the card idea did not work out. I am still proud of how these two pics came out.

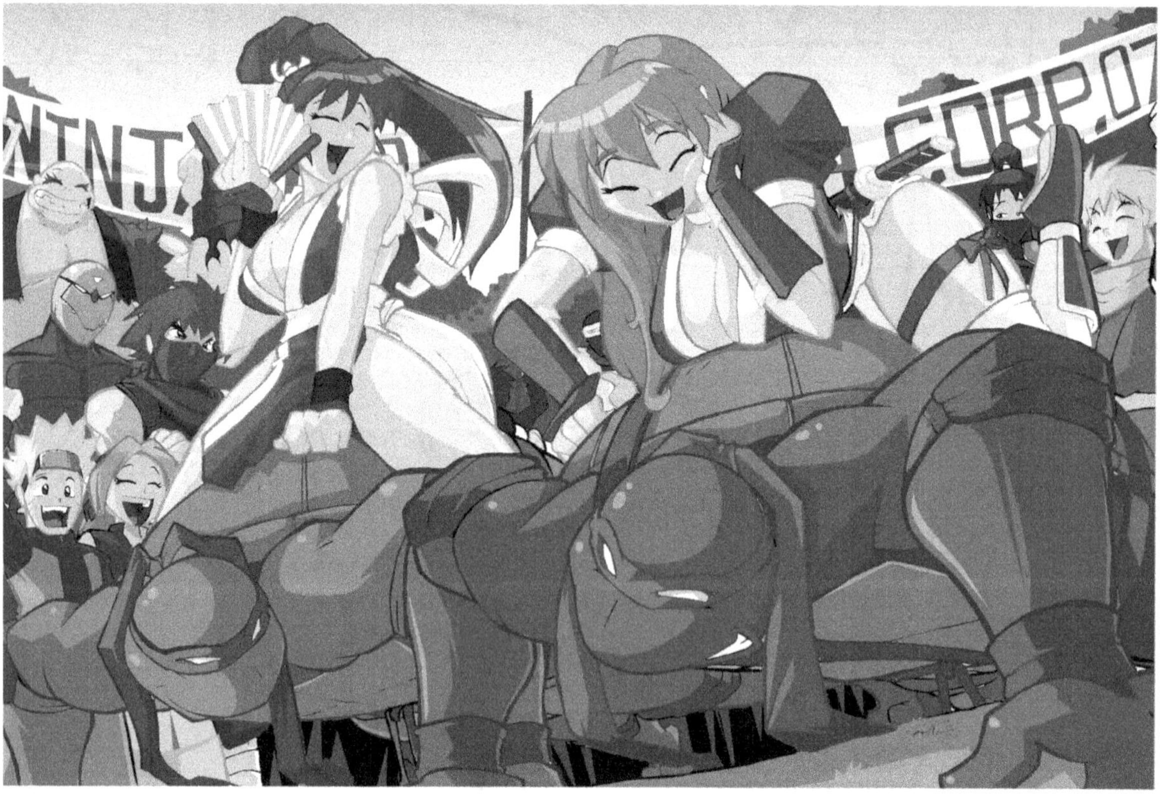

The 2007 Ninja cookout. The most ninja that I have ever drawn on one page ever.

# PIRATE VS NINJA

Pirates -vs- Ninja Pics drawn for fun.

# FAMILIAR CHARACTERS

Remember the Shirt-Tales. This is the Shirt-Tales gone Extreme.

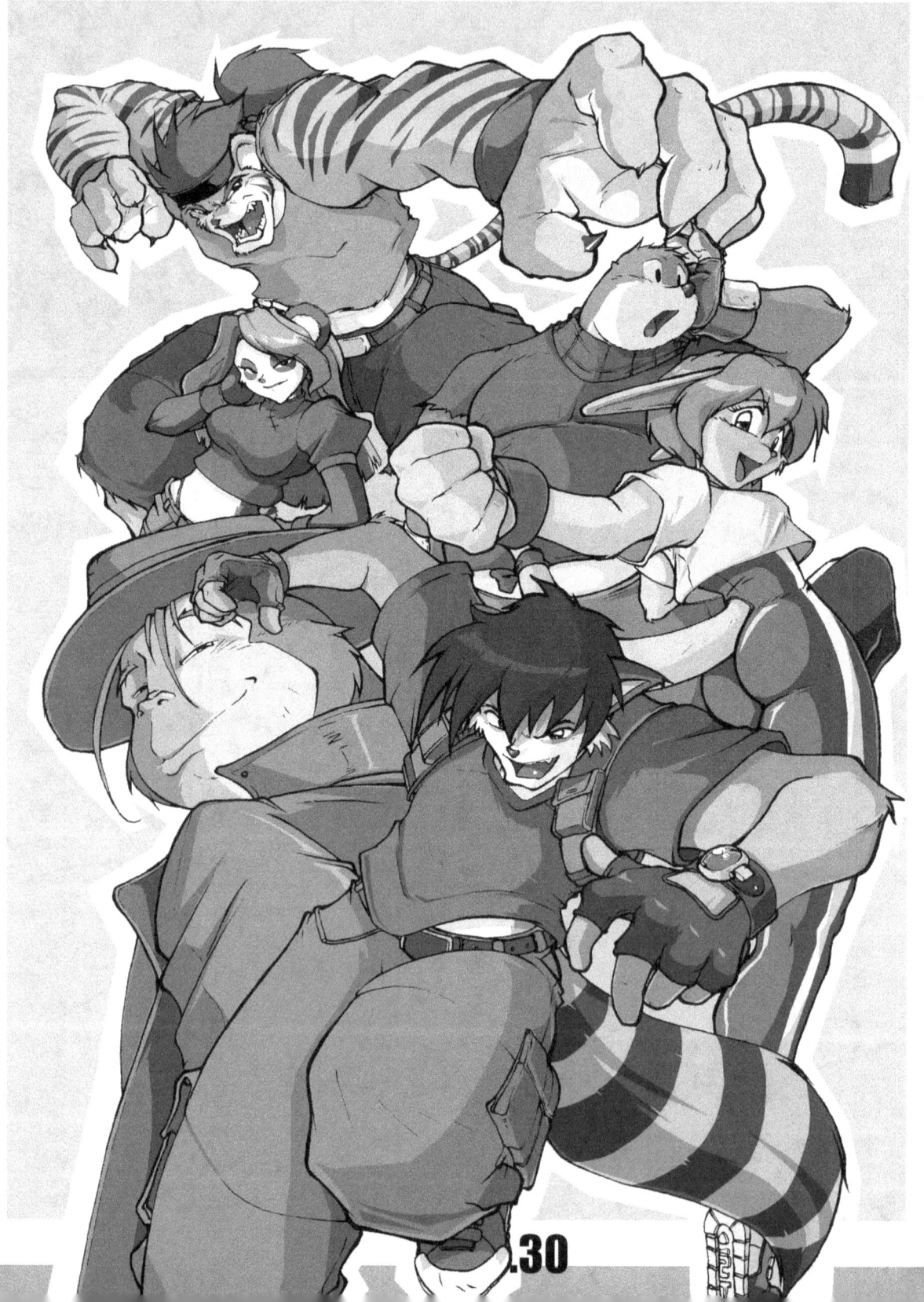

My first attempt at drawing any character from
Star Wars. I loved how the light-sabre effects came out.

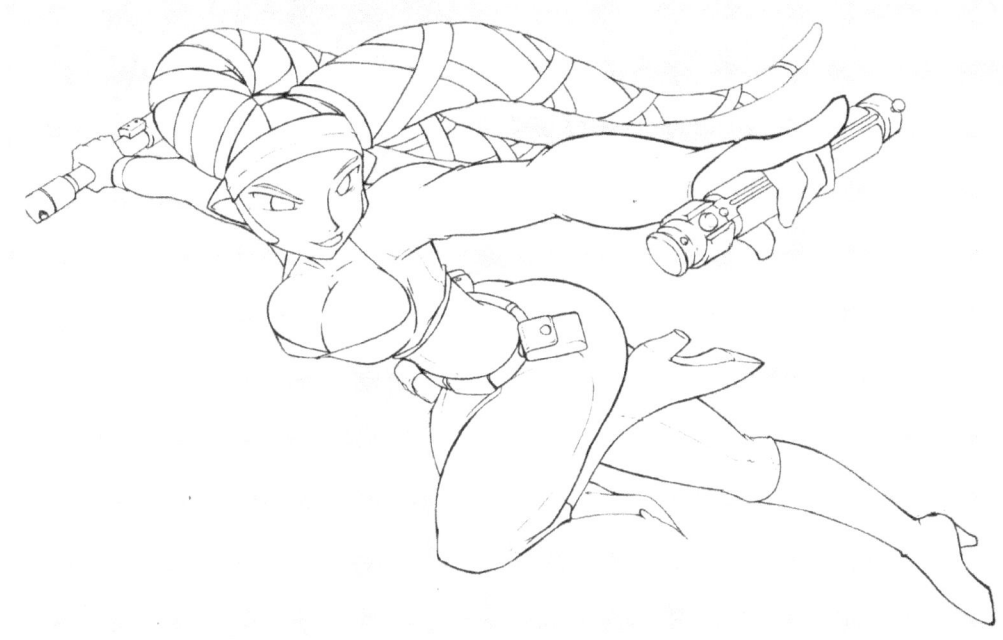

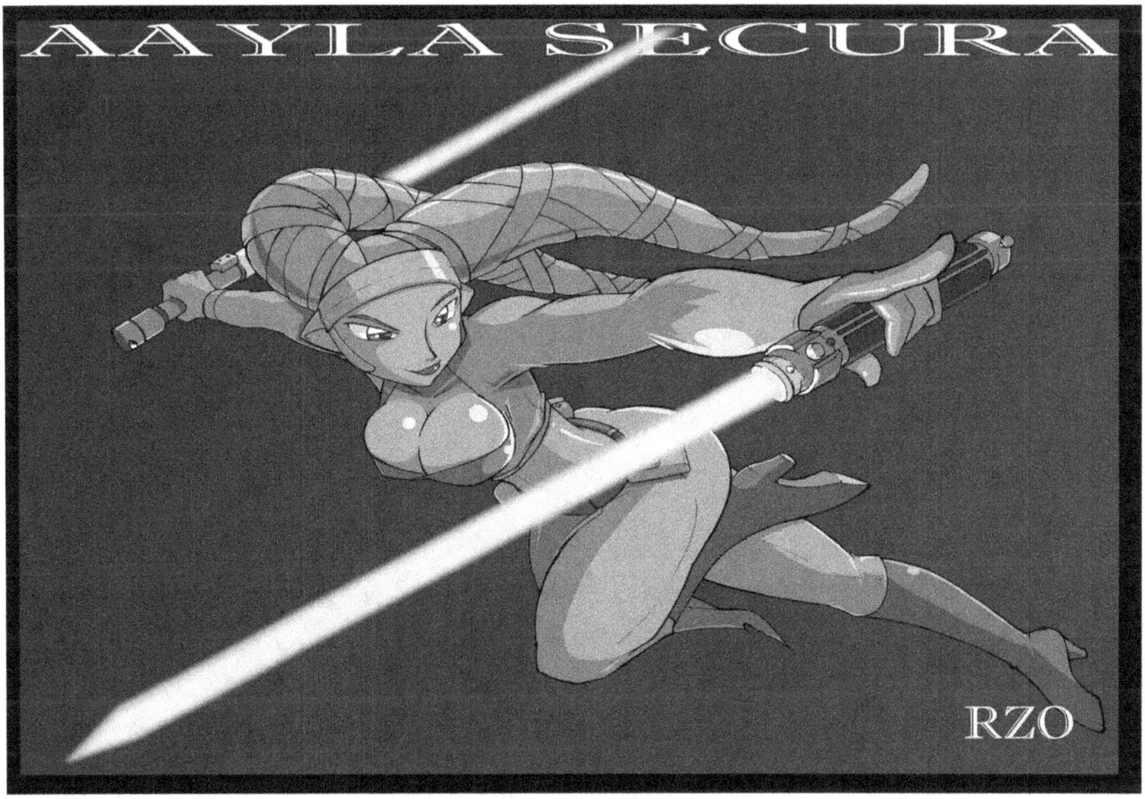

AAYLA SECURA

RZO

The "Acrobat" Diana from the old cartoon. Dungeons and Dragons. I was going for a if they were ever to remake the series look.

Sonja and Cleo. although they were on the same show. the two never met.

Maple Town's Bobby Bear and Patty Rabbit all grown up.

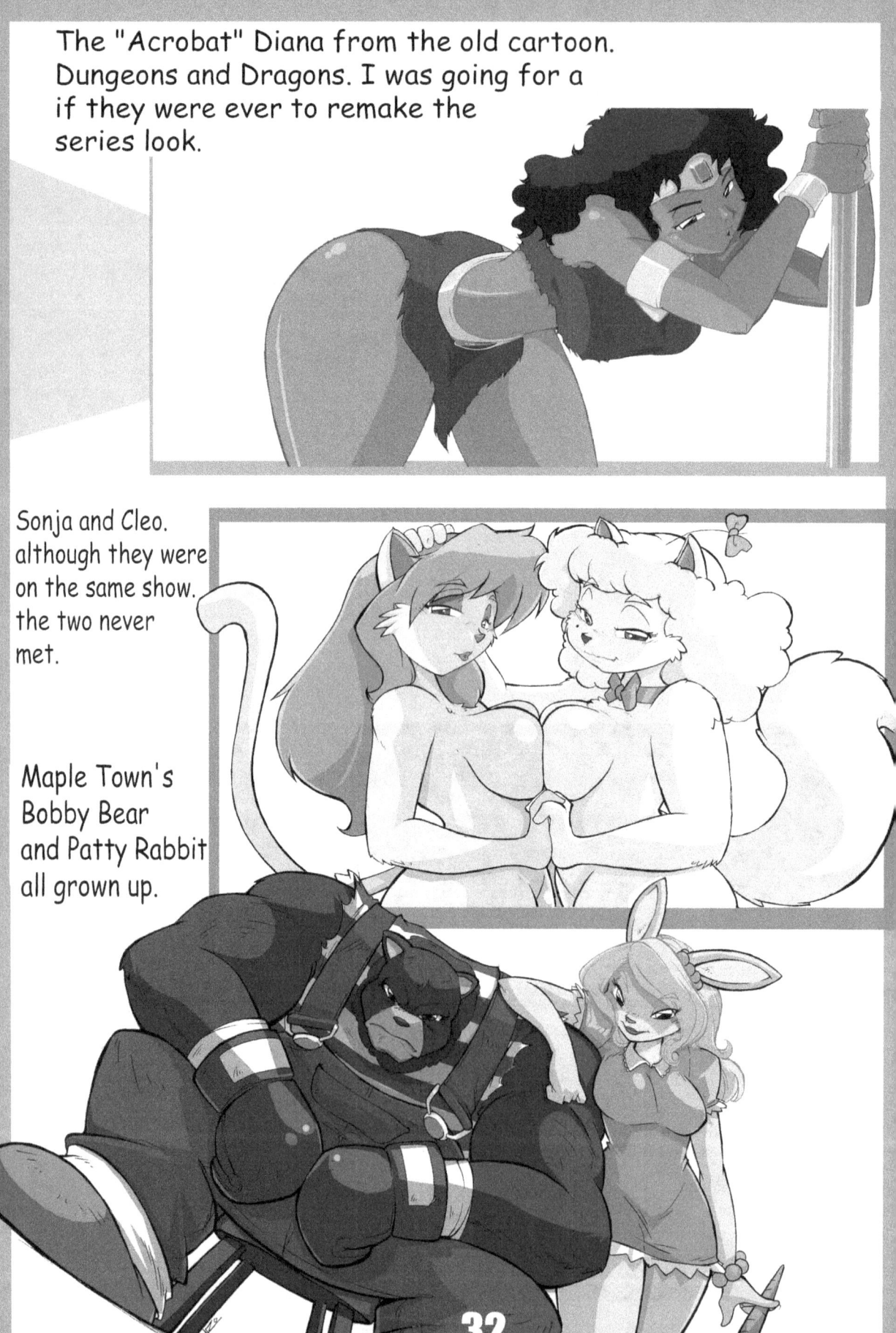

HongKong Phooey re-make Inspired from the Cartoon Network flash cartoon.

This was the first and only page in a short story I had planned with H.K.P and his encounter with the Cadillac Cats. I love how the cats came out.

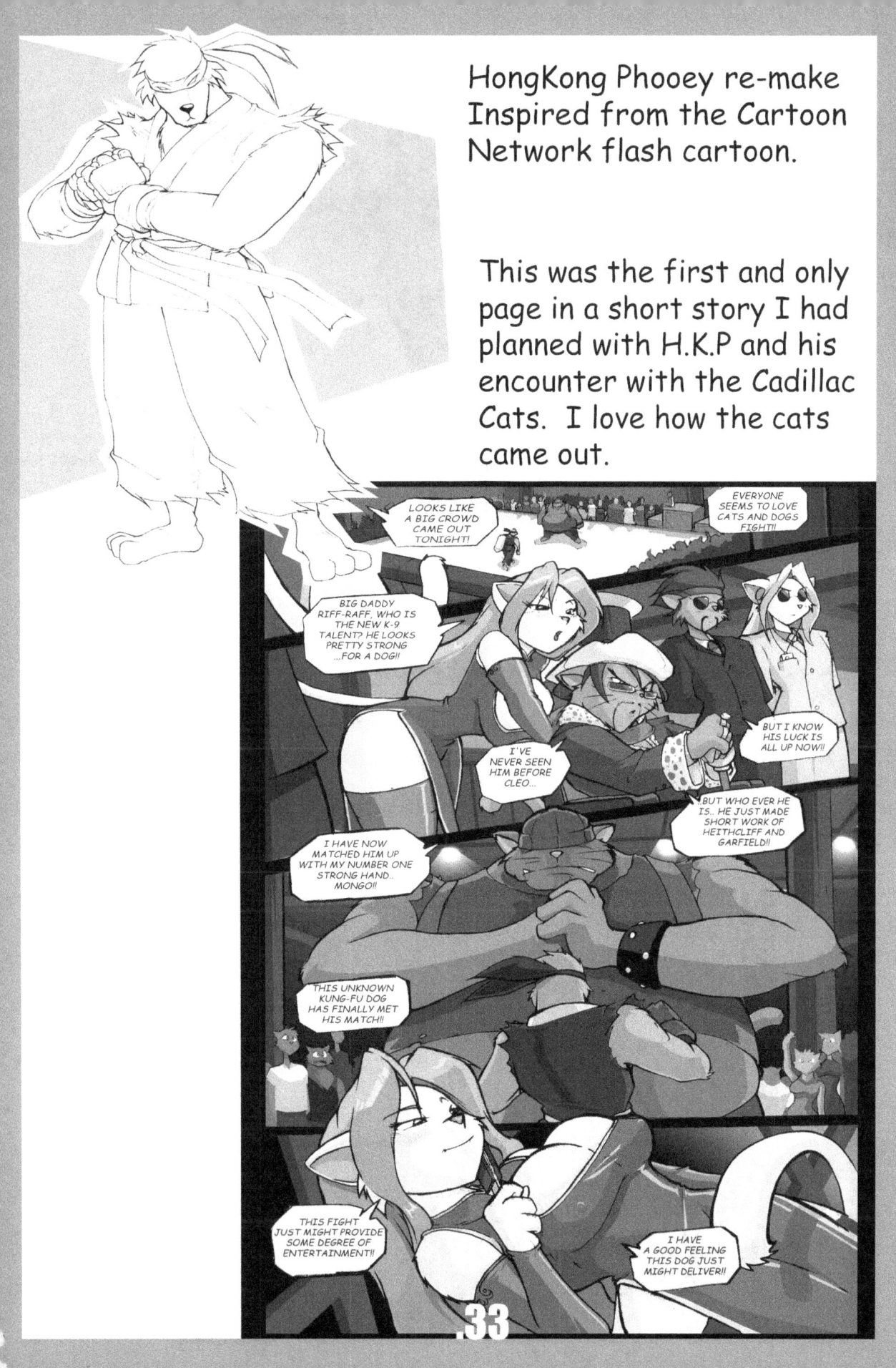

When I first saw the movie
"The Road to El Dorado" I
thought it was going to be
really bad, but when I saw
Chel, I thought she was
going to be the next
Jessica Rabbit...with
larger hips.

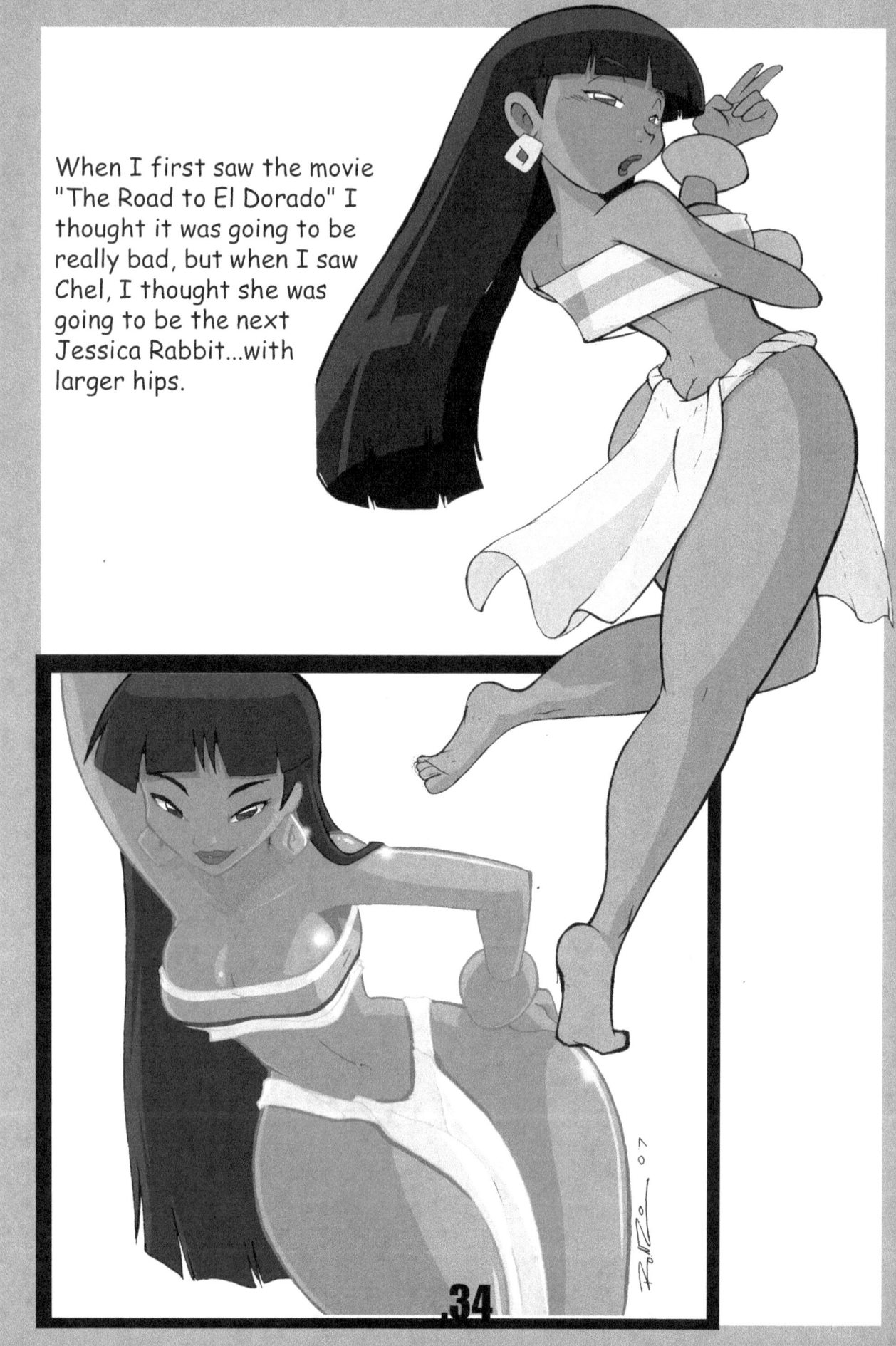

Of all the characters that I get requested to re-create the most it has to be Tinkerbell. In this pic I drew her in a futruistic version of her green outfit.

...think Cyber-Happy thoughts!!

This one of Tink is my favorite. Tink as a pirate .

Tigerlilly all grown up.. and in the right places.

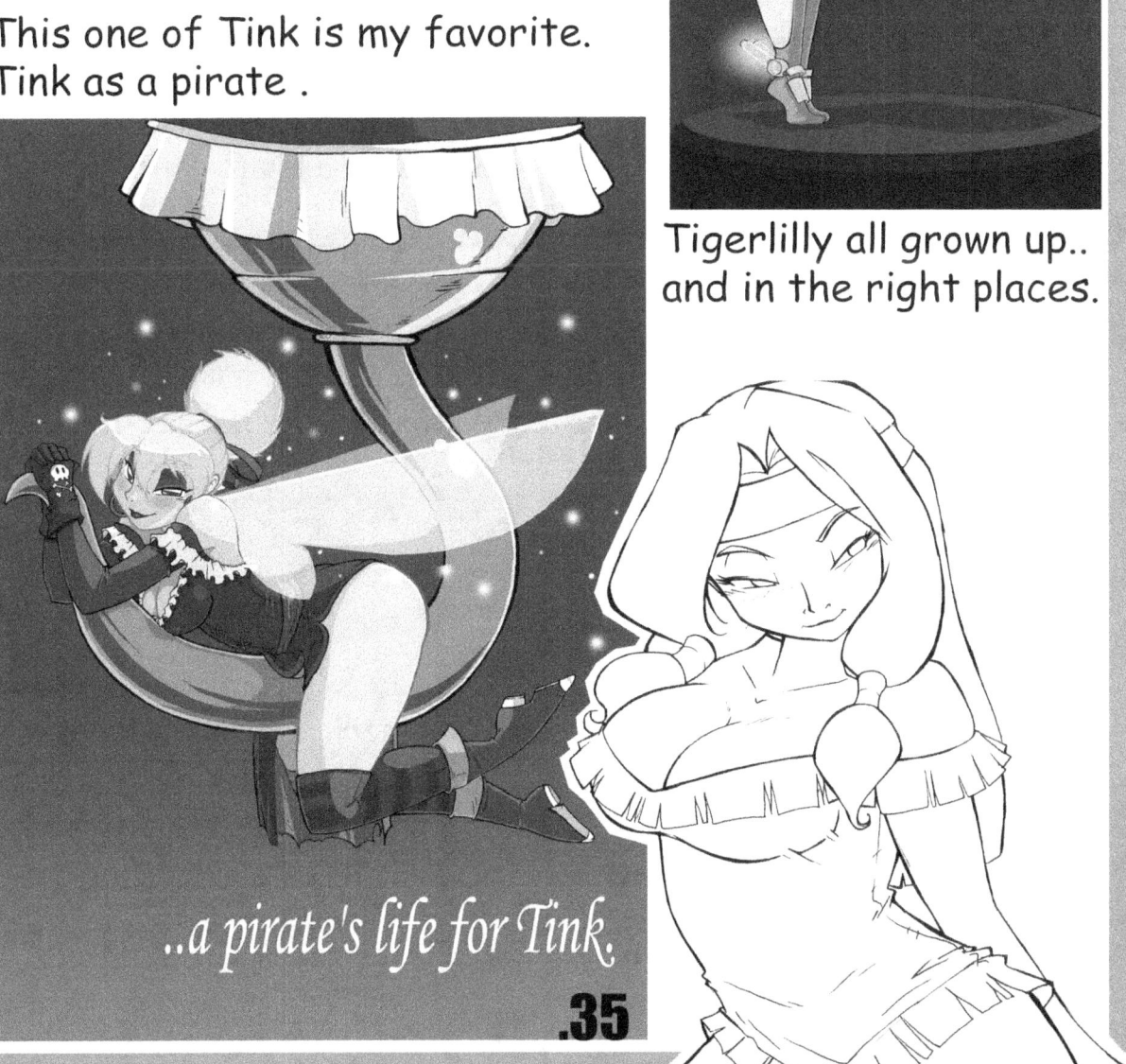

*..a pirate's life for Tink.*

Renamon from the Digimon anime.

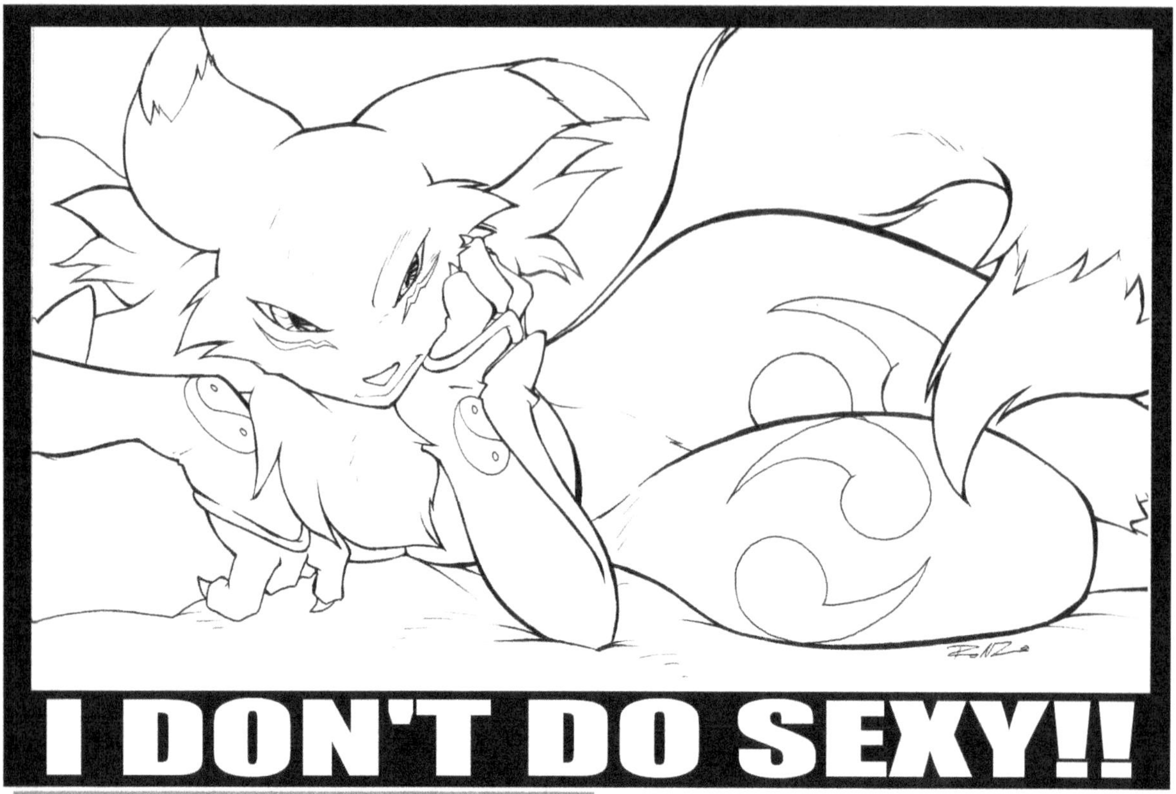

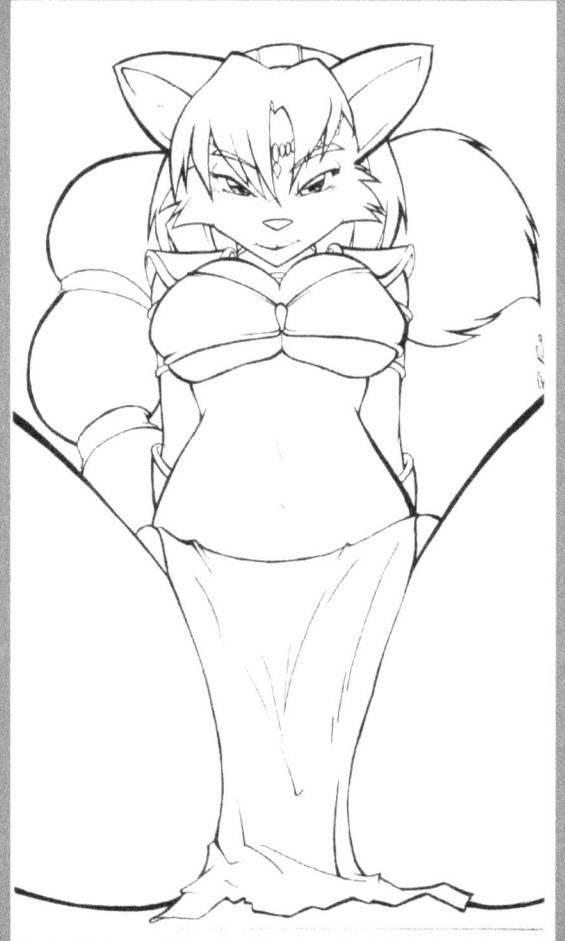

# I DON'T DO SEXY!!

I was never a big fan of Digimon show and especially of the Renamon character which I thought was a bit overhyped. When I drew this requested picture I titled it "I don't do sexy" because Renamon would never pose for a picture like this.

Krystal from the game Starfox, another character I thought to be drawn way too many times. At the time of this pic, I wanted to put her in a shocking position because I was in a shocking position mood.

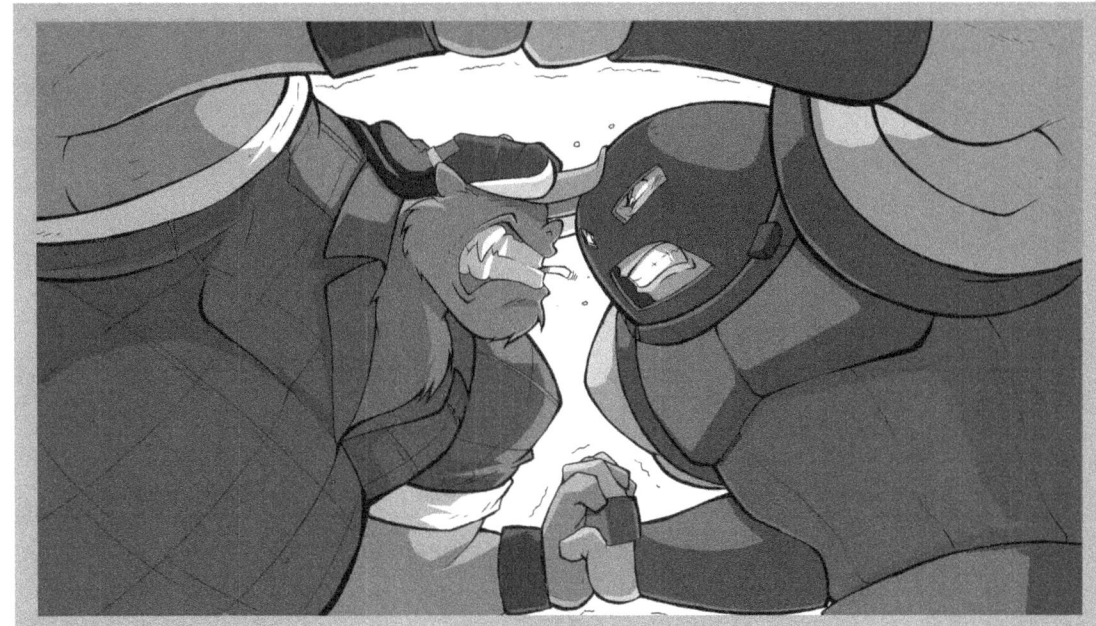

The "Battle of the Big Men" The Juggernaut versus Mr. Bull, This pic was to show his size and strength comparison.

image of Spider-Girl for my portfolio.

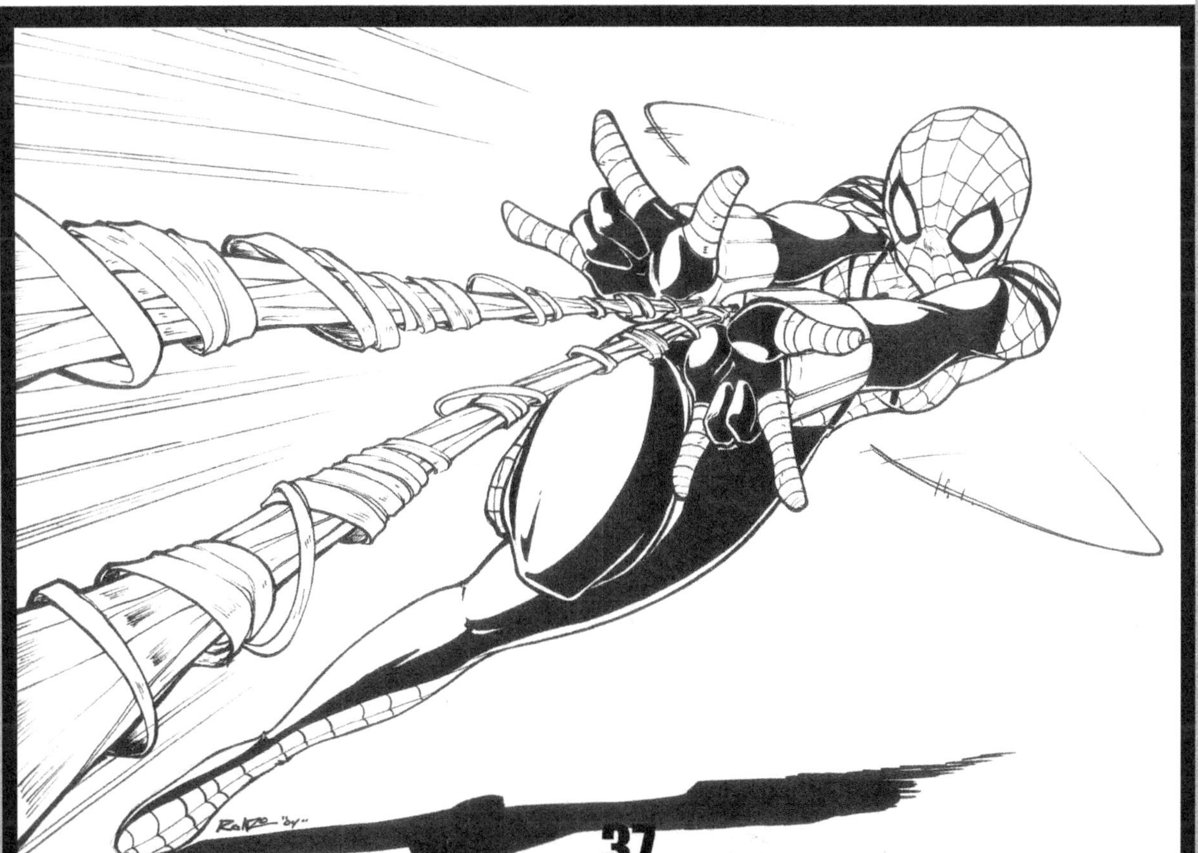

.37

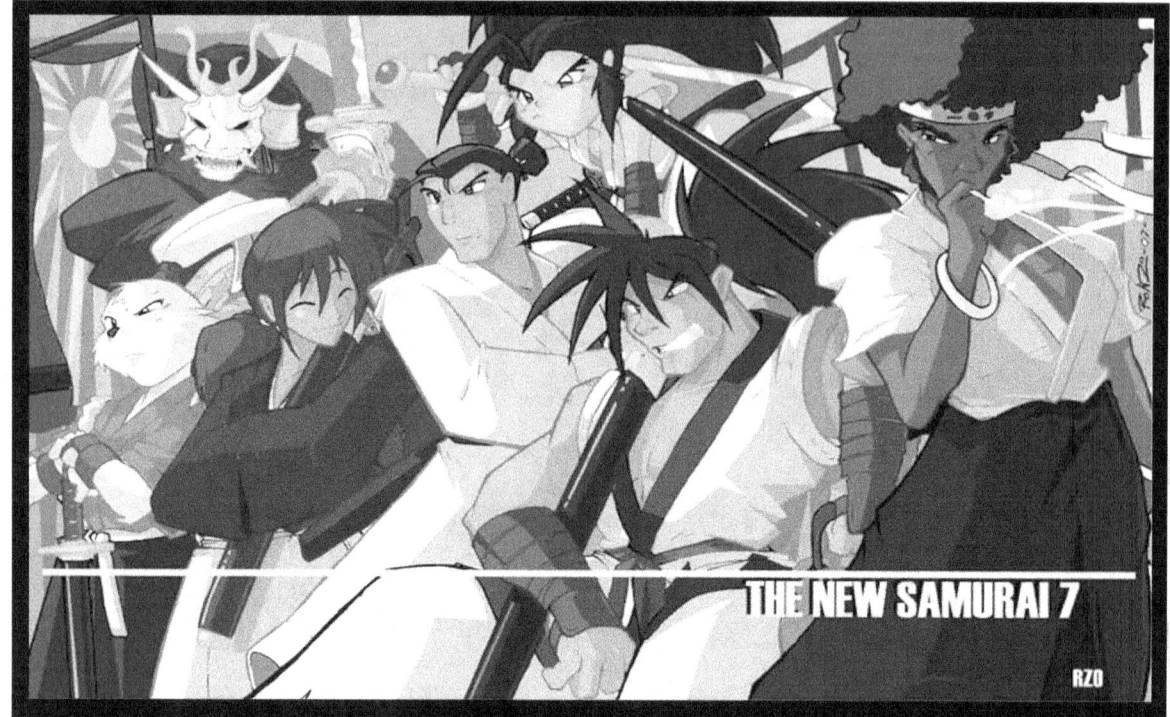

THE NEW SAMURAI 7

RZO

An all-star cast
that I designed to
be the new
7 Samurai.

Intress from the
cartoon Card game
"Chaotic" I was told
that I made her look
hotter than she looks
on the actual show.

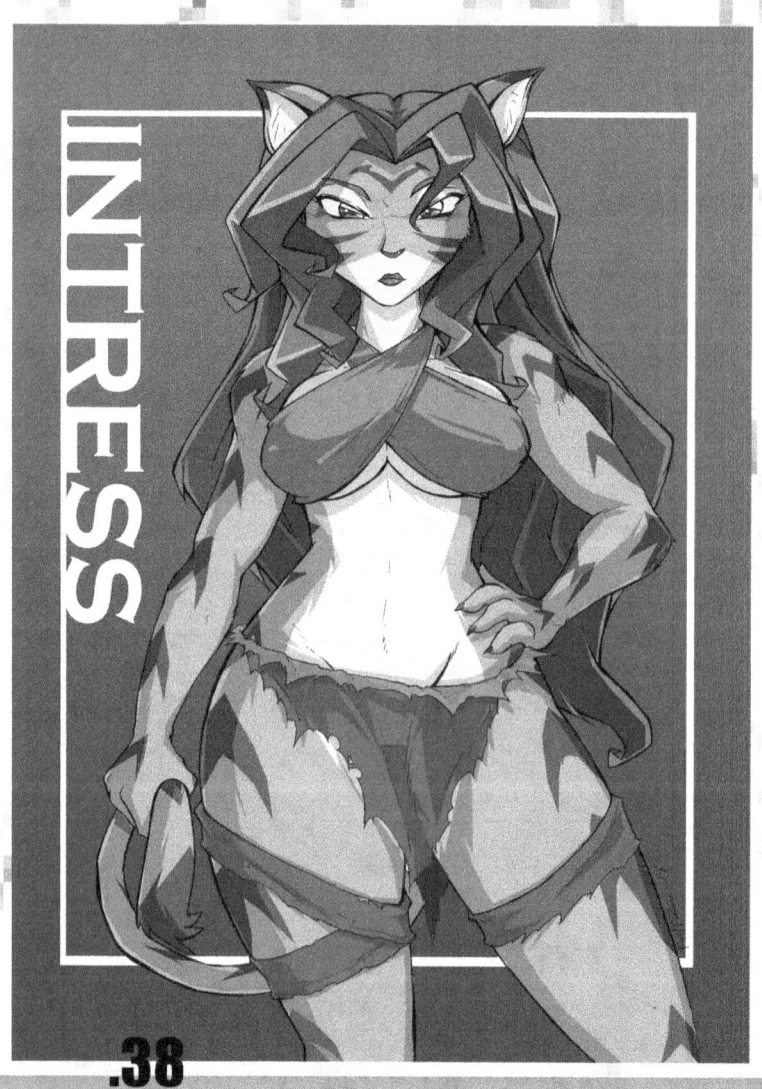

INTRESS

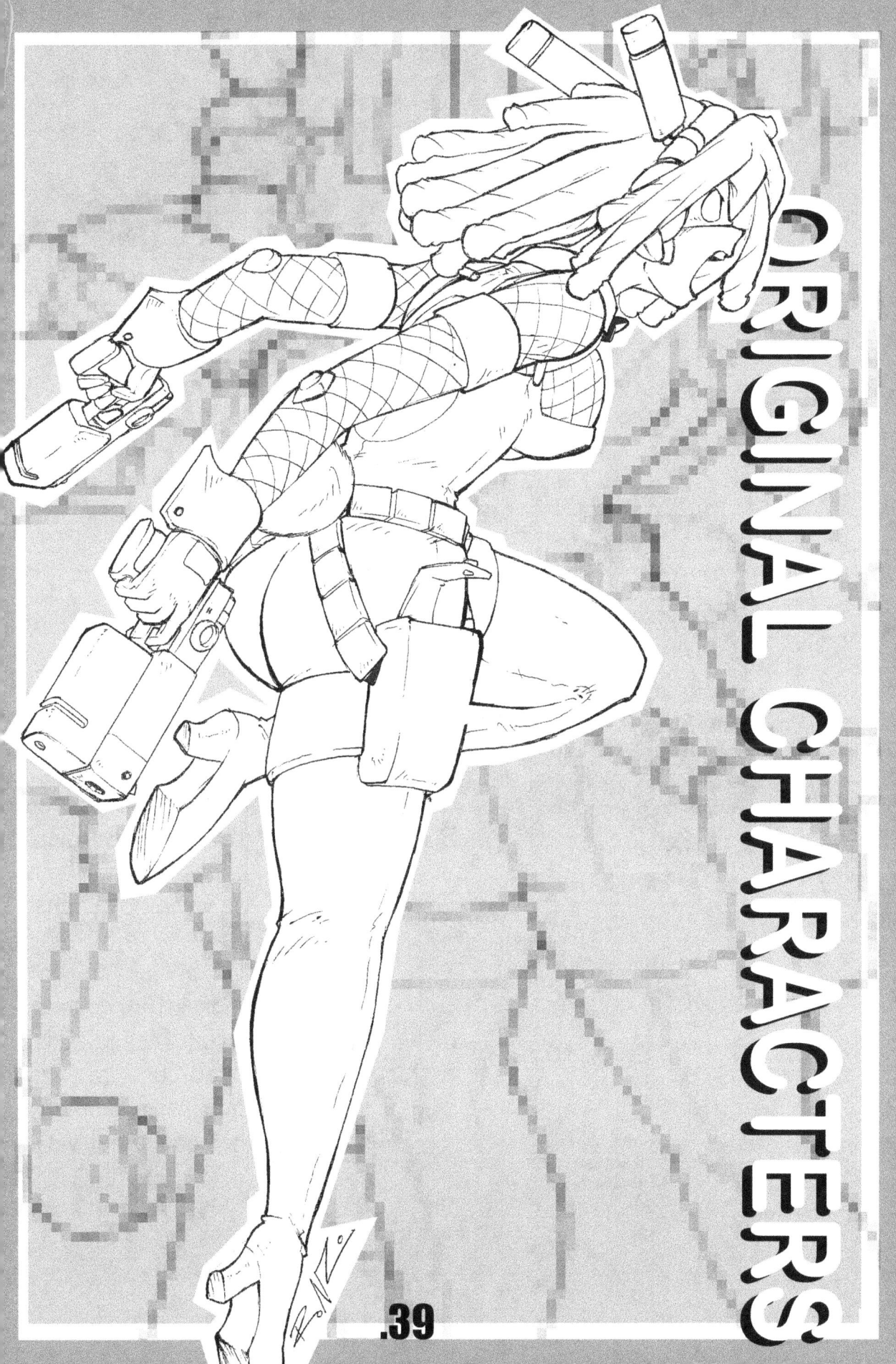

ORIGINAL CHARACTERS

.39

# Coco Gun-Bun

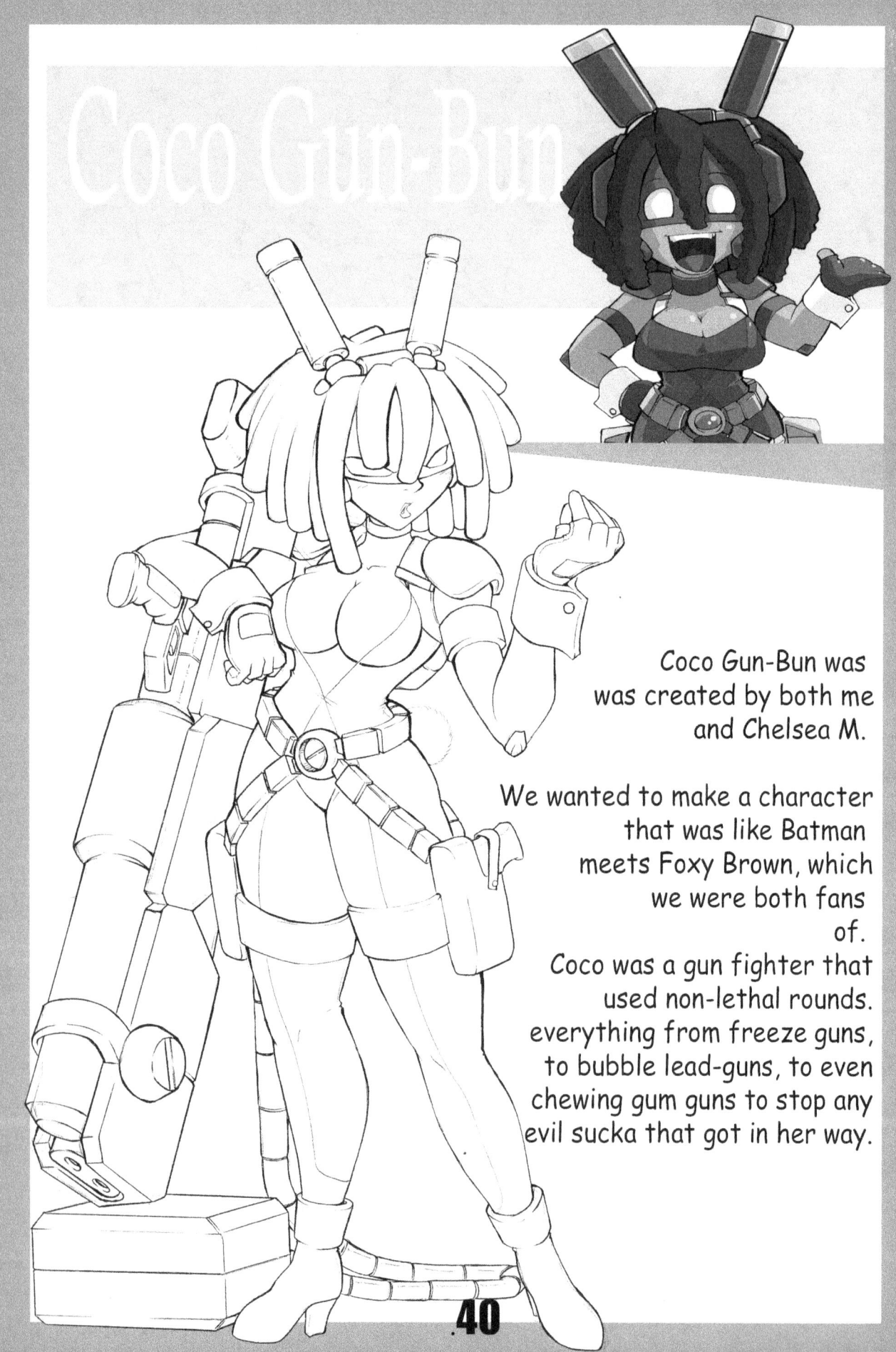

Coco Gun-Bun was was created by both me and Chelsea M.

We wanted to make a character that was like Batman meets Foxy Brown, which we were both fans of.
Coco was a gun fighter that used non-lethal rounds. everything from freeze guns, to bubble lead-guns, to even chewing gum guns to stop any evil sucka that got in her way.

**40**

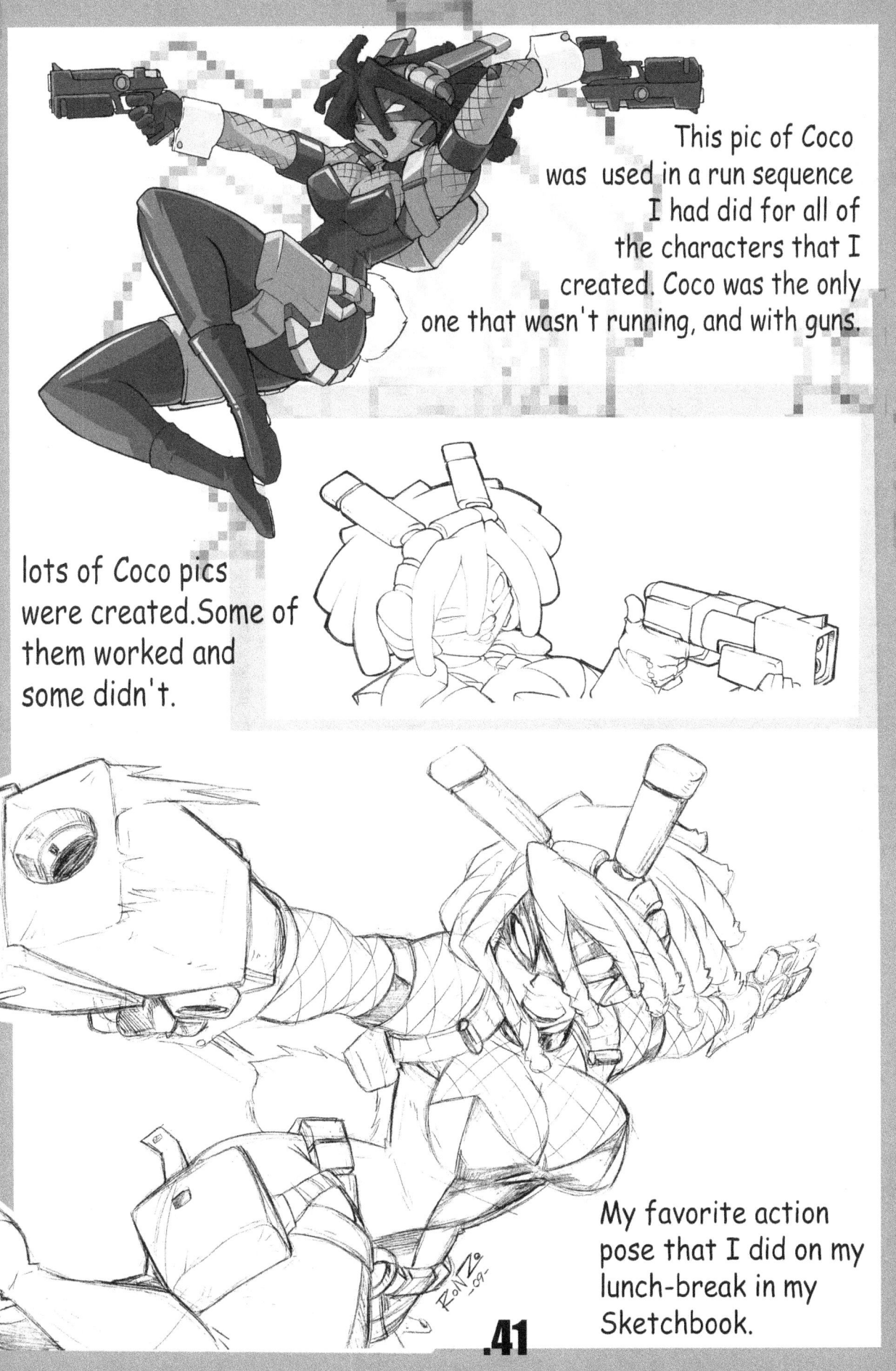

This pic of Coco was used in a run sequence I had did for all of the characters that I created. Coco was the only one that wasn't running, and with guns.

lots of Coco pics were created. Some of them worked and some didn't.

My favorite action pose that I did on my lunch-break in my Sketchbook.

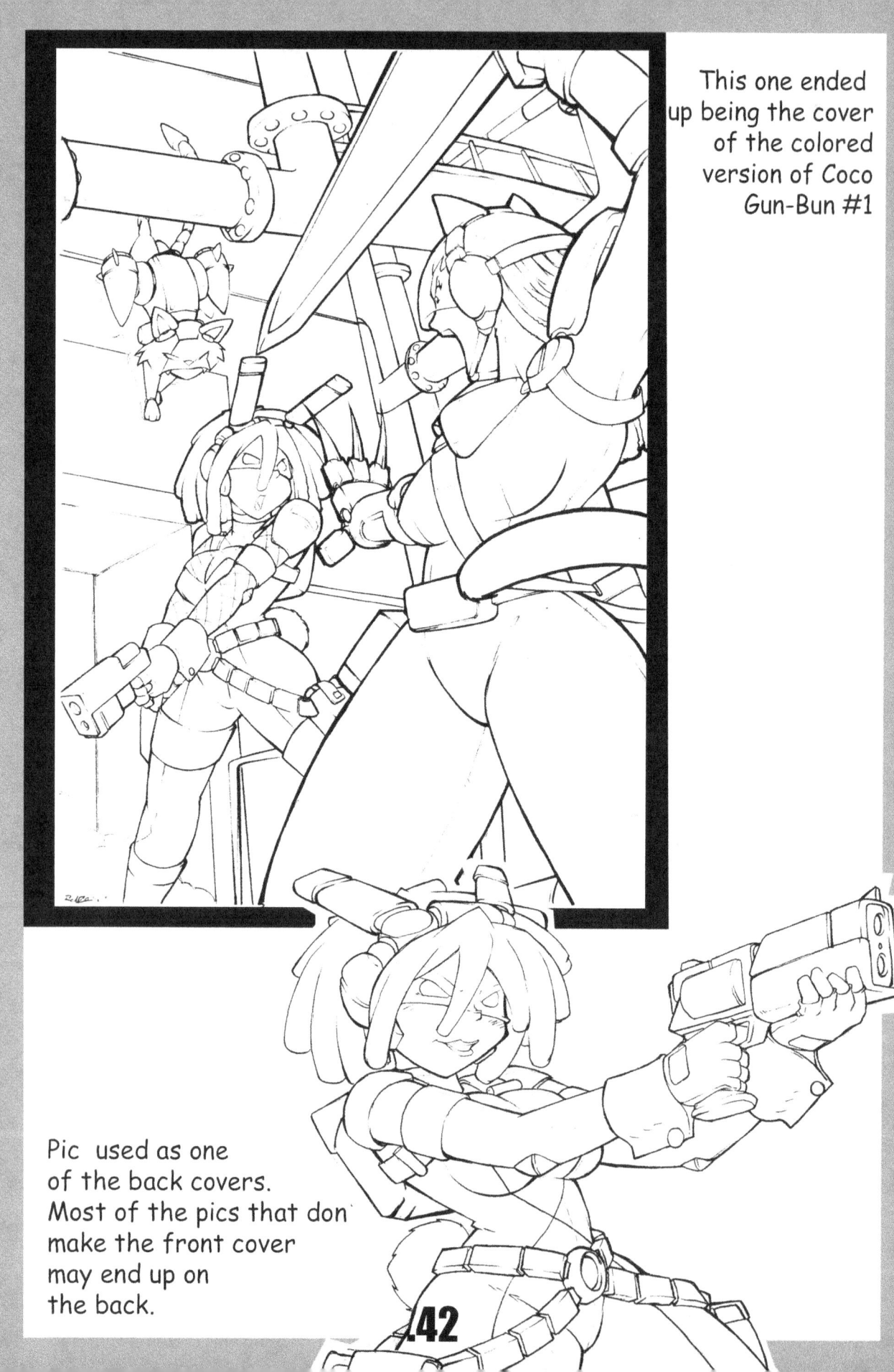

This one ended
up being the cover
of the colored
version of Coco
Gun-Bun #1

Pic used as one
of the back covers.
Most of the pics that don'
make the front cover
may end up on
the back.

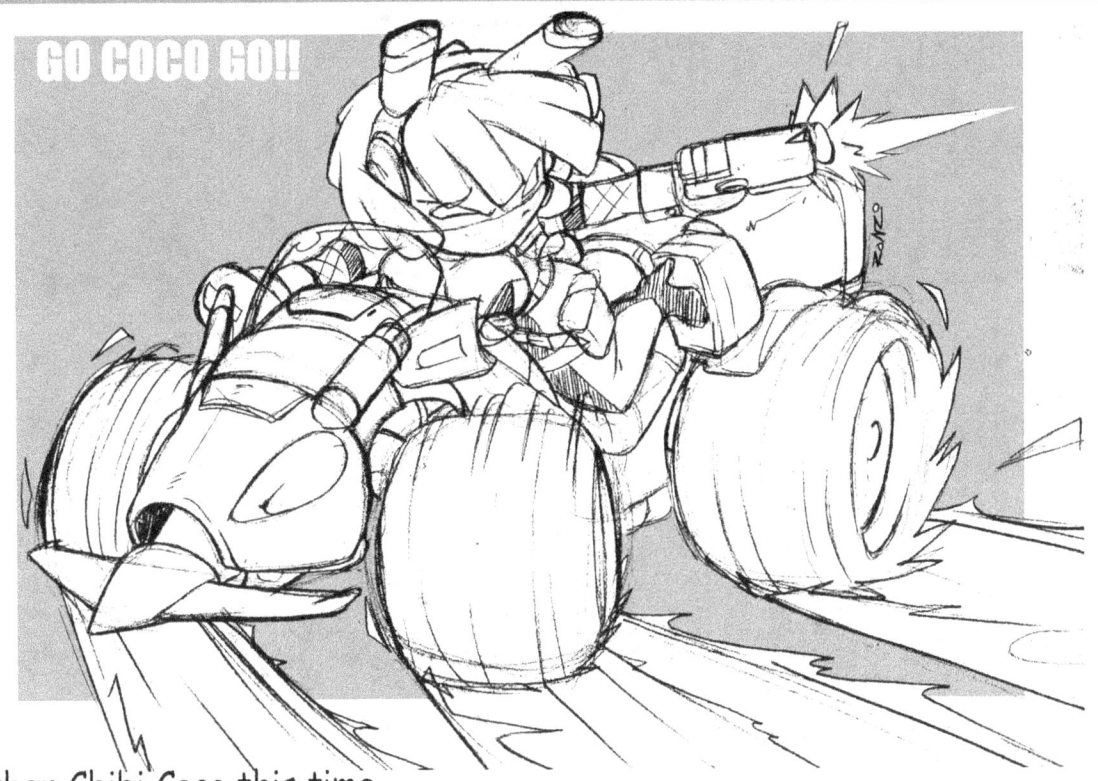

GO COCO GO!!

Another Chibi Coco this time on her four-wheeler. I never got around to giving the vehicle a name.

This was one of the Business card designs that I did like and got printed.

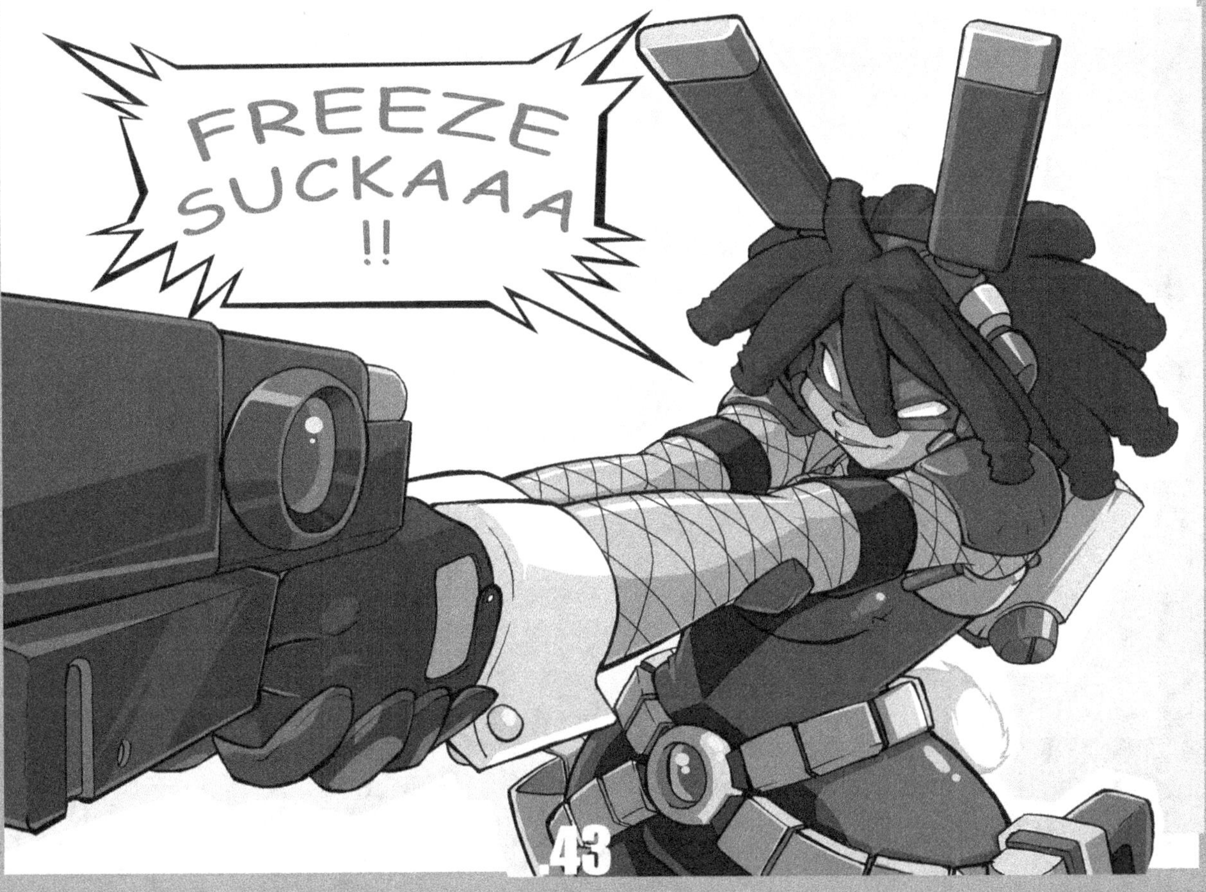

FREEZE SUCKAAA!!

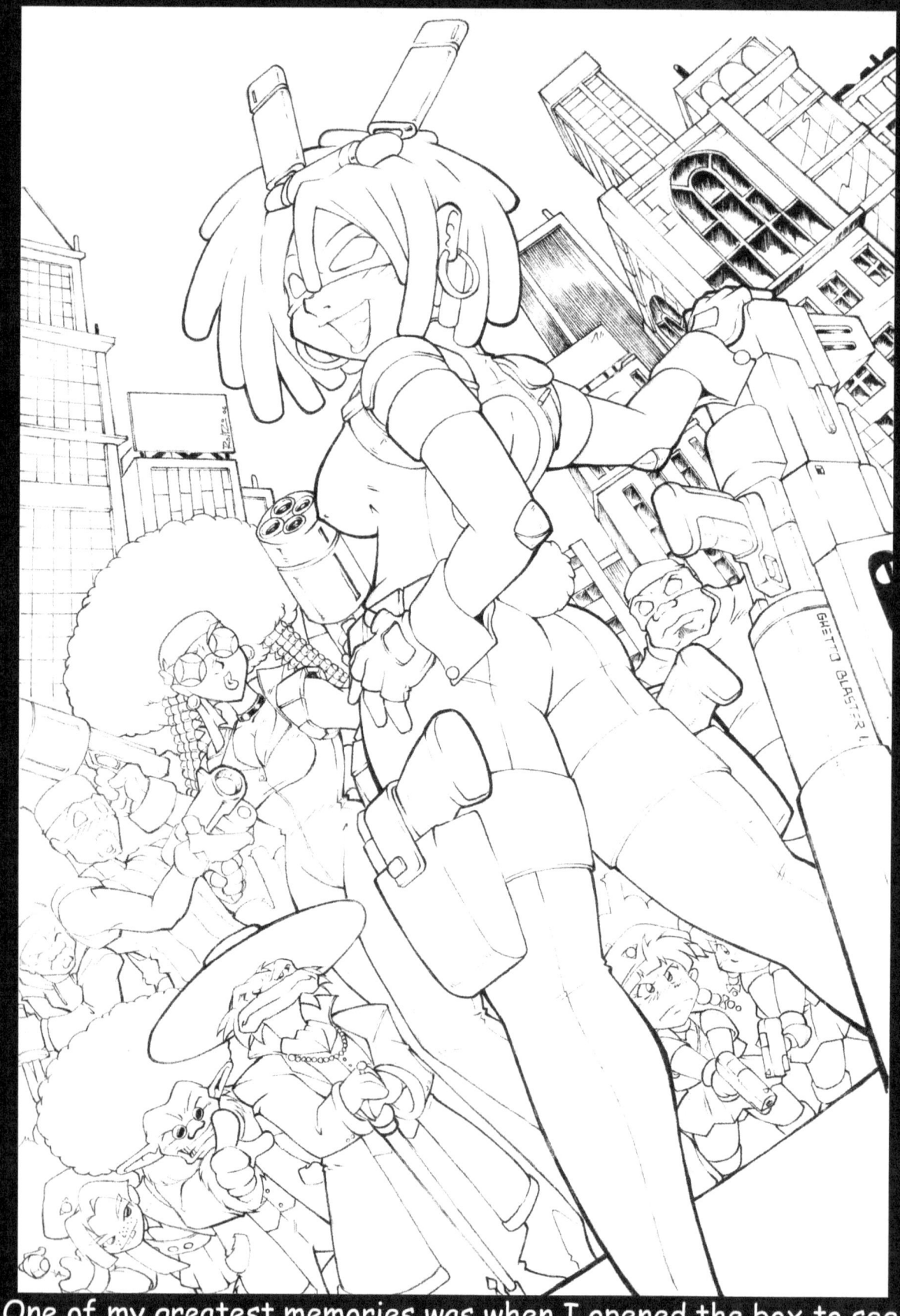

One of my greatest memories was when I opened the box to see this. The first copies of Coco Gun-Bun.

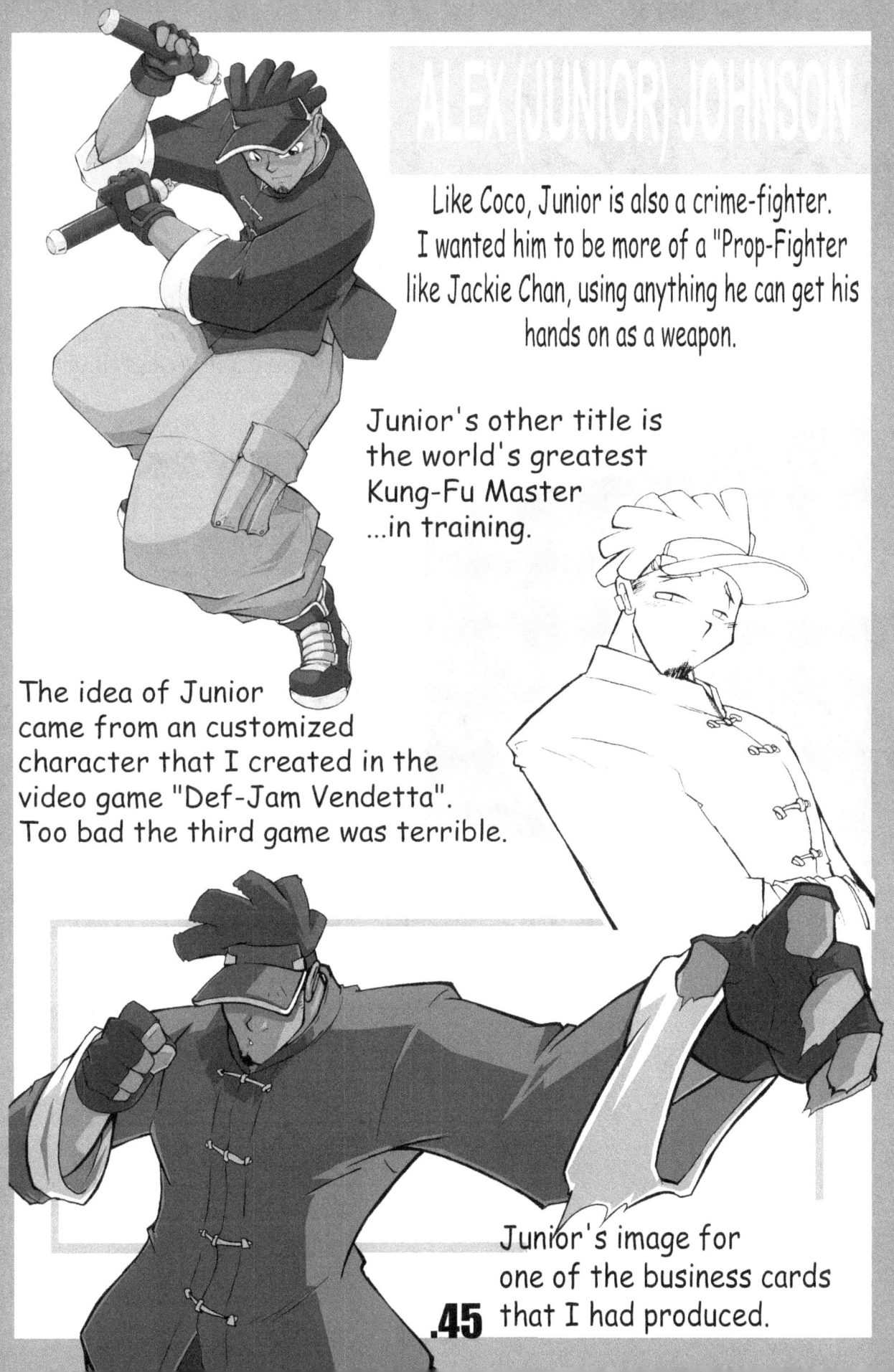

# ALEX (JUNIOR) JOHNSON

Like Coco, Junior is also a crime-fighter. I wanted him to be more of a "Prop-Fighter like Jackie Chan, using anything he can get his hands on as a weapon.

Junior's other title is the world's greatest Kung-Fu Master ...in training.

The idea of Junior came from an customized character that I created in the video game "Def-Jam Vendetta". Too bad the third game was terrible.

Junior's image for one of the business cards that I had produced.

.45

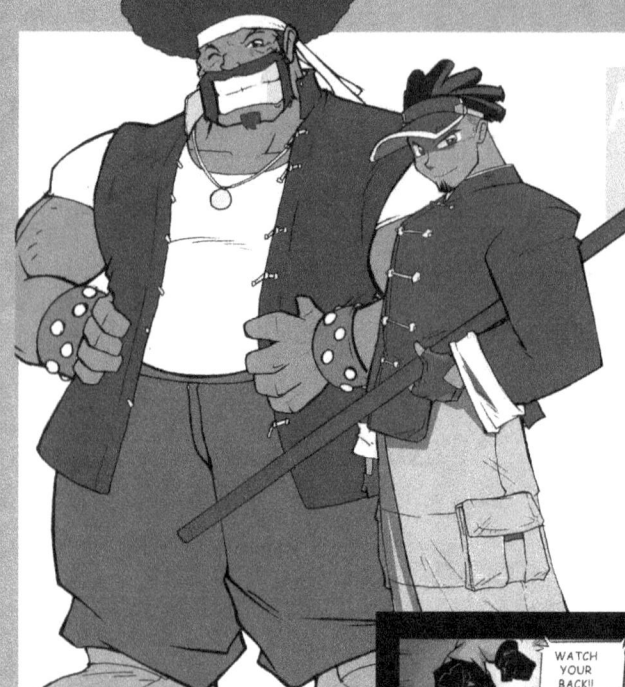

# ALEX (DRAGON-KICK) JOHNSON SR.

Like Father Like Son.
Alex (Dragon-Kick) Johnson is the father of Junior and is considered Neo-Metro city's greatest Kung-Fu master..back in the 70's and he is also a world-class rib-grilling champion.

His way of training his son is putting him right in the heart of danger, while he sits back and plays on his portable game system.

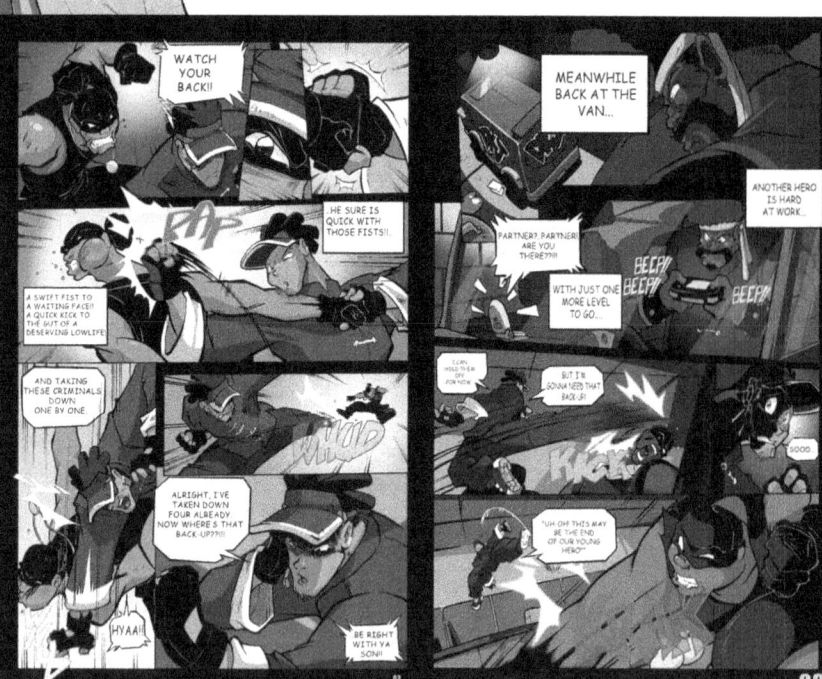

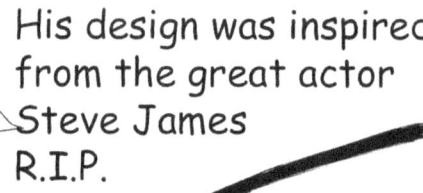

His design was inspired from the great actor Steve James R.I.P.

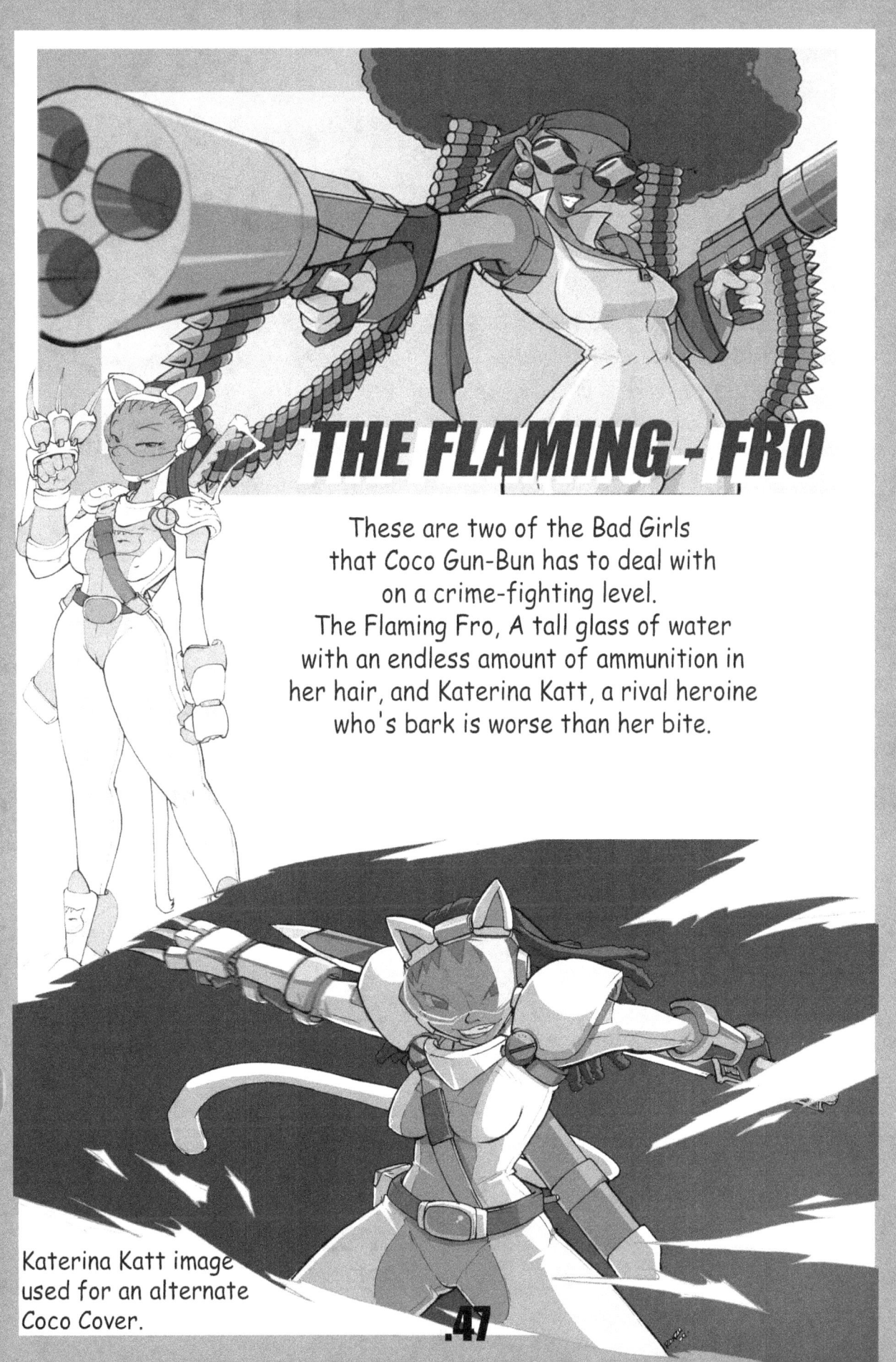

# THE FLAMING - FRO

These are two of the Bad Girls
that Coco Gun-Bun has to deal with
on a crime-fighting level.
The Flaming Fro, A tall glass of water
with an endless amount of ammunition in
her hair, and Katerina Katt, a rival heroine
who's bark is worse than her bite.

Katerina Katt image
used for an alternate
Coco Cover.

# Hula-Girl

The defender of Paradise, Hula-Gurl began as a silly concept super hero that I started to like to draw a lot. As time went on I never had a plot for her other than she would protect her island from evil-doers, and collect money from visitors on vacation on the island.

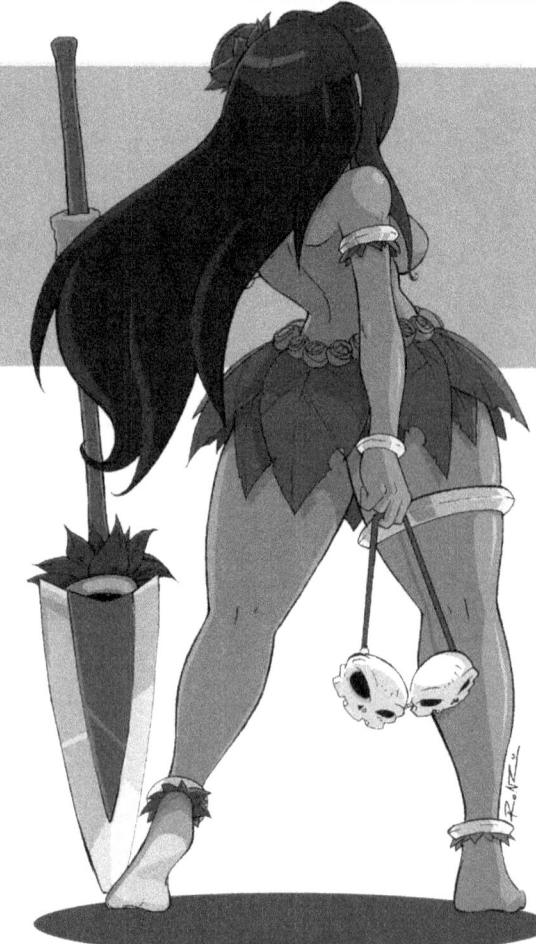

a sketch of Hula-Girl from one of my sketch books. Not all of the sketched that I do of her come out as good as this one.

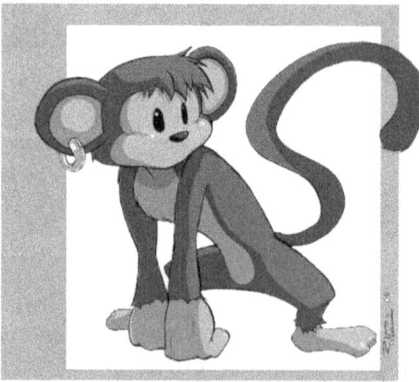

Hula-Girl's monkey sidekick, Hangtime.

This Hula-Girl sketch
was originally made
for the big run sequence
I made of all of the
characters that I created.
By the time I finished it
I was on to the next
pair of commissions.

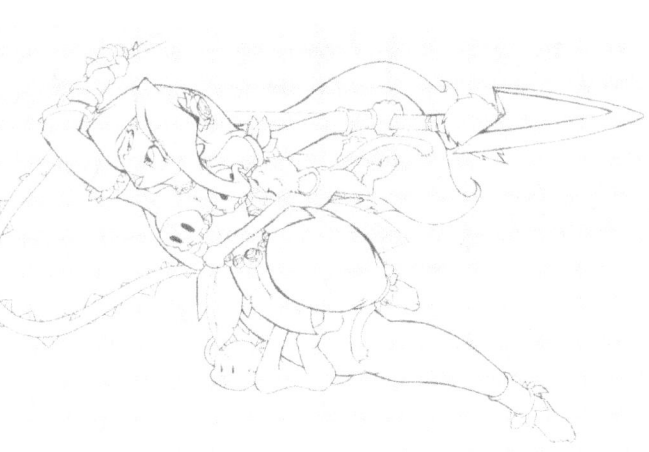

Bored Hula-Girl done on my Lunch break.

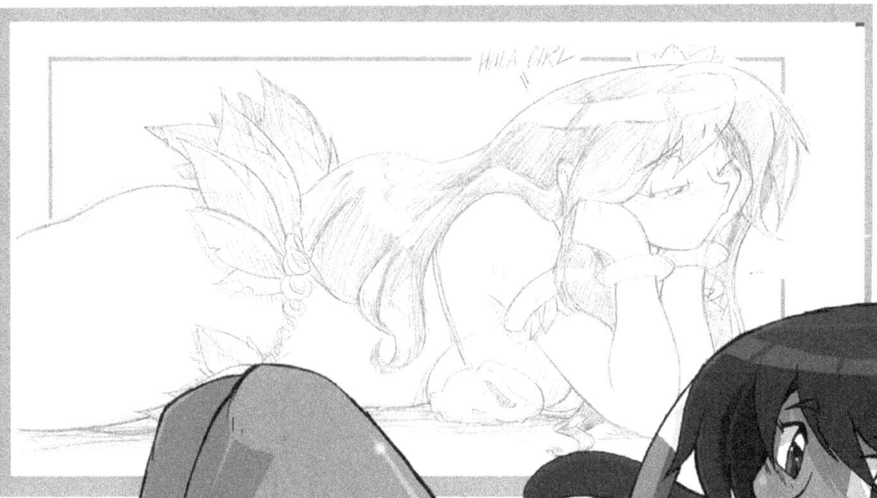

Poster Image
I did for a series
of cards I sold.
This is by far my
favorite.

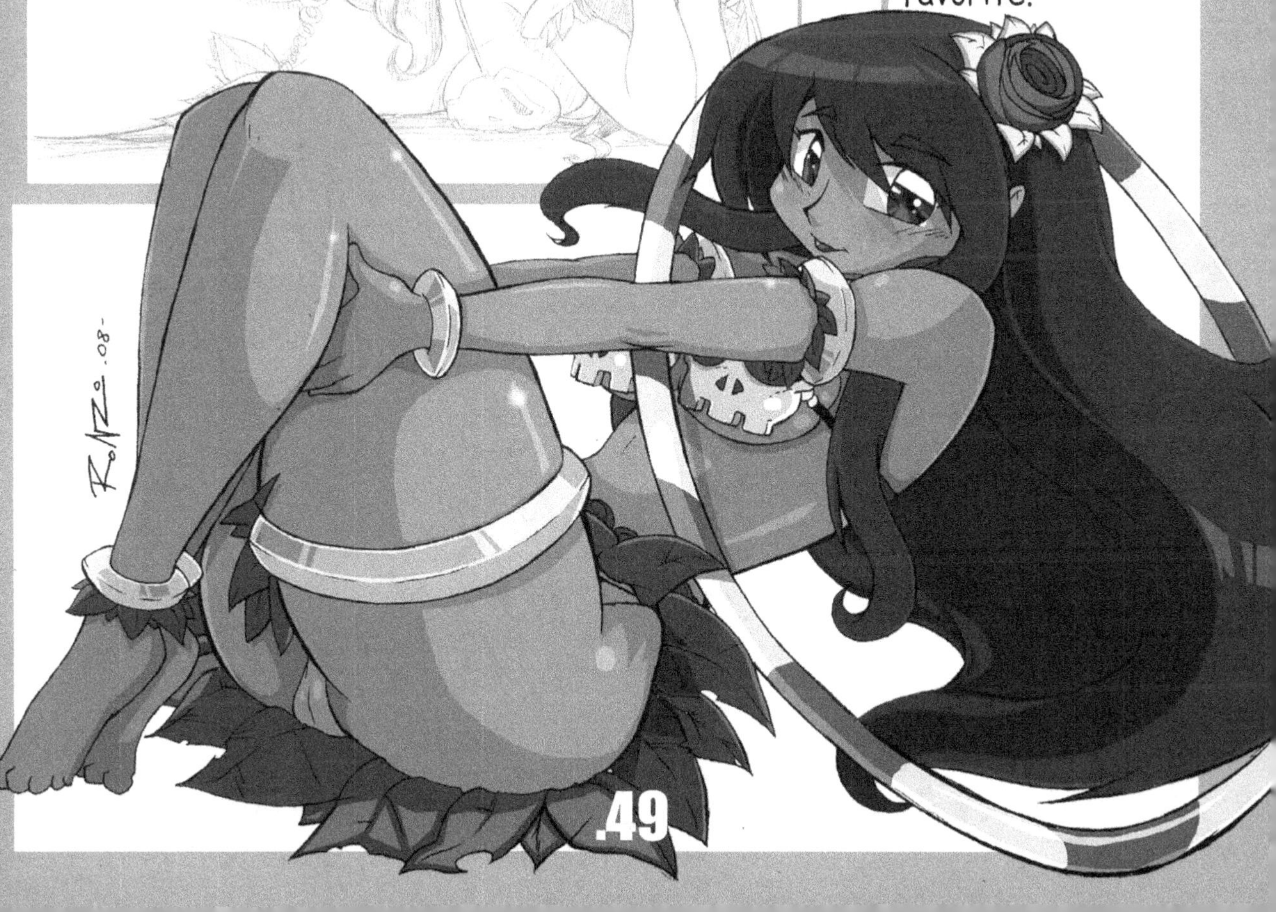

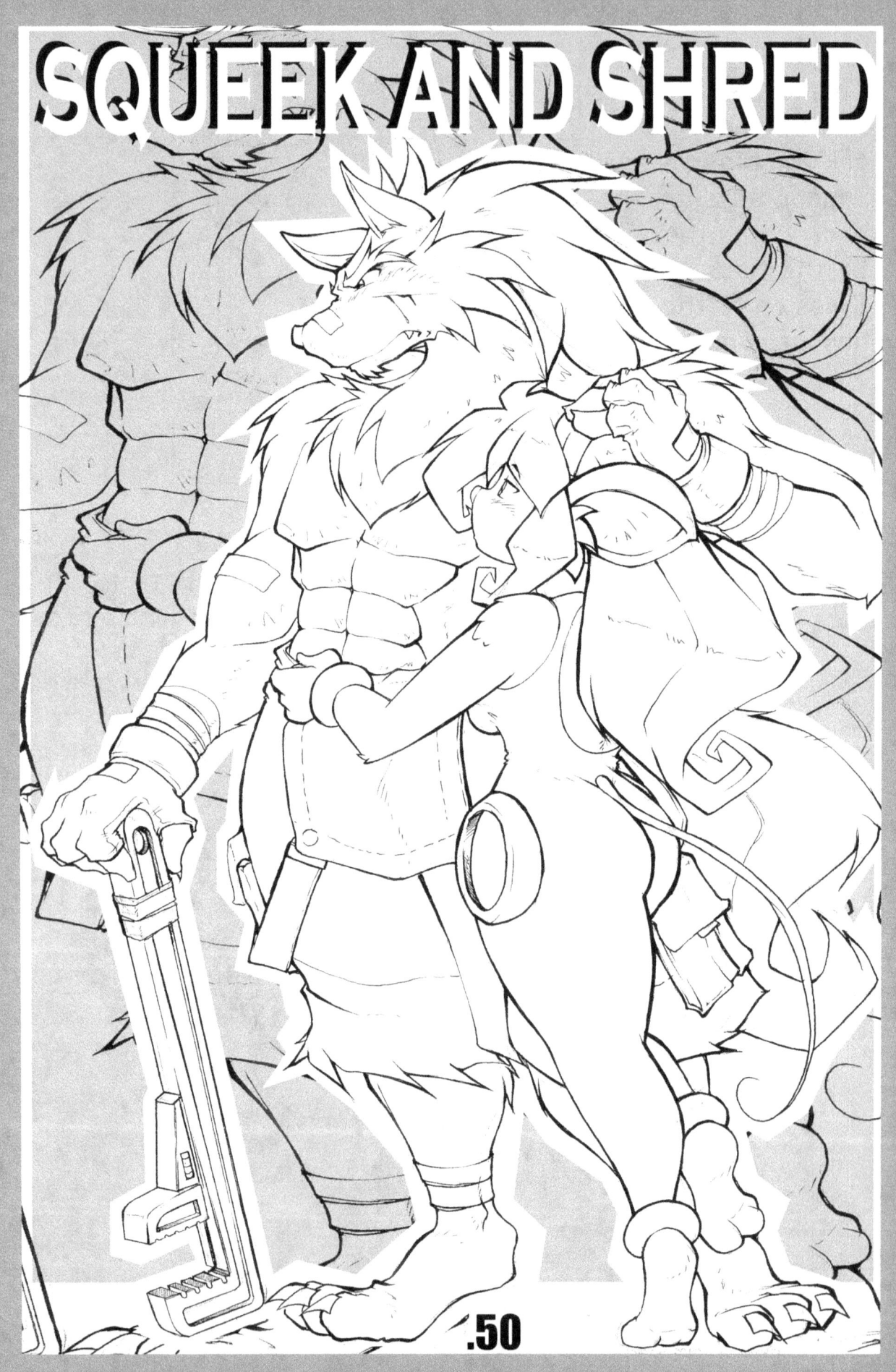

# SQUEEK AND SHRED

.50

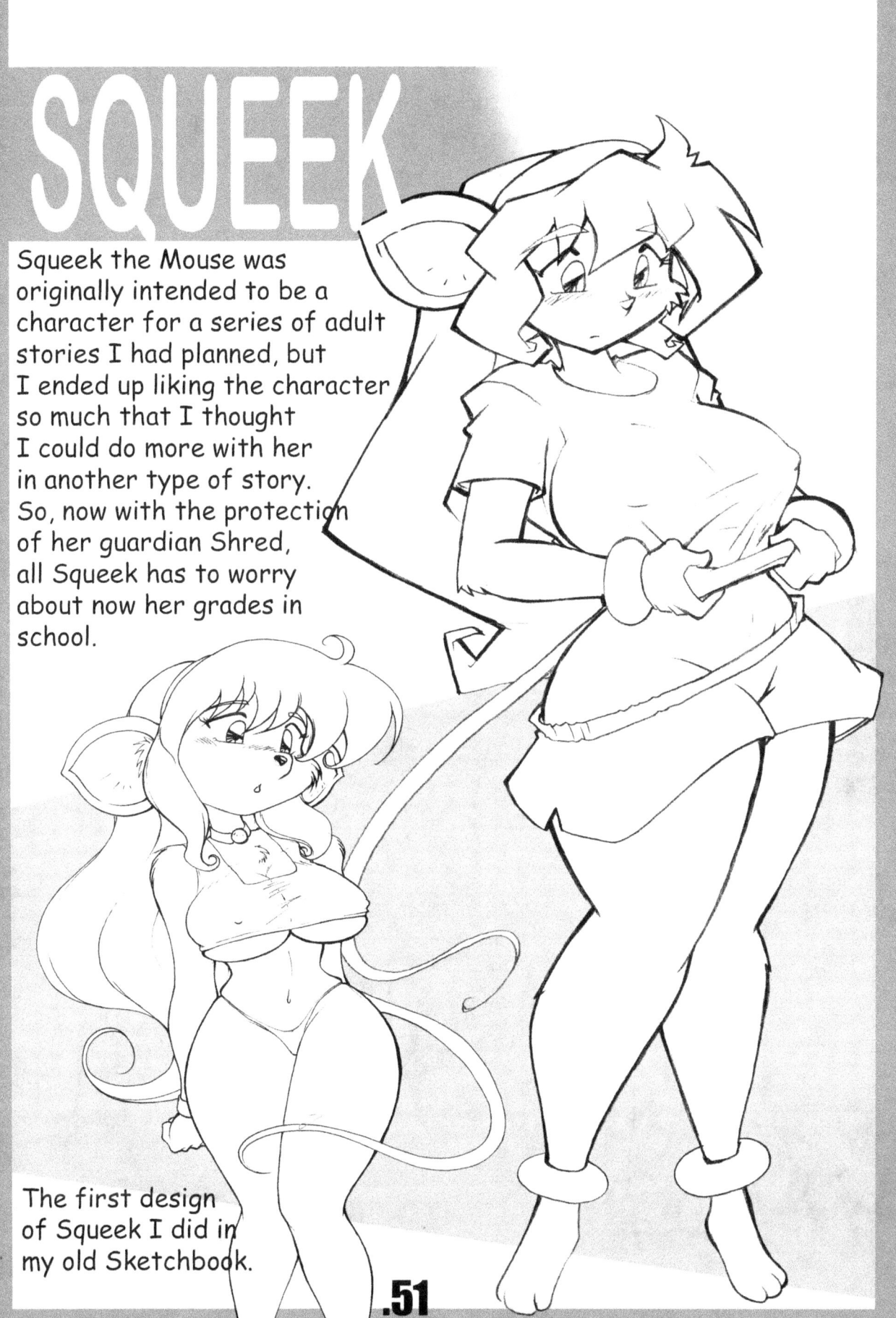

# SQUEEK

Squeek the Mouse was originally intended to be a character for a series of adult stories I had planned, but I ended up liking the character so much that I thought I could do more with her in another type of story. So, now with the protection of her guardian Shred, all Squeek has to worry about now her grades in school.

The first design of Squeek I did in my old Sketchbook.

.51

One of the questions that I
get the most about Squeek is why
I made her thighs so big.  I did this
to make her stick out from other
teenage mice with petite legs.

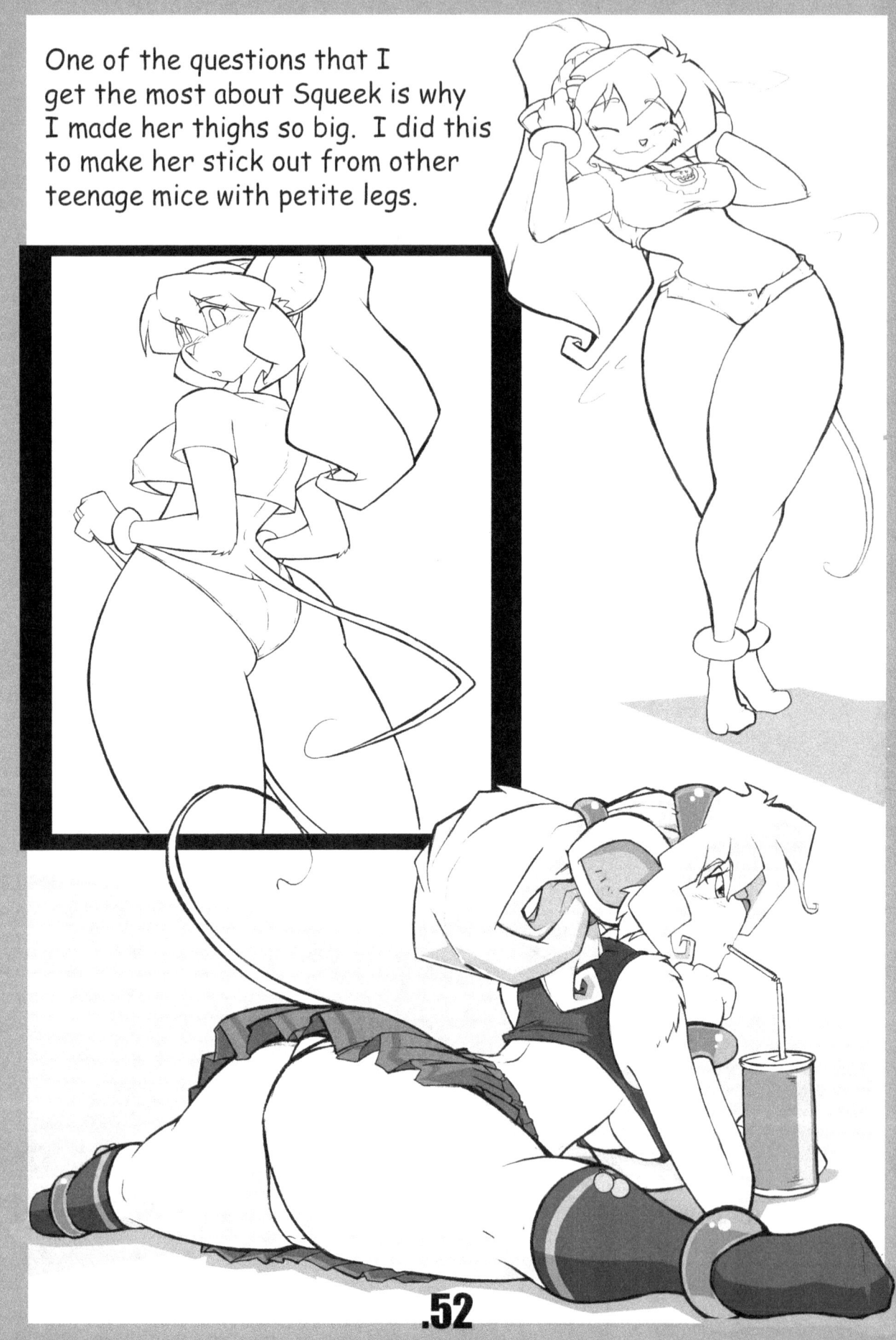

Over the years, I drew Squeek in various outfits. Some were back-burner ideas, while others were put into color and seen on some of the galleries that I have online.

Squeek in the white Dangermouse type outfit.

Savage cavegirl Squeek that never left the pages of my sketchbook.

Valkyrie Squeek.

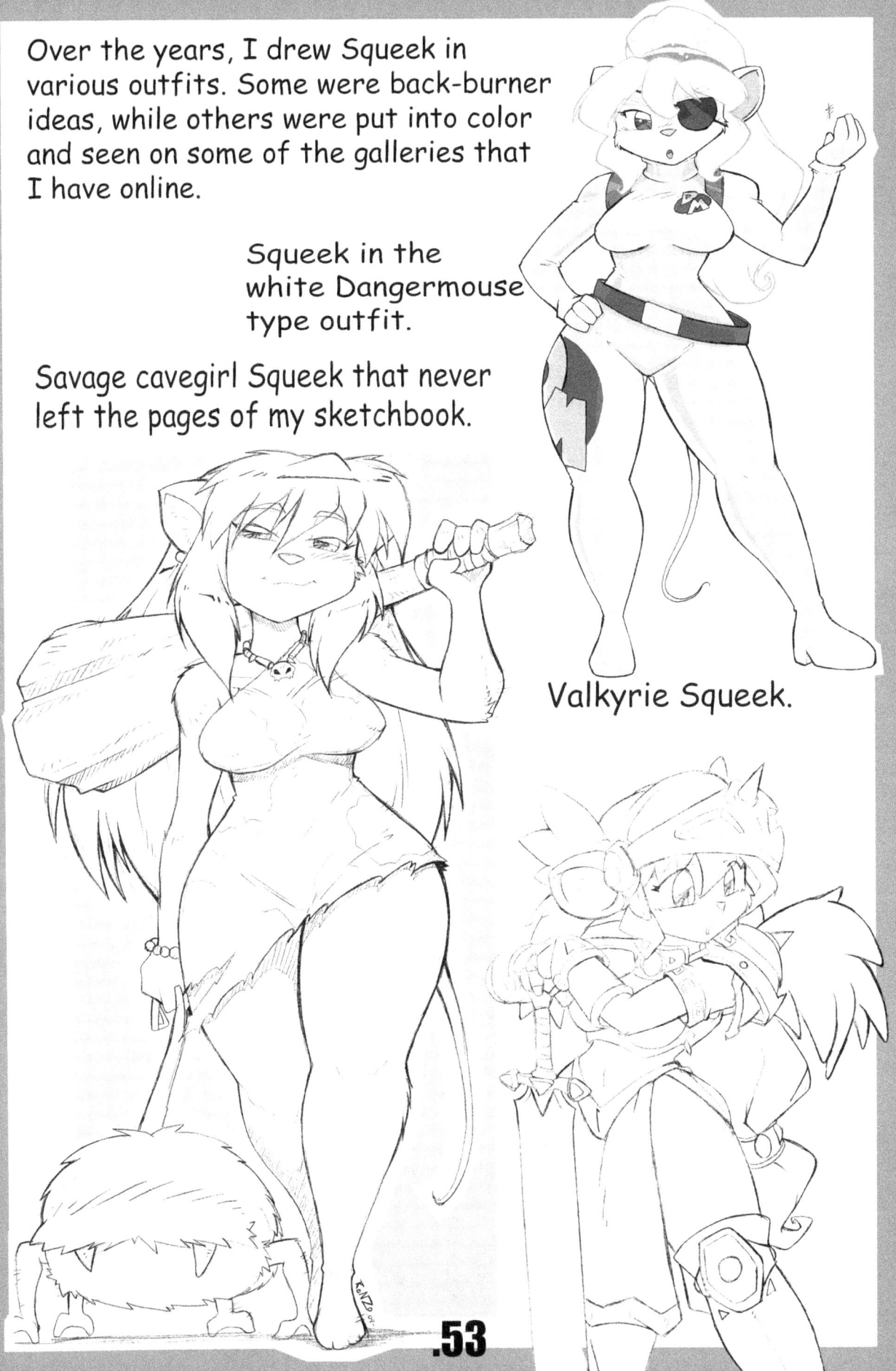

Squeek in the
Bill Raizer outfit
from NEO Contra.
At the time I was
obsessed with
beating that game
with an "S" ranking.
I eventually did.

Squeek in Shred's
original outfit looking
very bad-ass.

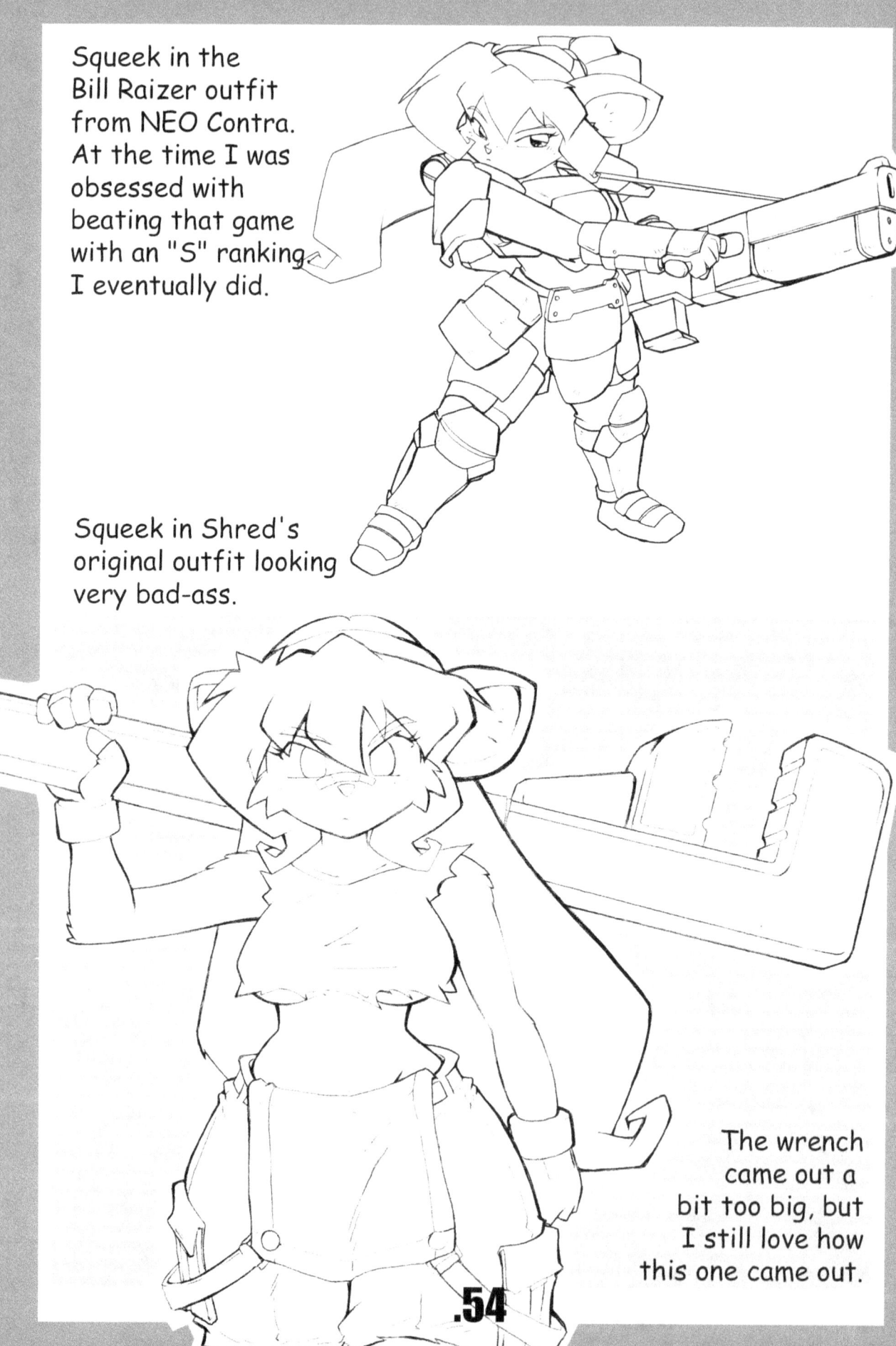

The wrench
came out a
bit too big, but
I still love how
this one came out.

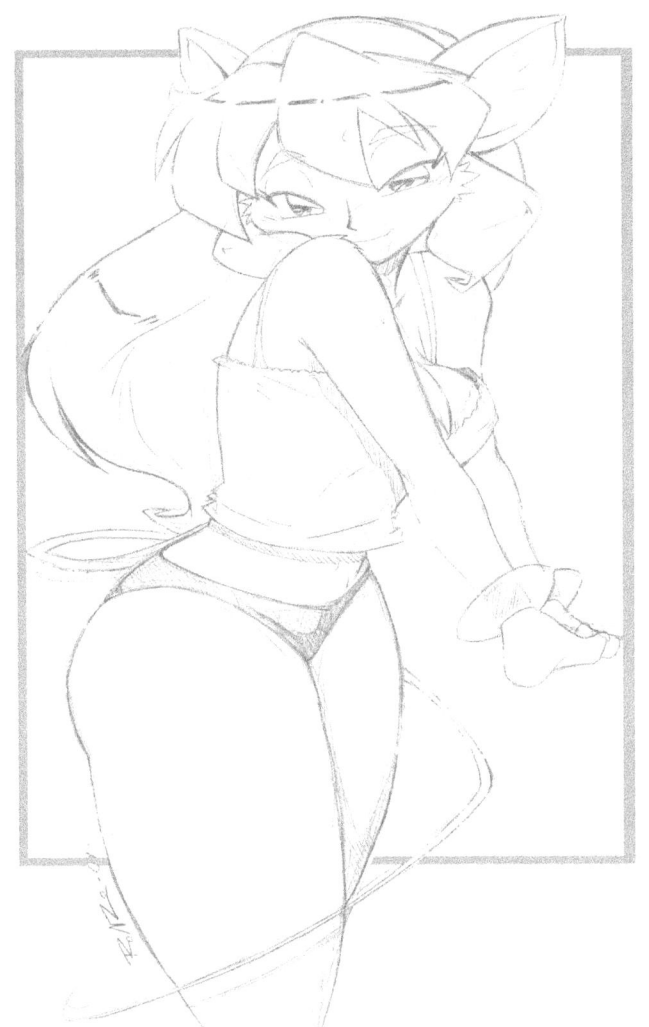

Drew this one in my sketch-book during a dry spell that I was having. It was intended to be inked and colored in. I never got around to doing it because of all of the commissions I had set up to do.

Squeek with Shred in their fighting Win stance.

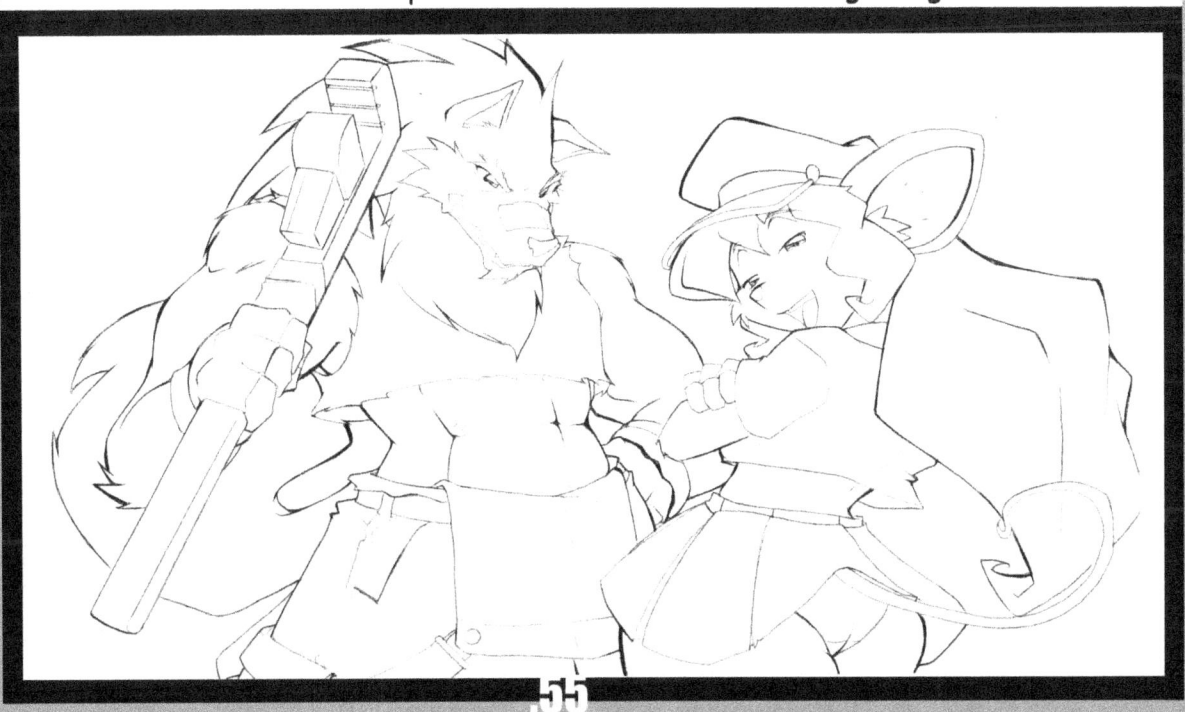

# SHRED

In the beginning, Shred the Wolf had it all. Money, Girls, and all of the beer that he could drink. Next he finds himself with no money, a beertab that is almost impossible to pay off. and to top it all off, he finds himself playing babysitter to a small blond mouse gets on his nerves.

Shred's was based in many of my favorite movie and video game personalities such as Terry Bogard, James Bond, John McClain (Die Hard), John Talbain, and Wade Garrett (Roadhouse).

Shred's occupation is to protect a mouse named Squeek from harm. His other occupation is Bouncer at a Bar called the "Brick-house" run by the now grown up three little pigs.

This is the first
official drawing that
I did of Shred the wolf.
This was going to be a design
for the back of one of
my leather jackets.
He was inspired from the Video
game "Dark Stalker's fighter named Gallon
I did not think at the time that
I would go as far as I
have with a character like this.

An unused pic of Shred
with his favorite weapon,
a large wrentch.

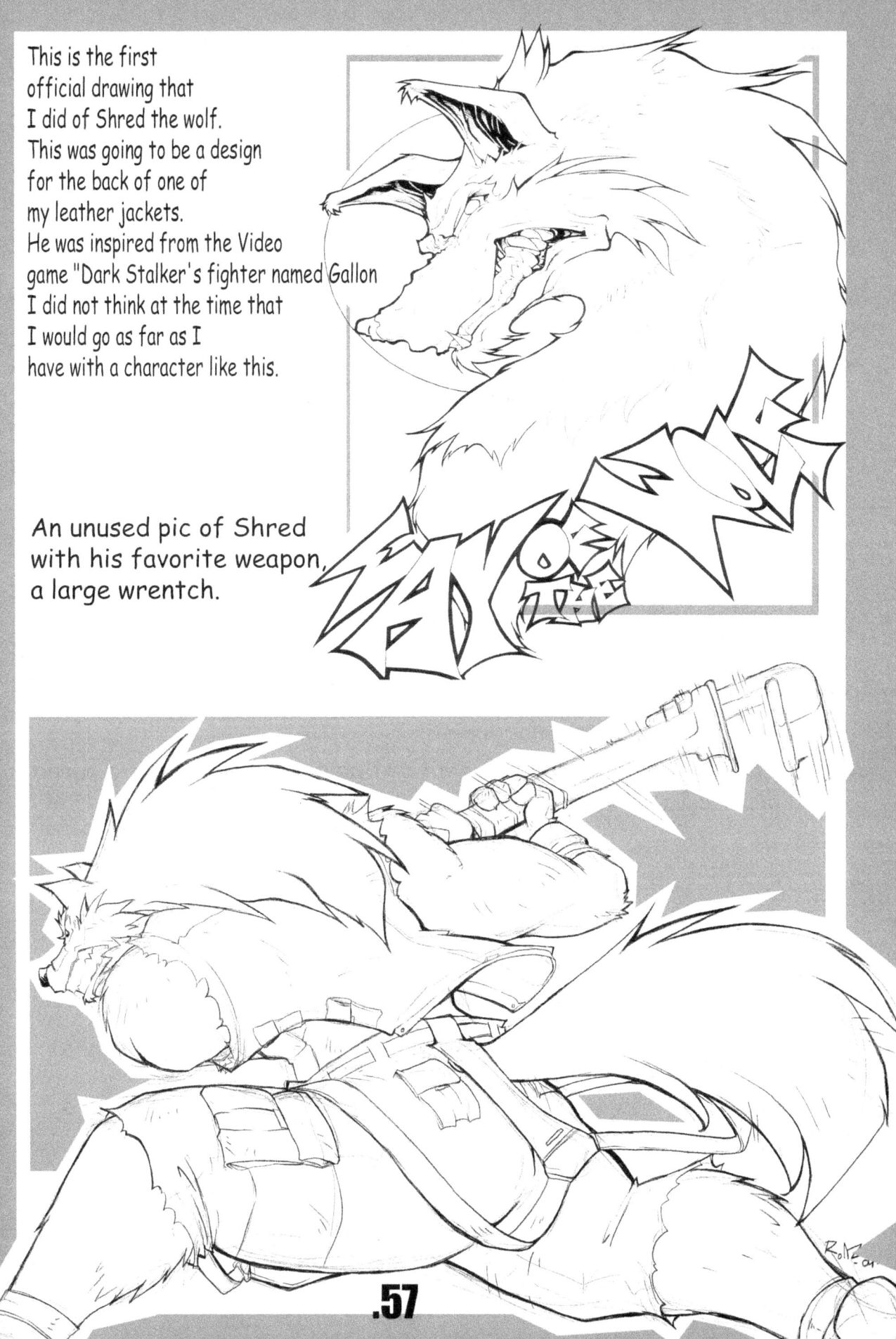

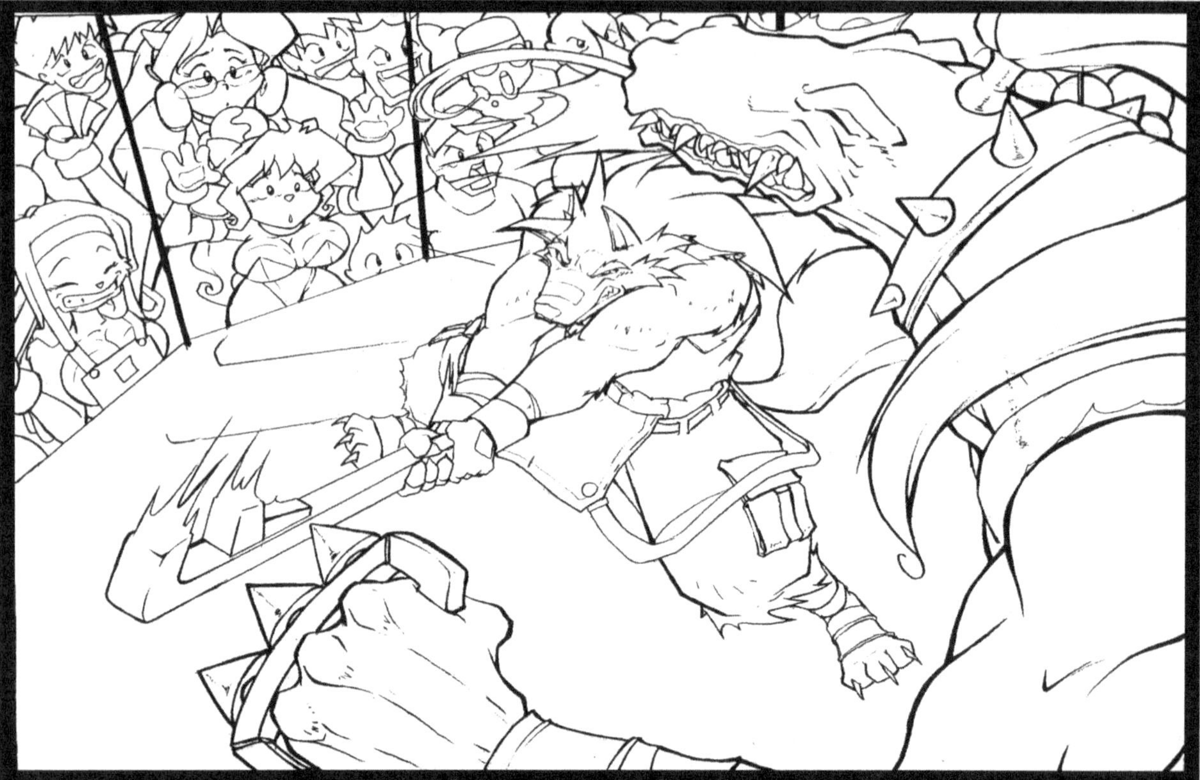

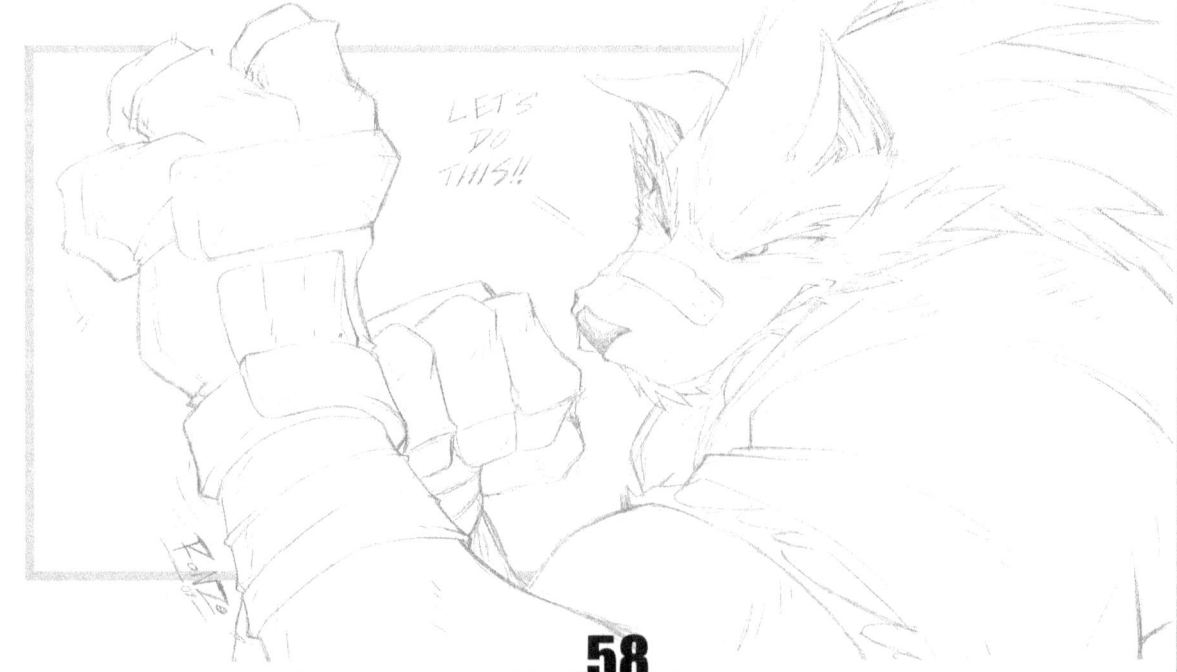

Shred the wolf in an anything goes full-weapon cage fight that was never fully colored in because of lack of time. The design of the cage was to be added in after the pic was colored. Might not happen now.

A lunchtime sketch of Shred  in a fighting pose. The pose is a parody of a picture I saw in a fighting game book called "Fatal-Fury".

LET'S
DO
THIS!!

Not all of Shred's encounters with the opposite sex are successful. Take these series of pics. Like his encounter with Jessica Rabbit.

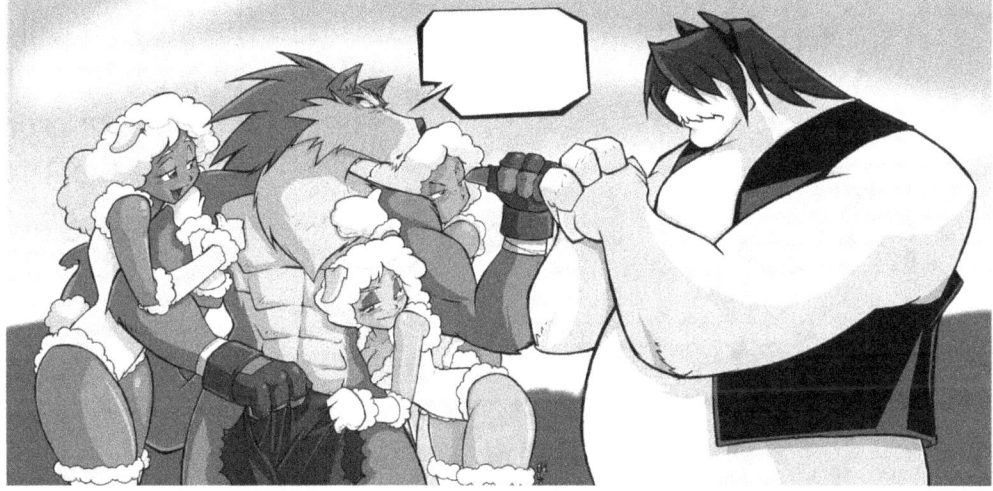

Or the famous sheep herder, Sam the Sheep-Dog.

Shred also finds out never to mess with a queen bee that has a honey crazed bear on her side.

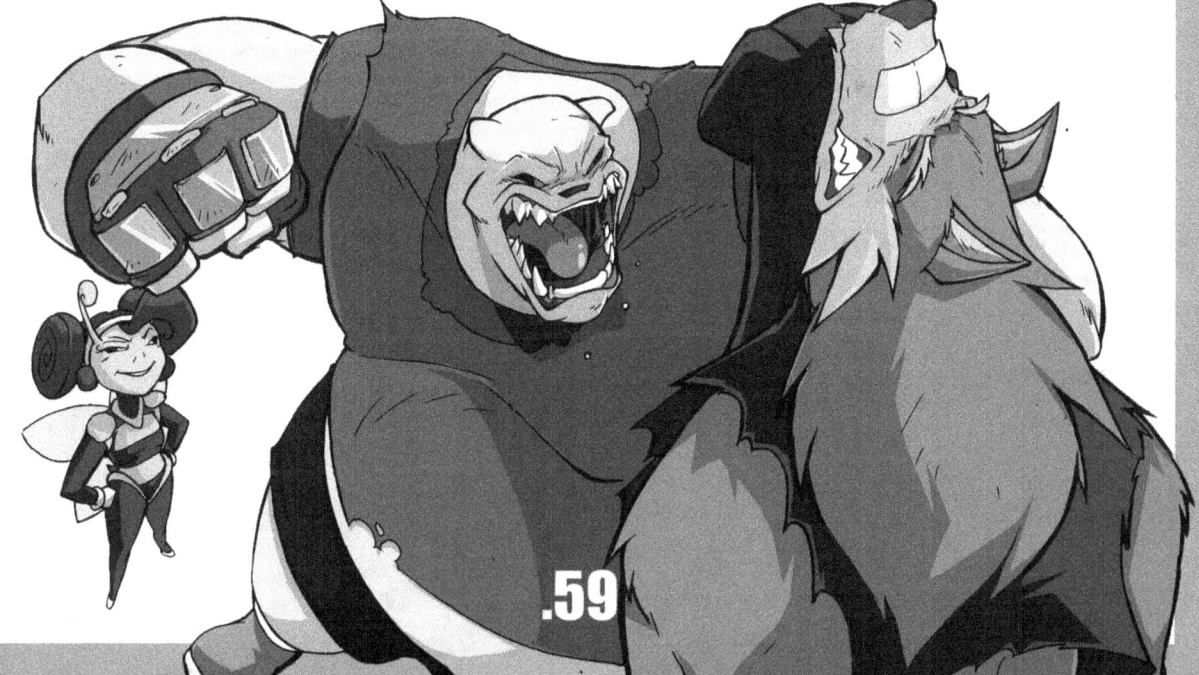

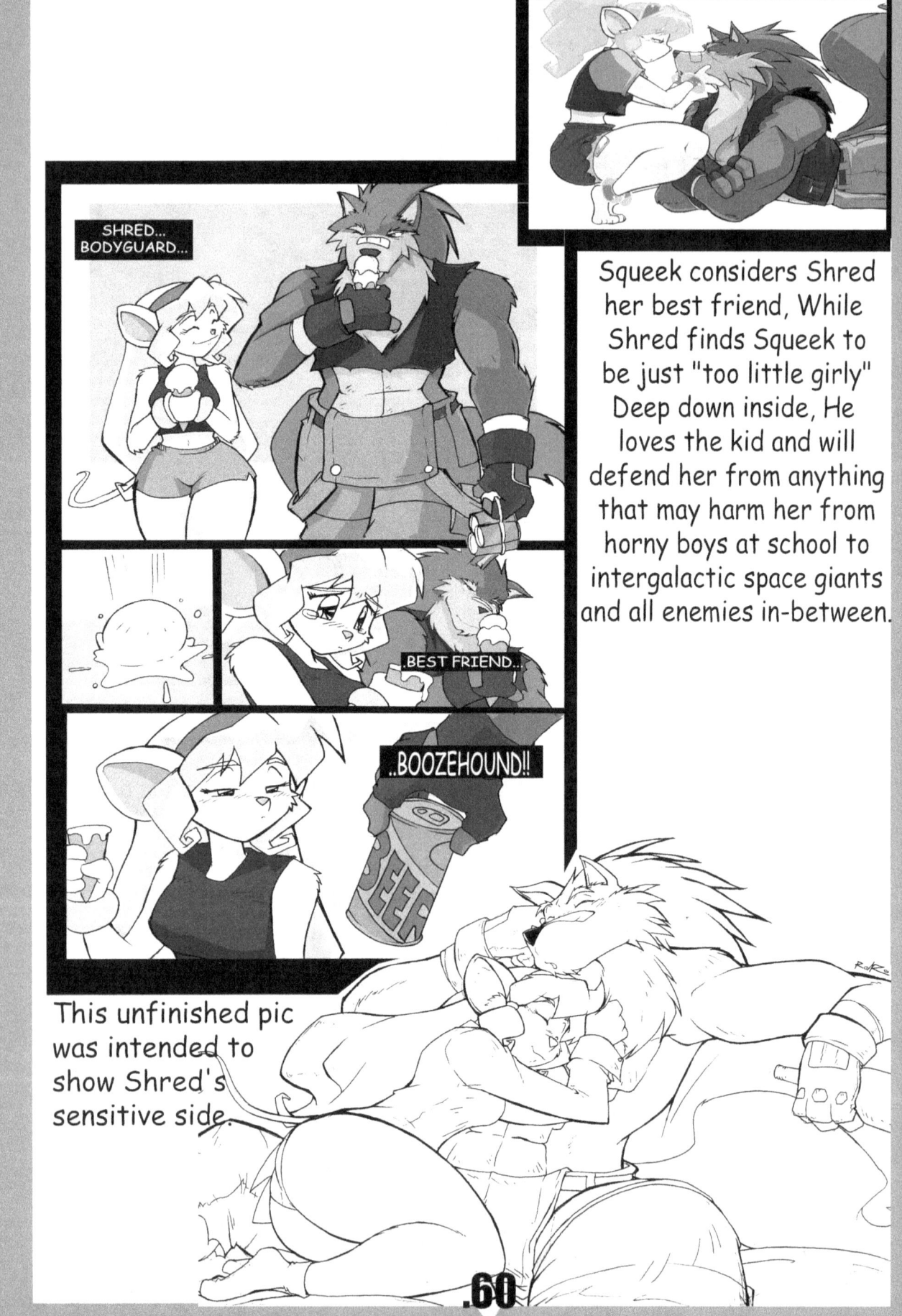

SHRED... BODYGUARD...

..BEST FRIEND...

..BOOZEHOUND!!

BEER

Squeek considers Shred her best friend, While Shred finds Squeek to be just "too little girly" Deep down inside, He loves the kid and will defend her from anything that may harm her from horny boys at school to intergalactic space giants and all enemies in-between.

This unfinished pic was intended to show Shred's sensitive side.

# FRIZZY

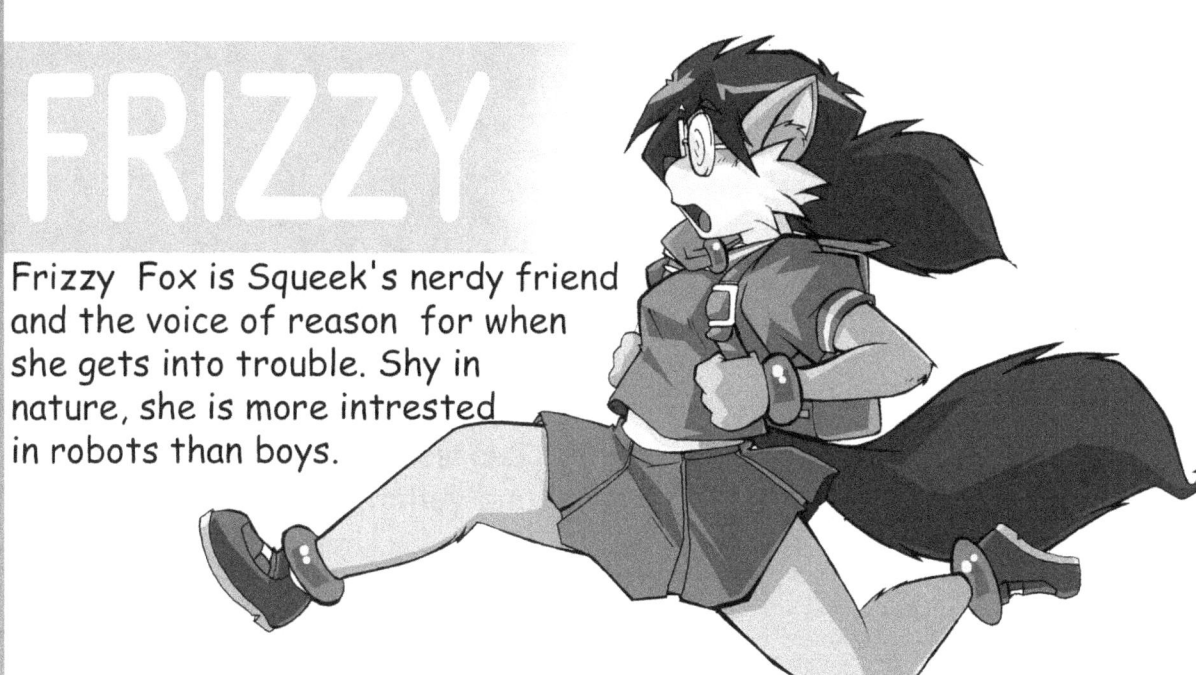

Frizzy Fox is Squeek's nerdy friend and the voice of reason for when she gets into trouble. Shy in nature, she is more intrested in robots than boys.

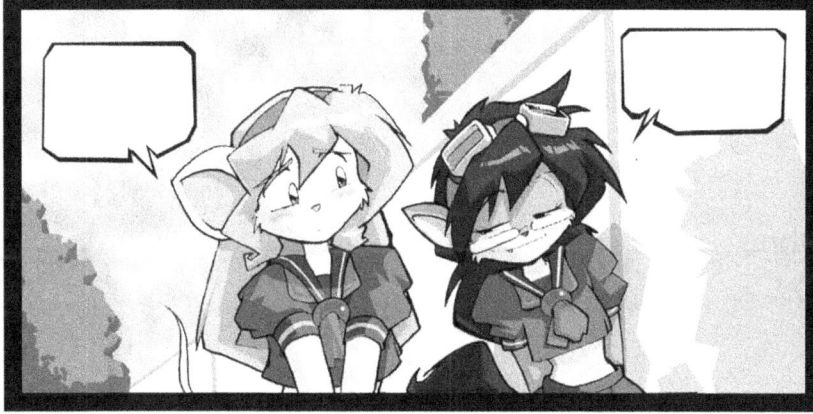

For the original look for Frizzy, I gave her small glasses and goggles, later I decieded to take out the goggles and give her the thick bifocals look insted.

Frizzy dressed like Penfold from the Dangermouse cartoon. In the original pic, she was staring at a bomb.

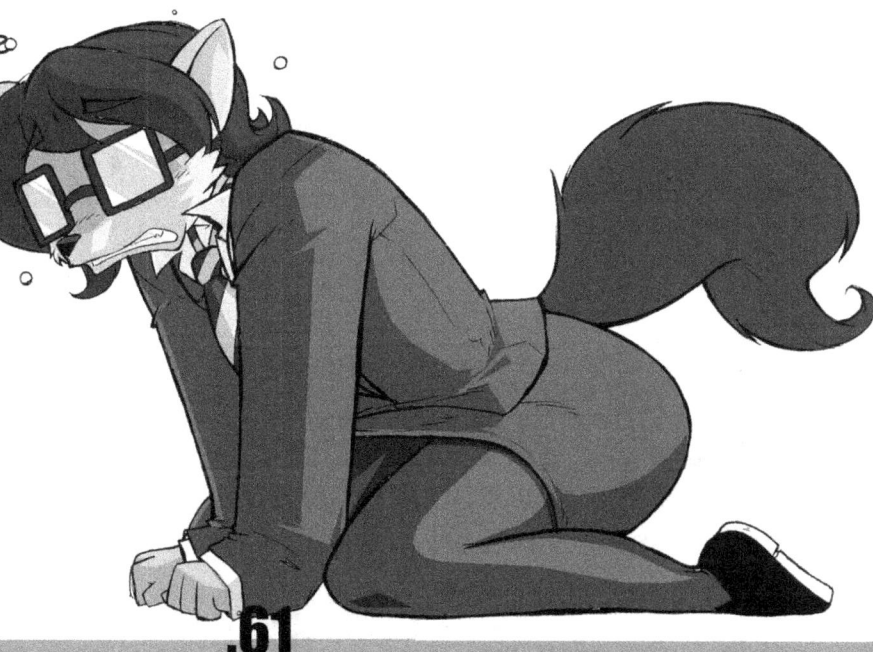

# Lenora-Pig

The oldest of the three not so little pigs and the most aggressive. She likes to argue and yell at people while serving them drinks.

I wanted to put some of my characters in evening outfits and this is the one I did for Lenora.

Lenora sketch I did while I was at a lounge in D.C.

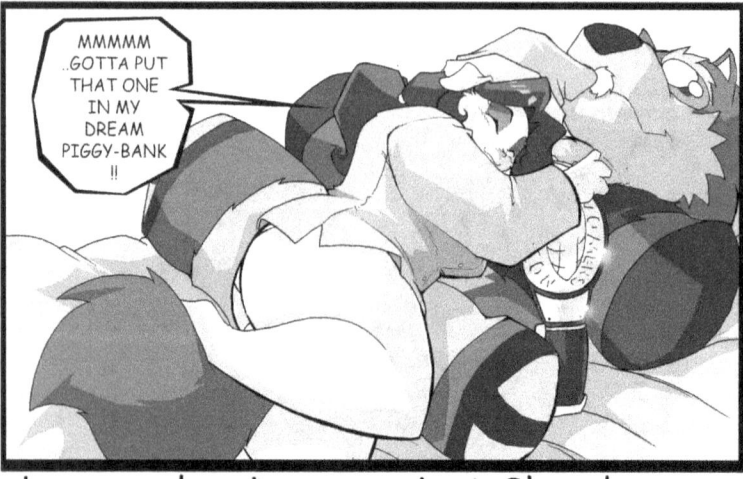

MMMMM ..GOTTA PUT THAT ONE IN MY DREAM PIGGY-BANK !!

Lenora sleeping on a giant Shred doll. I think someone has a secret crush on a certain wolf.

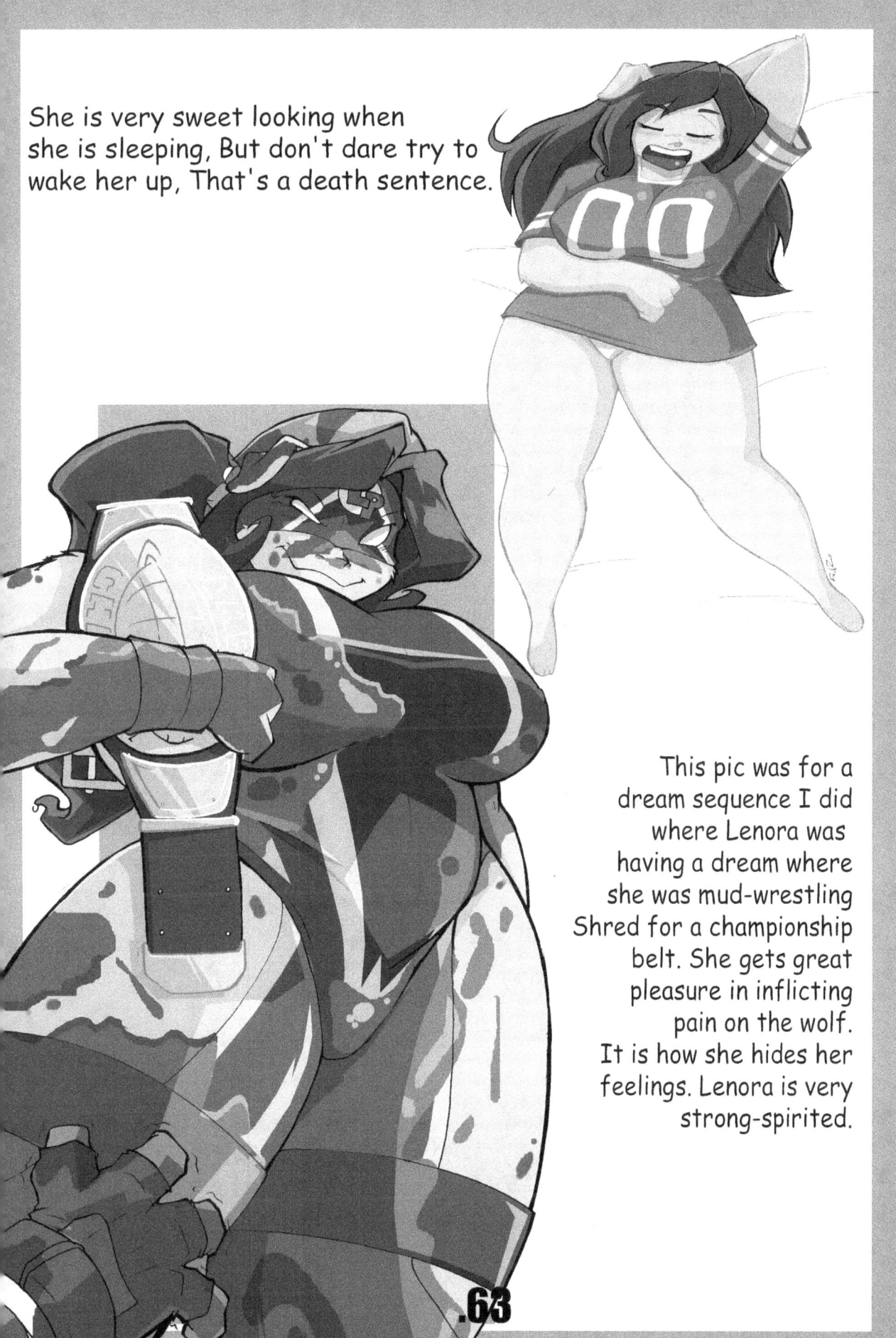

She is very sweet looking when she is sleeping, But don't dare try to wake her up, That's a death sentence.

This pic was for a dream sequence I did where Lenora was having a dream where she was mud-wrestling Shred for a championship belt. She gets great pleasure in inflicting pain on the wolf. It is how she hides her feelings. Lenora is very strong-spirited.

# VICTORIA

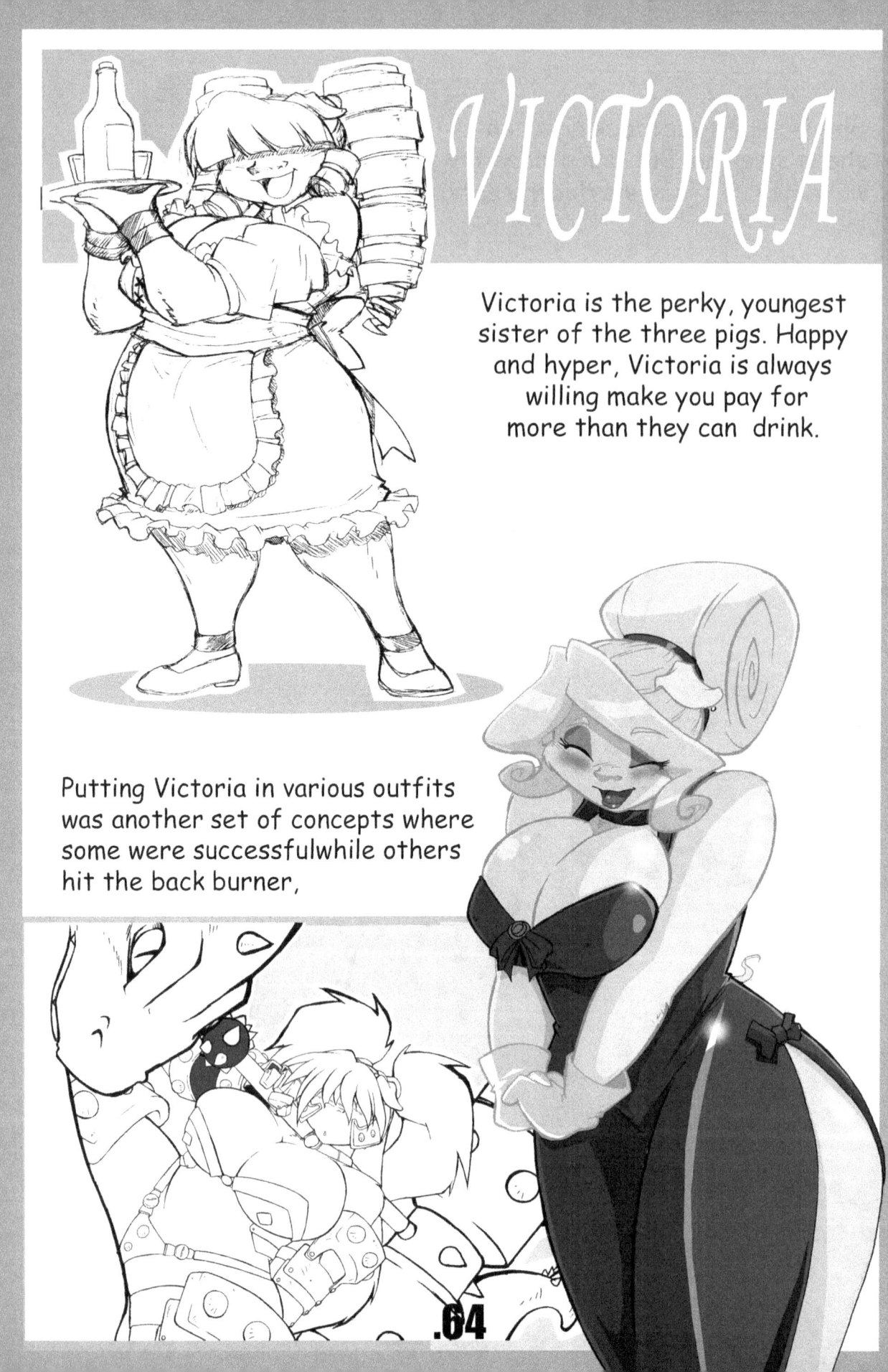

Victoria is the perky, youngest sister of the three pigs. Happy and hyper, Victoria is always willing make you pay for more than they can drink.

Putting Victoria in various outfits was another set of concepts where some were successfulwhile others hit the back burner,

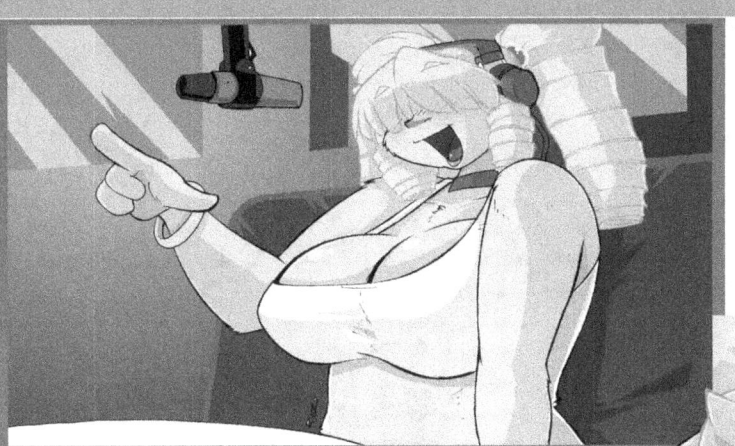

Vikki's Radio interview pic.

Sleepy Vikki used for a series of pics of sleeping characters.

This image of Victoria was for my deviantart site. I gave the audience the choice of deciding what Shred was thinking.

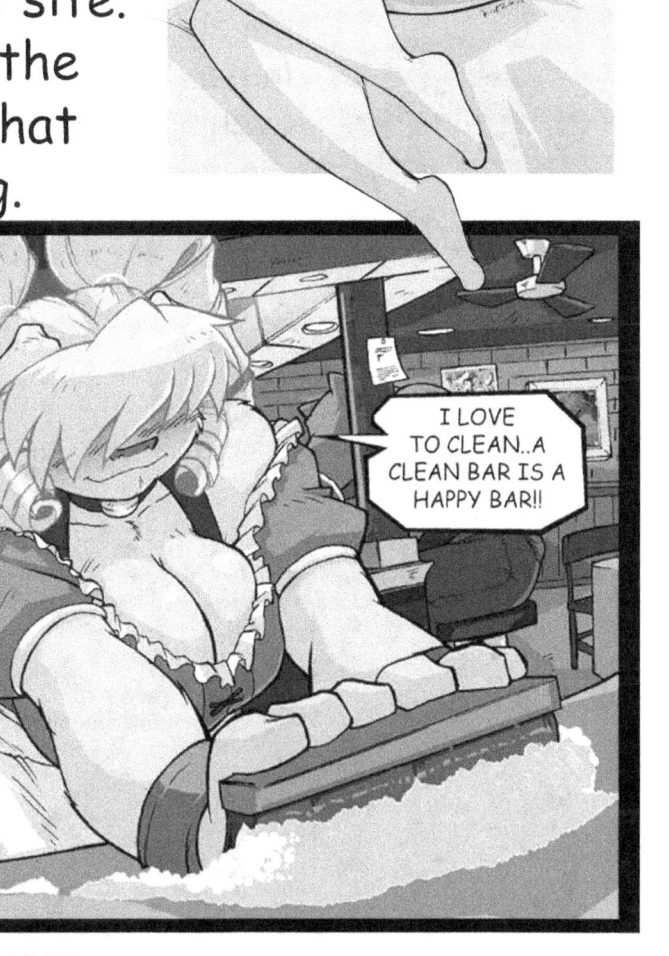

I LOVE TO CLEAN..A CLEAN BAR IS A HAPPY BAR!!

..AND WHAT ARE YOU THINKING ABOUT, SHRED!?

# PANDORA-PIG

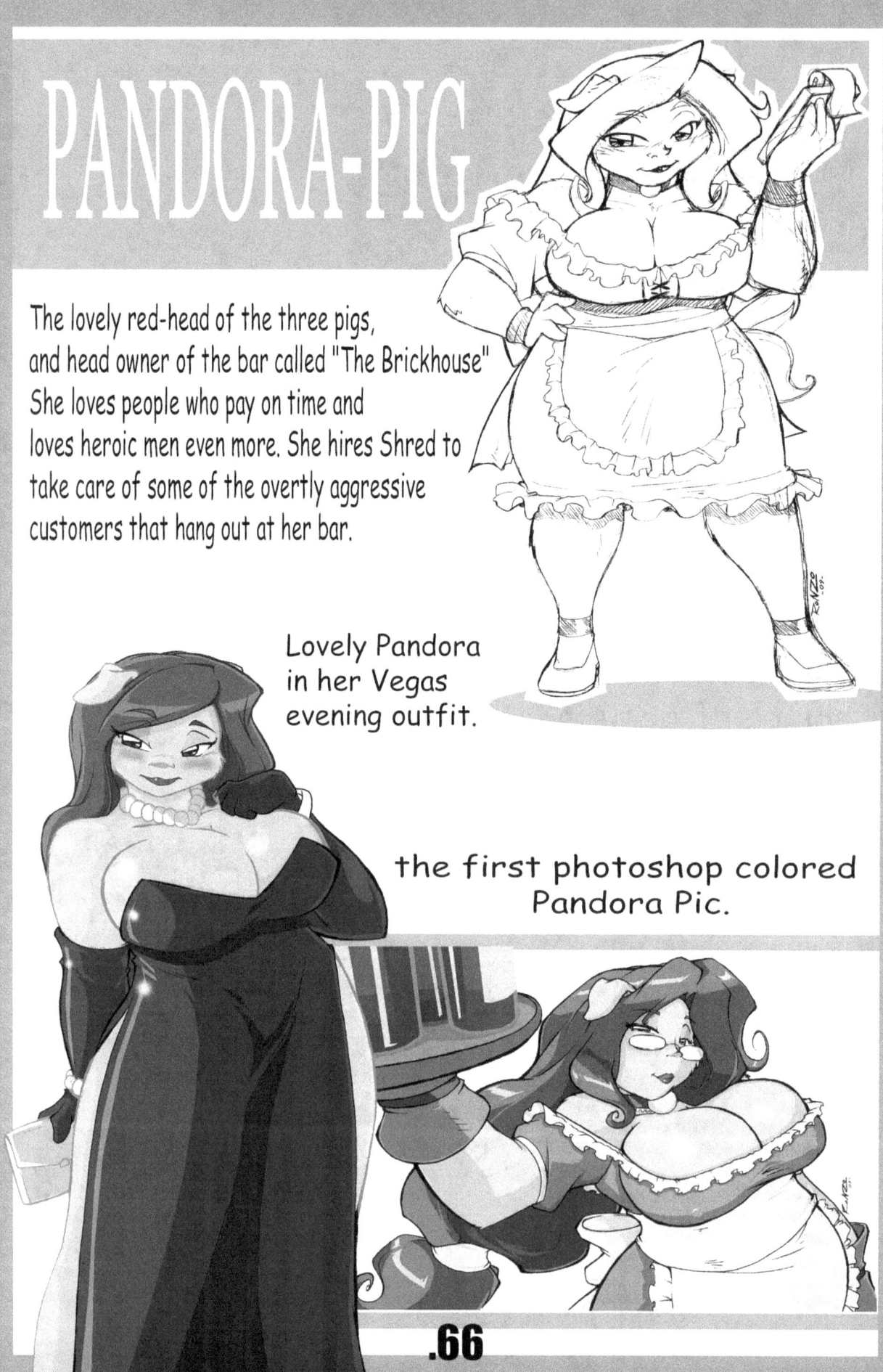

The lovely red-head of the three pigs, and head owner of the bar called "The Brickhouse" She loves people who pay on time and loves heroic men even more. She hires Shred to take care of some of the overtly aggressive customers that hang out at her bar.

Lovely Pandora in her Vegas evening outfit.

the first photoshop colored Pandora Pic.

Piggies with wings.
This was more a
series of spoof
Victoria's
Secret
Pics
that I
with girls in
lingere with wings.

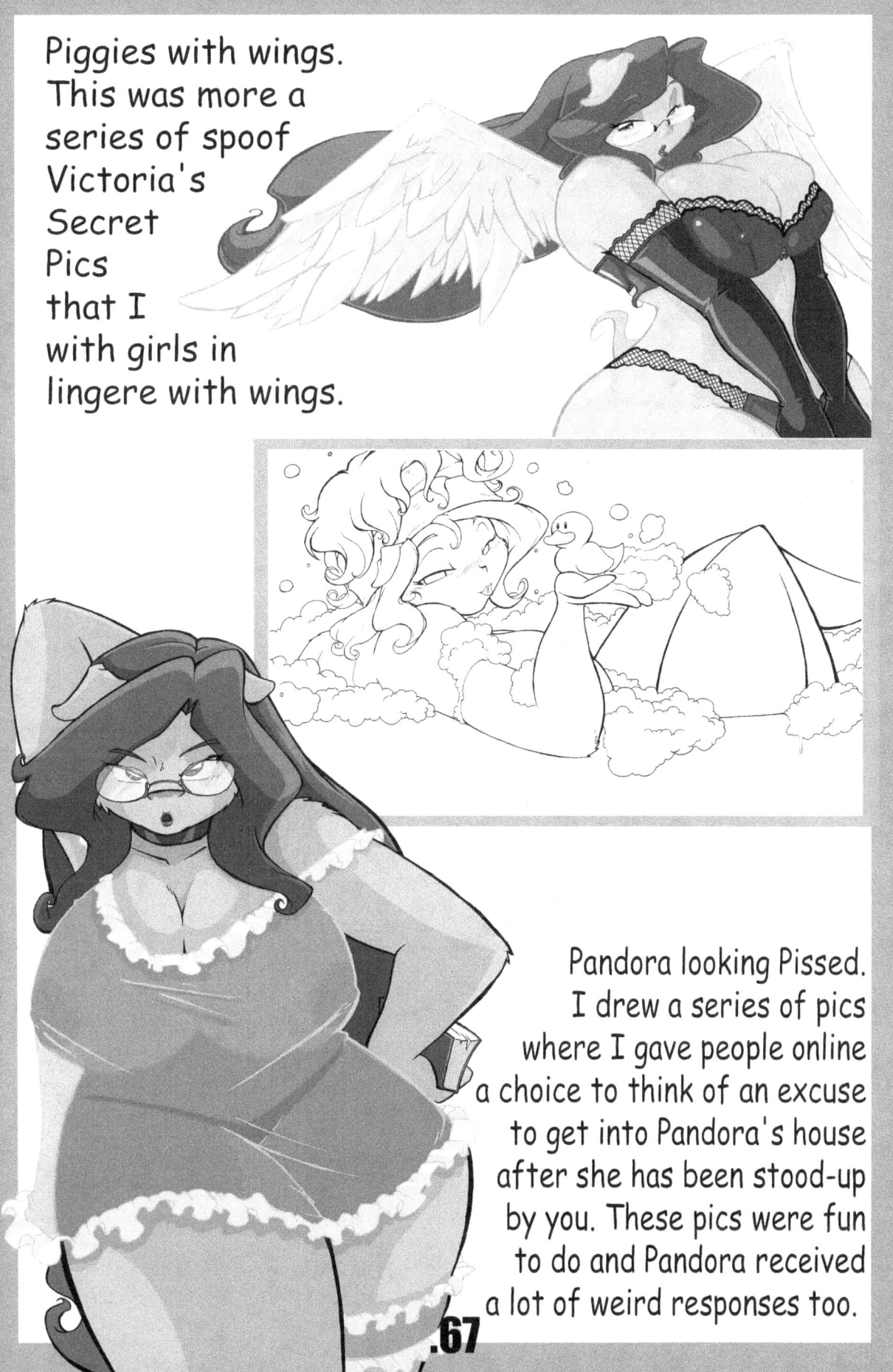

Pandora looking Pissed.
I drew a series of pics
where I gave people online
a choice to think of an excuse
to get into Pandora's house
after she has been stood-up
by you. These pics were fun
to do and Pandora received
a lot of weird responses too.

.67

Lunch-time sketch of Pandora while eating cheetos.

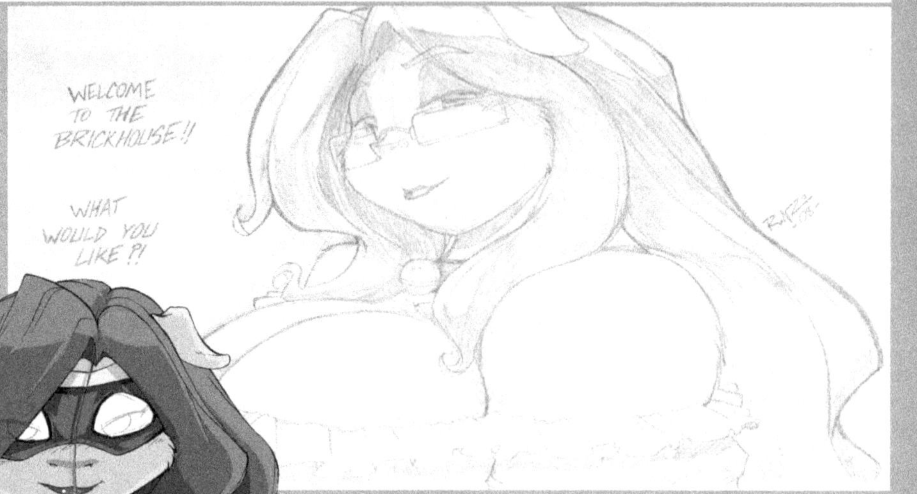

WELCOME TO THE BRICKHOUSE !!

WHAT WOULD YOU LIKE ?!

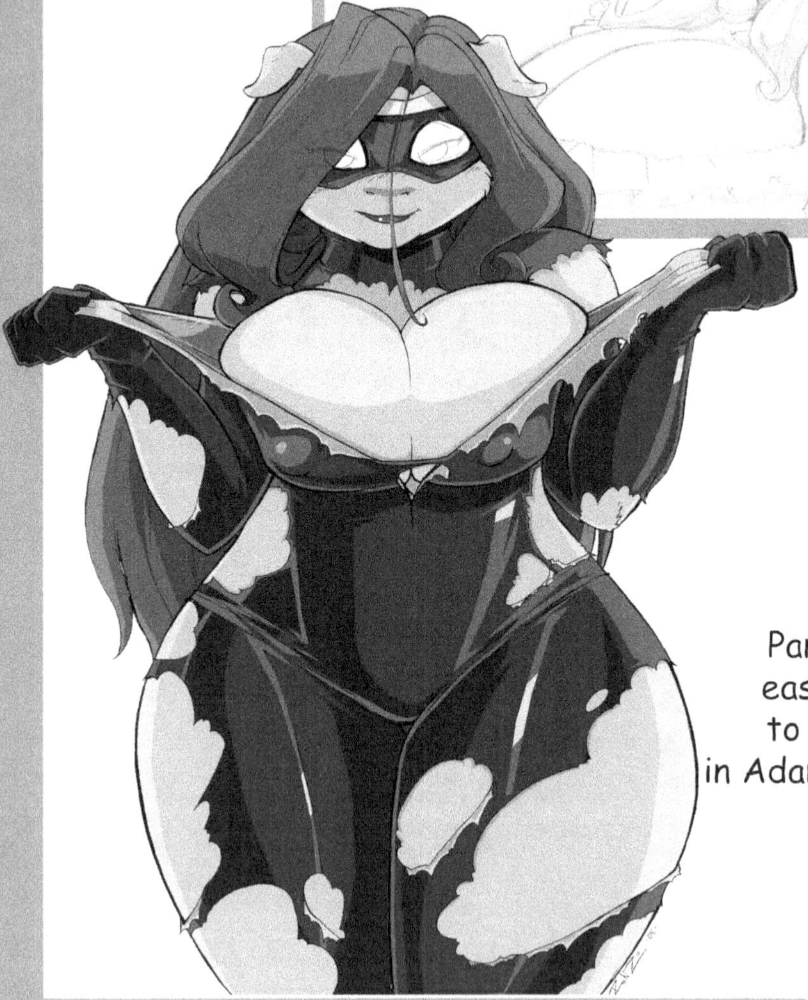

Pandora is probably the easiest of the three pigs to draw and putting her in Adam Warren's "Empowered" ripable super-suit is no acception.

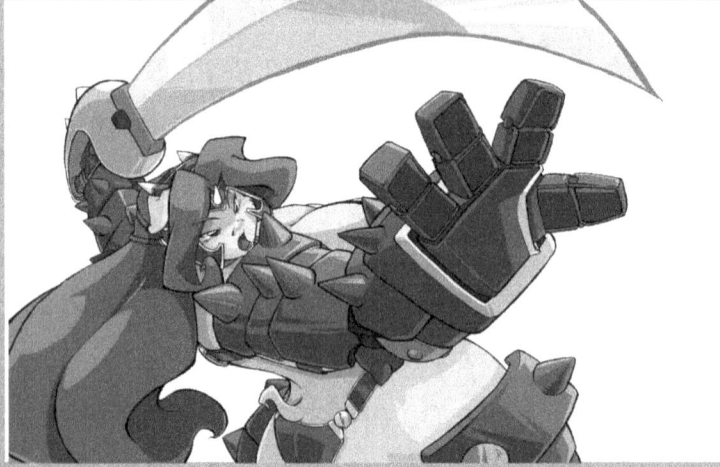

A Barbarian Pandora Picture I finished on my trip to West Virginia. A back burner idea hopefully i'll use for a future project.

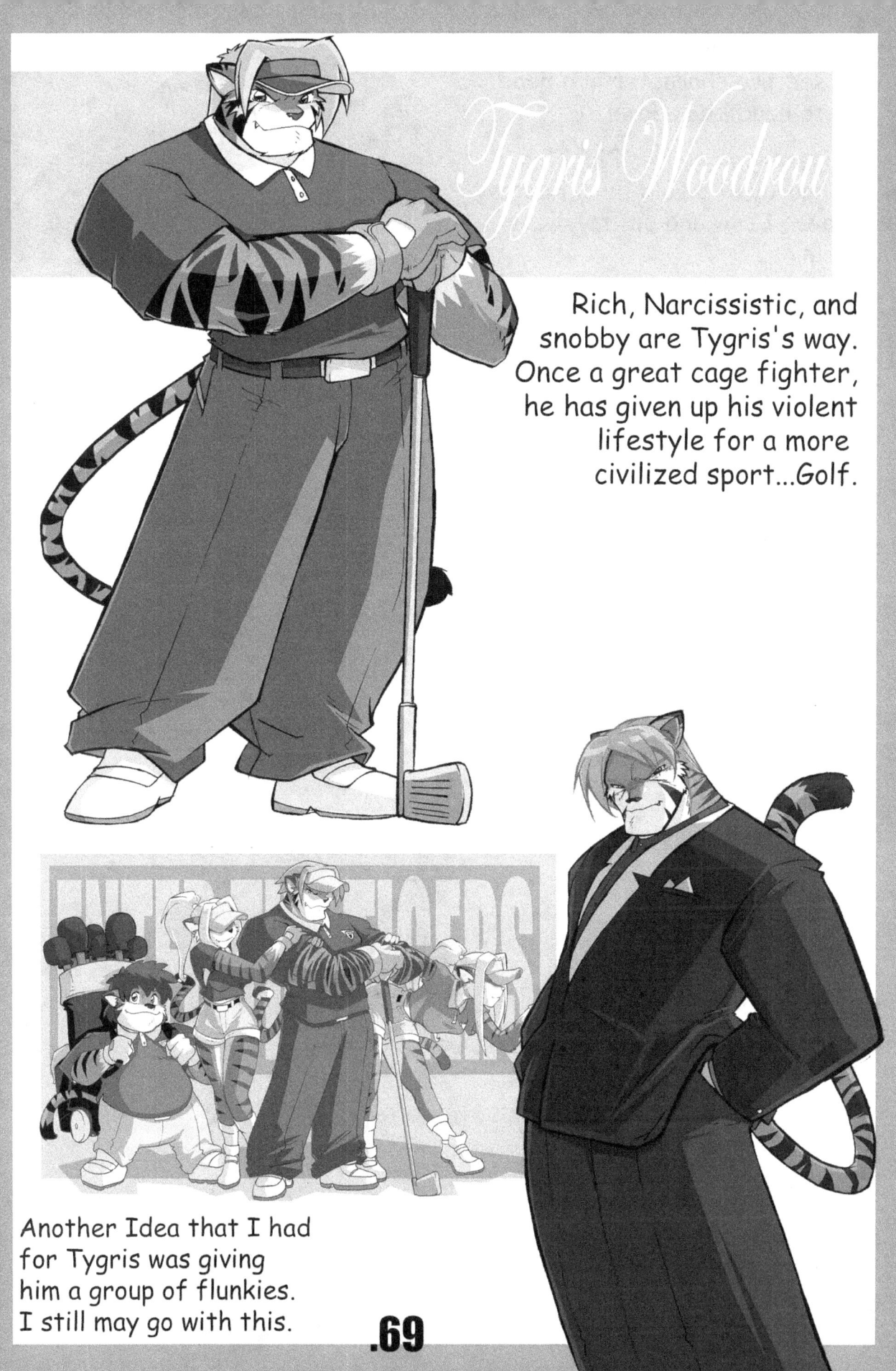

# Tygris Woodrou

Rich, Narcissistic, and snobby are Tygris's way. Once a great cage fighter, he has given up his violent lifestyle for a more civilized sport...Golf.

Another Idea that I had for Tygris was giving him a group of flunkies. I still may go with this.

I love drawing pics where you see two character in a head to head staredown.

Tigers -vs- Wolves Pic. This is a Paordy of an old Final Fantasy cover I saw and put my own spin on.

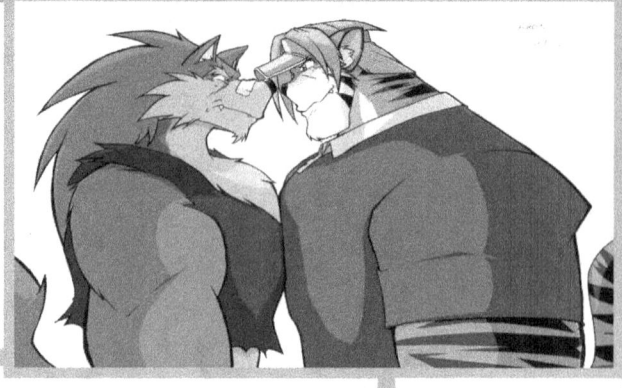

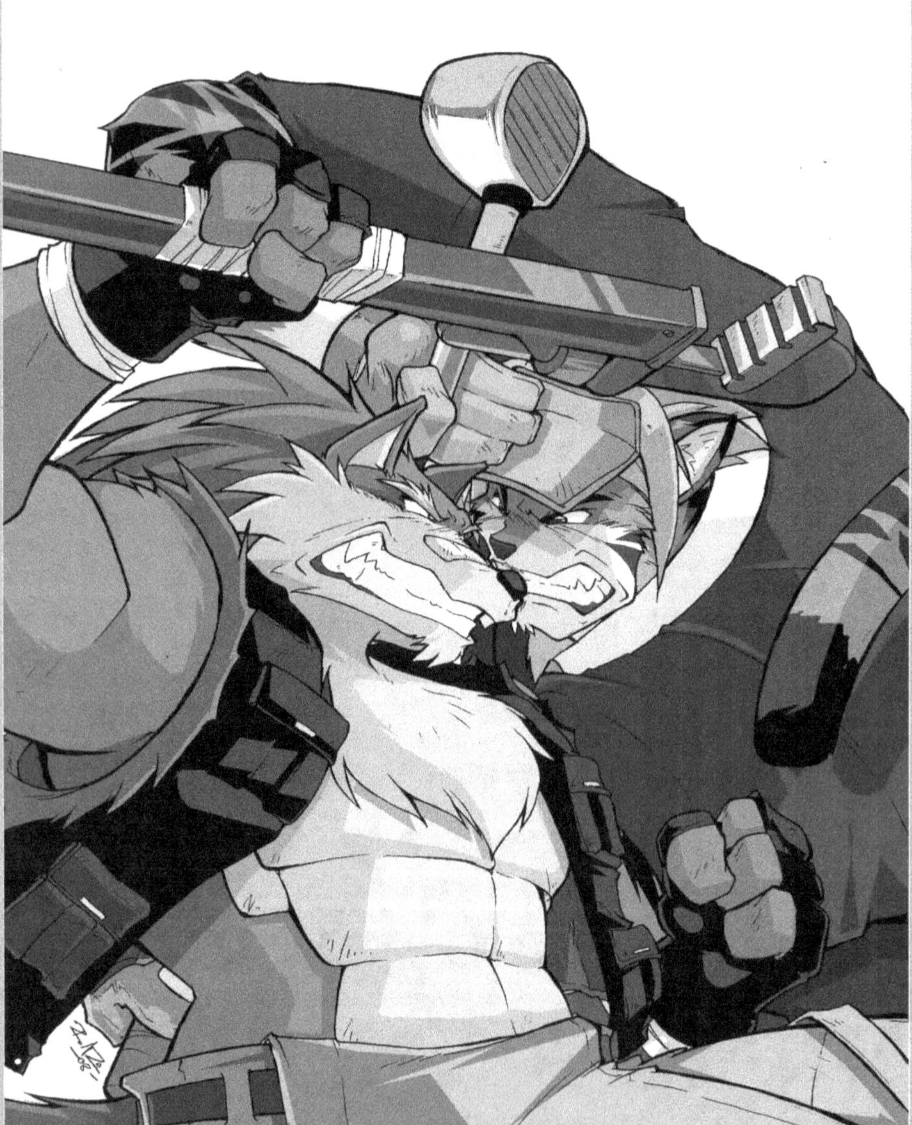

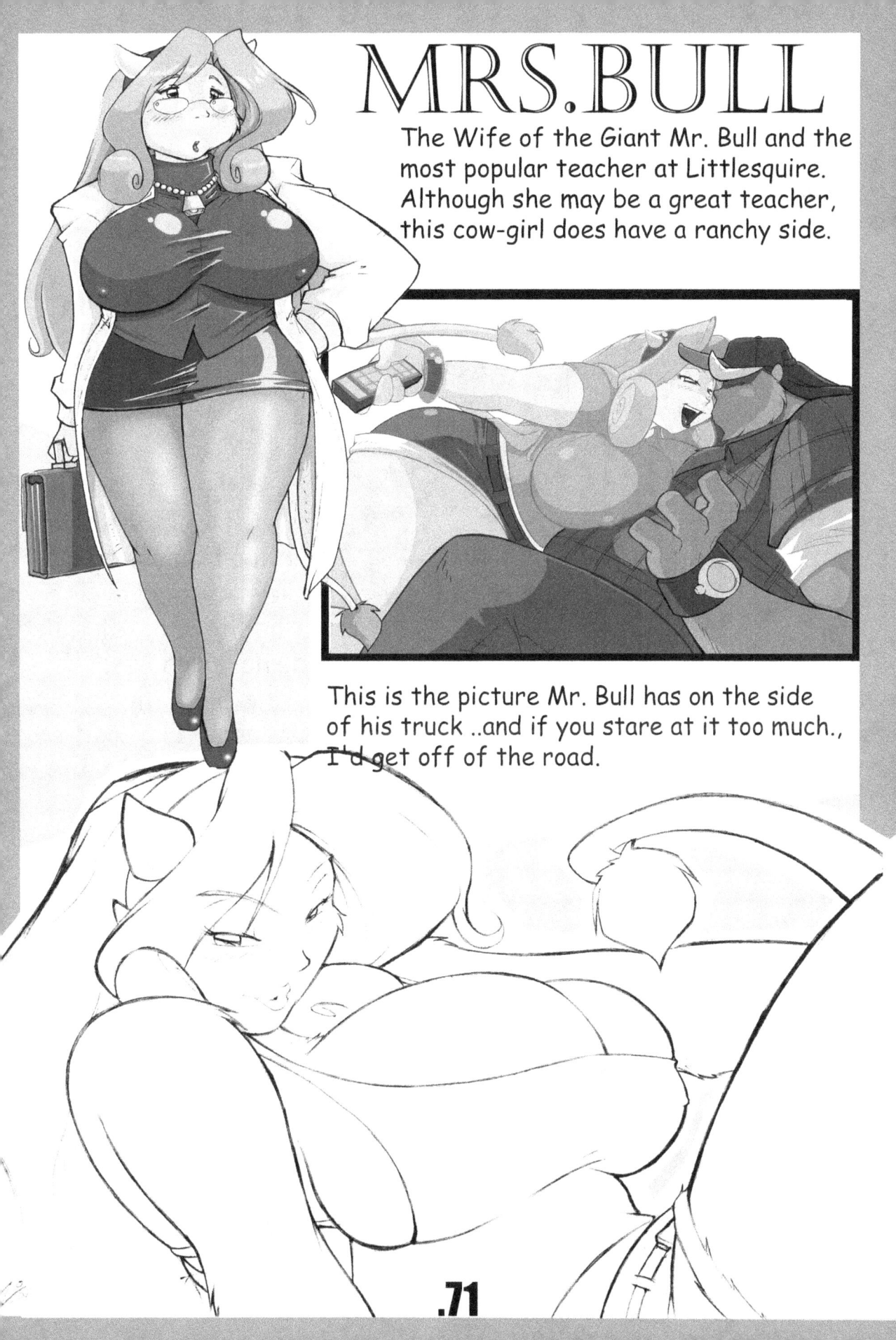

# MRS. BULL

The Wife of the Giant Mr. Bull and the most popular teacher at Littlesquire. Although she may be a great teacher, this cow-girl does have a ranchy side.

This is the picture Mr. Bull has on the side of his truck ..and if you stare at it too much., I'd get off of the road.

.71

Mrs. Bull pics a bra that is just too small for her...again.

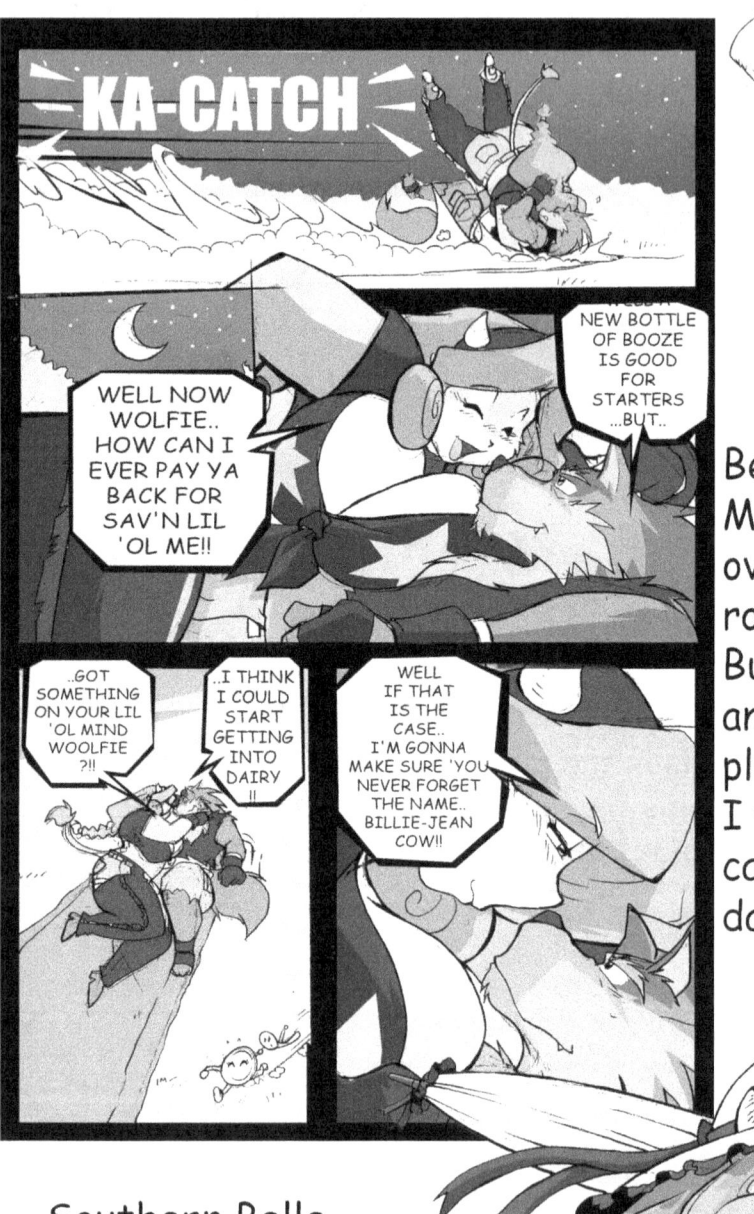

KA-CATCH

WELL NOW WOLFIE.. HOW CAN I EVER PAY YA BACK FOR SAV'N LIL 'OL ME!!

NEW BOTTLE OF BOOZE IS GOOD FOR STARTERS ...BUT..

..GOT SOMETHING ON YOUR LIL 'OL MIND WOOLFIE ?!!

..I THINK I COULD START GETTING INTO DAIRY !!

WELL IF THAT IS THE CASE.. I'M GONNA MAKE SURE 'YOU NEVER FORGET THE NAME.. BILLIE-JEAN COW!!

Before she was married, Mrs. Bull wanted to jump over the moon using a rocket-powered cycle. But hen the rocket failed and she found herself plummeting to her doom, I was good 'ol Shred that came in and caught the damsel in distress.

Southern Belle
Mrs. Bull

.72

# MR. BULL

They don't get any meaner
and more southern than Mr. Bull
He is what you get if you mix Hank
Hill from "King of the Hill" and put
him in the Juggernaught's body.
His Hulk-like aggressiveness is only
tamed by his lovely wife Mrs. Bull

Mr. Bull keeping an eye
on all of you people googl'n
at his wife.

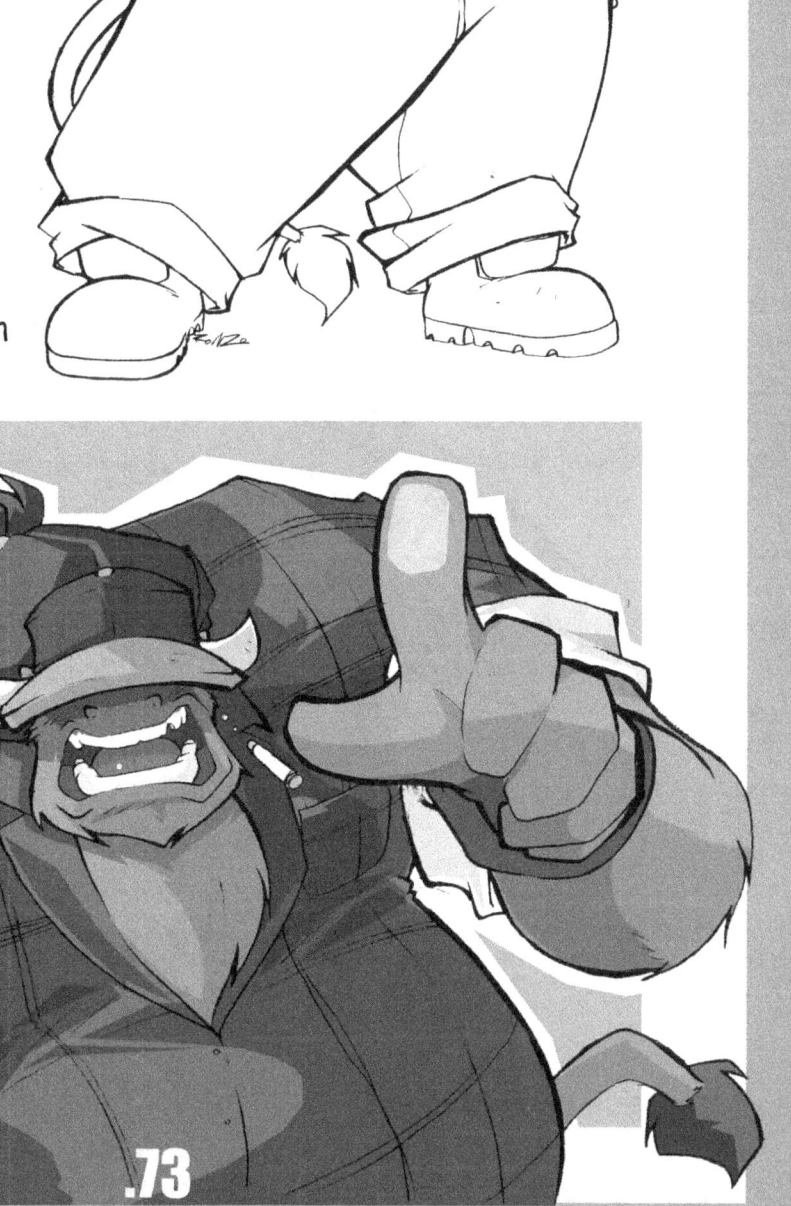

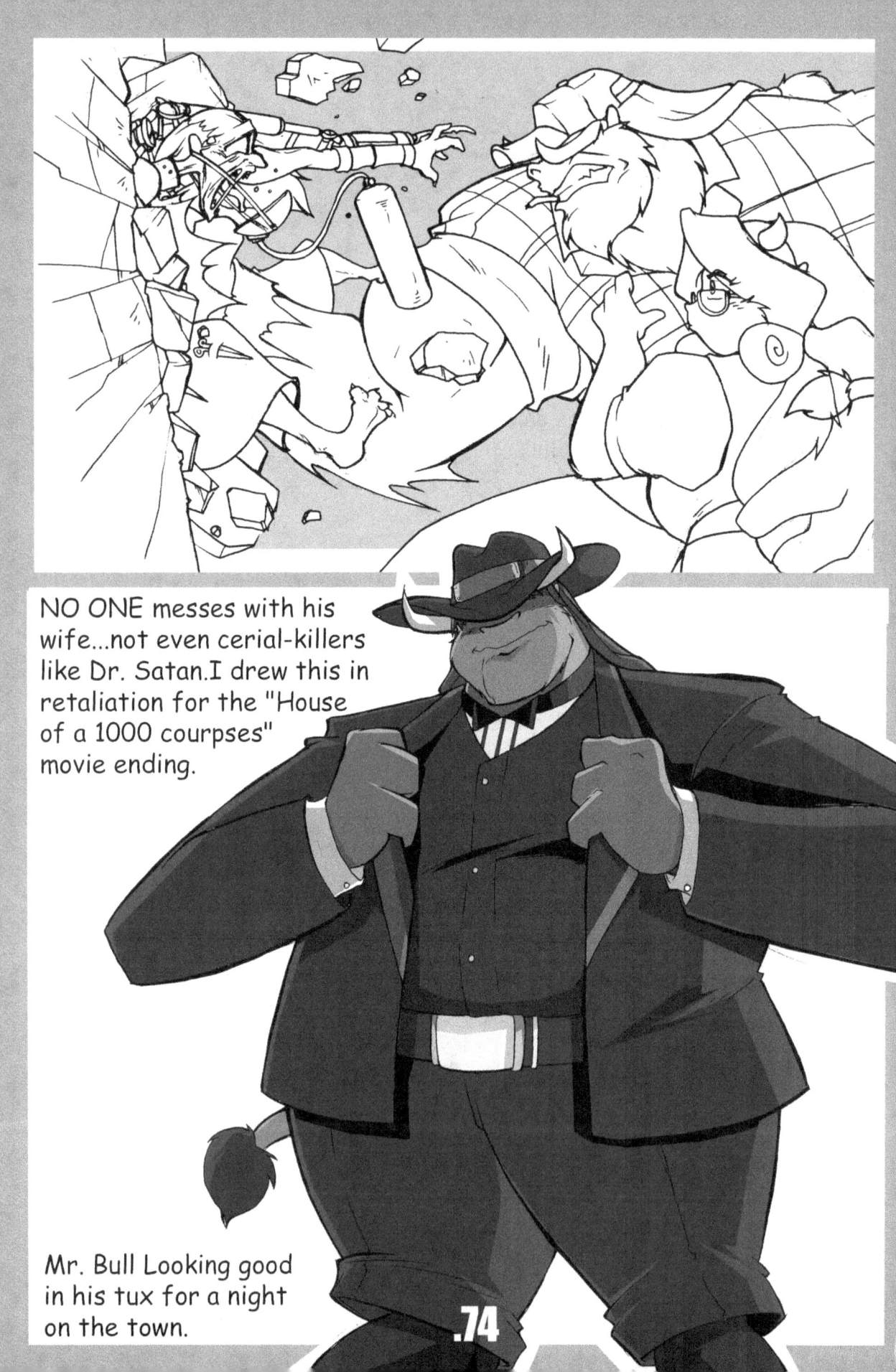

NO ONE messes with his wife...not even cerial-killers like Dr. Satan.I drew this in retaliation for the "House of a 1000 courpses" movie ending.

Mr. Bull Looking good in his tux for a night on the town.

# Ms. CHOCO

The Chocolate flavored Ms. Choco is the school's Science teacher. She loves inventing things from robots to new types of perfume, but has no luck in finding a suitable husband like her cousin.

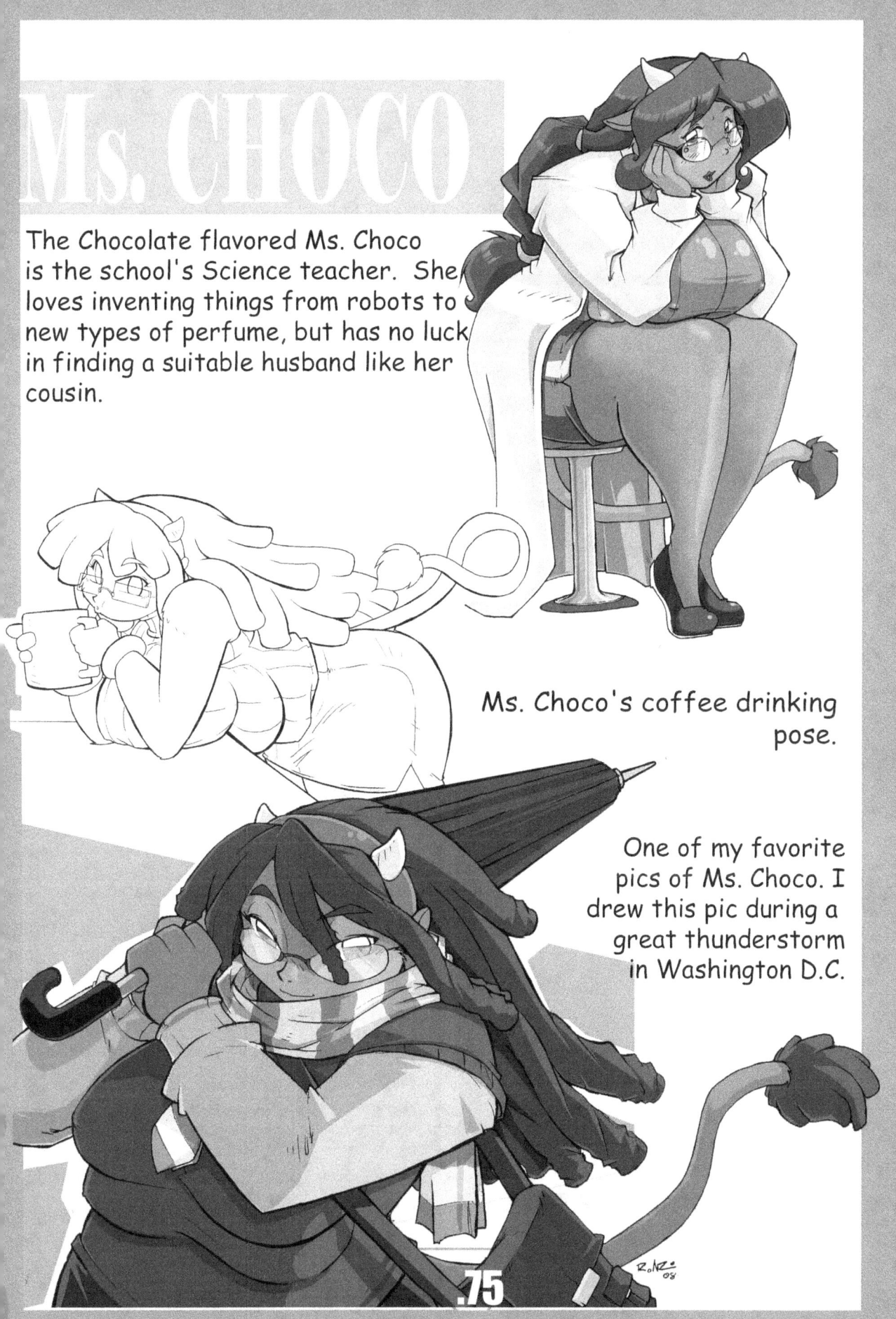

Ms. Choco's coffee drinking pose.

One of my favorite pics of Ms. Choco. I drew this pic during a great thunderstorm in Washington D.C.

# Ms. BATTLEBERRY

Ms. Battleberry was originally going to be Geisha Girl type, then I thought why not make her the most athletic, ruthless, gym teacher cow ever. No one is ever prepared to take P.E. when she is teaching the class.

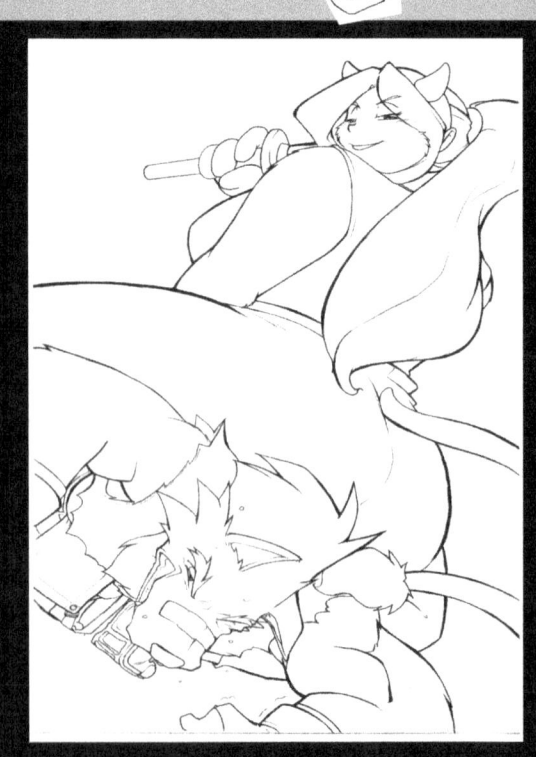

Ms. Battleberry approves the consumption of the other white meat.

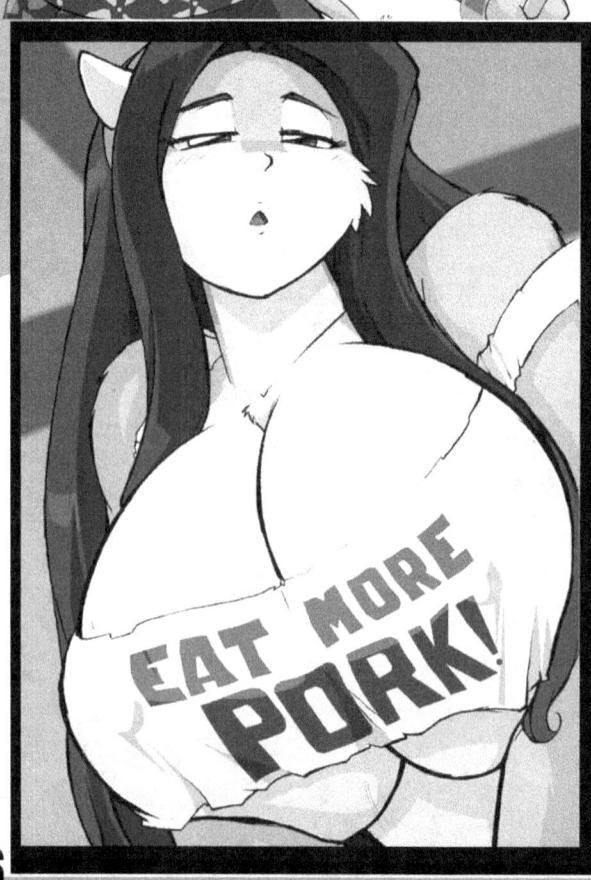

# Ms. Woodly & Ms. Sweetcorn

Woodly and Sweetcorn are the teaching assistants of Ms. Battleberry whom they both idolize. Drawing duos like this is one thing I like to create. The tall thin/ short chubby combo never gets old to me.

Although she may be chubby, Sweetcorn is one of the most athletic Squirrels to dawn a pair of gym shorts.

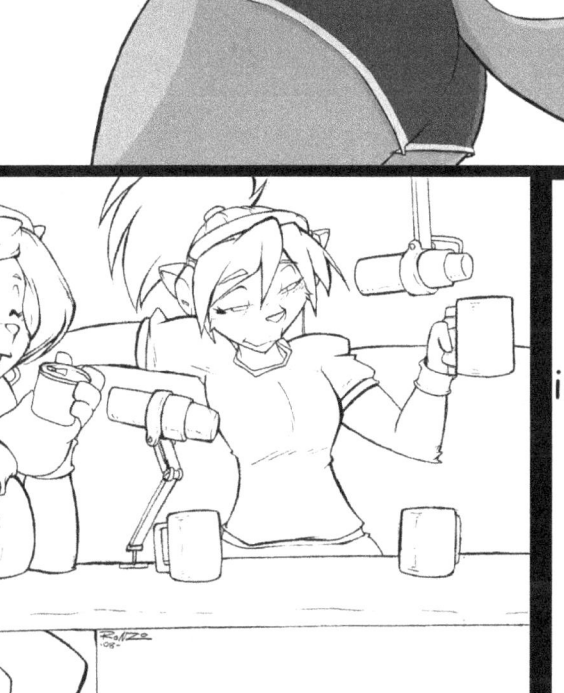

Woodly and Sweetcorn's interview pic.

# SYNNABUNN

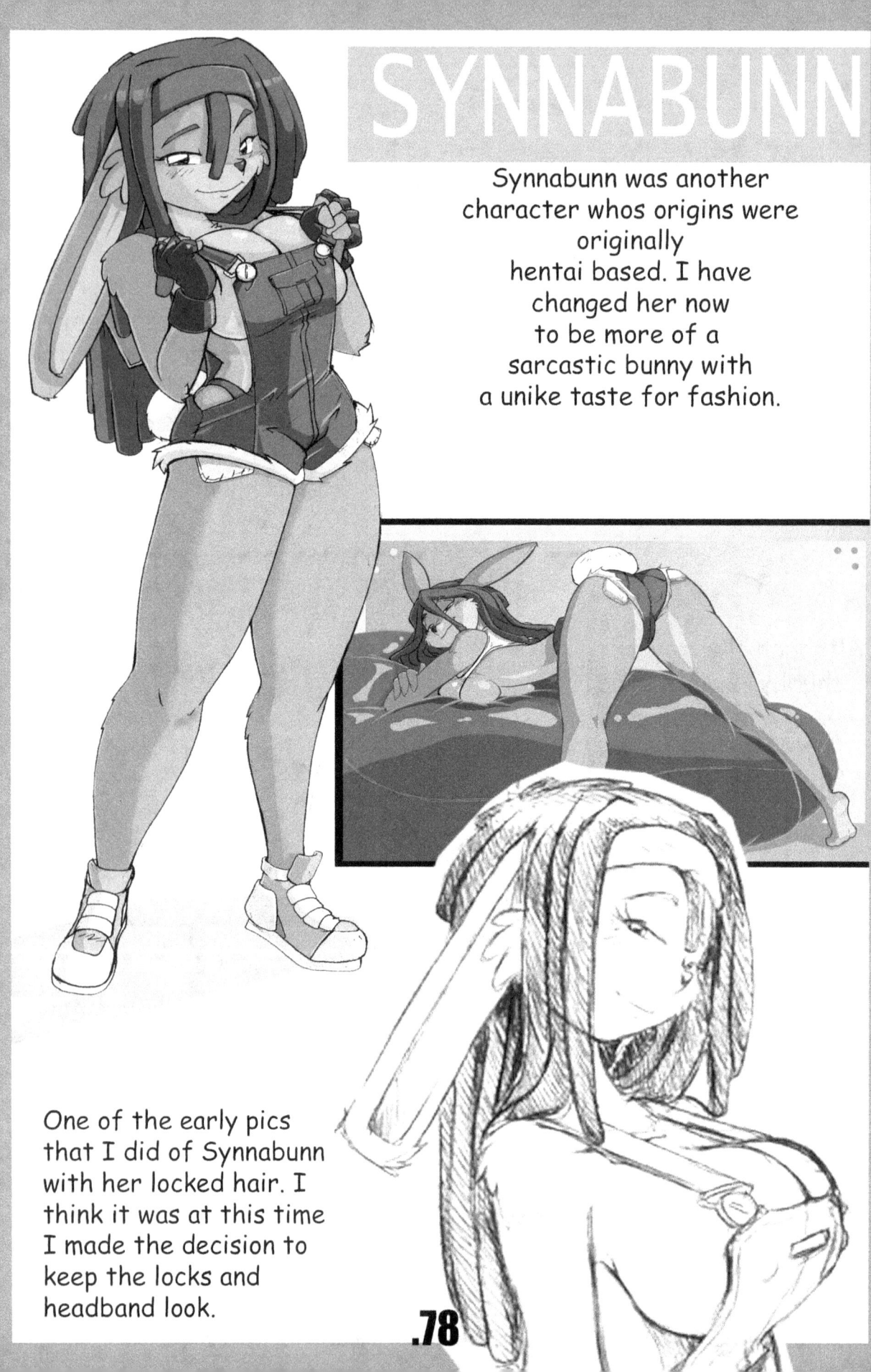

Synnabunn was another character whos origins were originally hentai based. I have changed her now to be more of a sarcastic bunny with a unike taste for fashion.

One of the early pics that I did of Synnabunn with her locked hair. I think it was at this time I made the decision to keep the locks and headband look.

.78

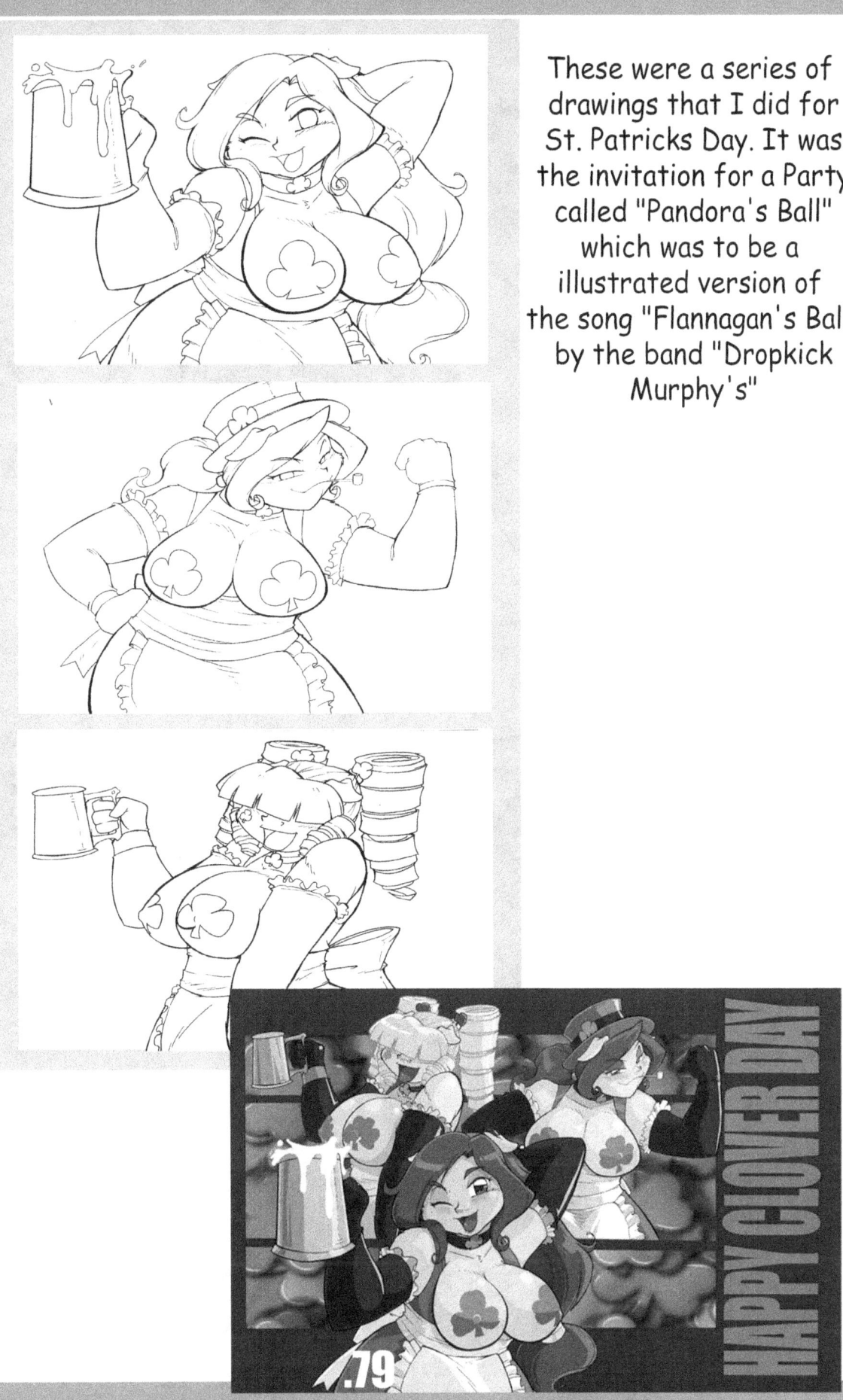

These were a series of drawings that I did for St. Patricks Day. It was the invitation for a Party called "Pandora's Ball" which was to be a illustrated version of the song "Flannagan's Ball" by the band "Dropkick Murphy's"

HAPPY CLOVER DAY

.79

# CONCEPTS & IDEAS

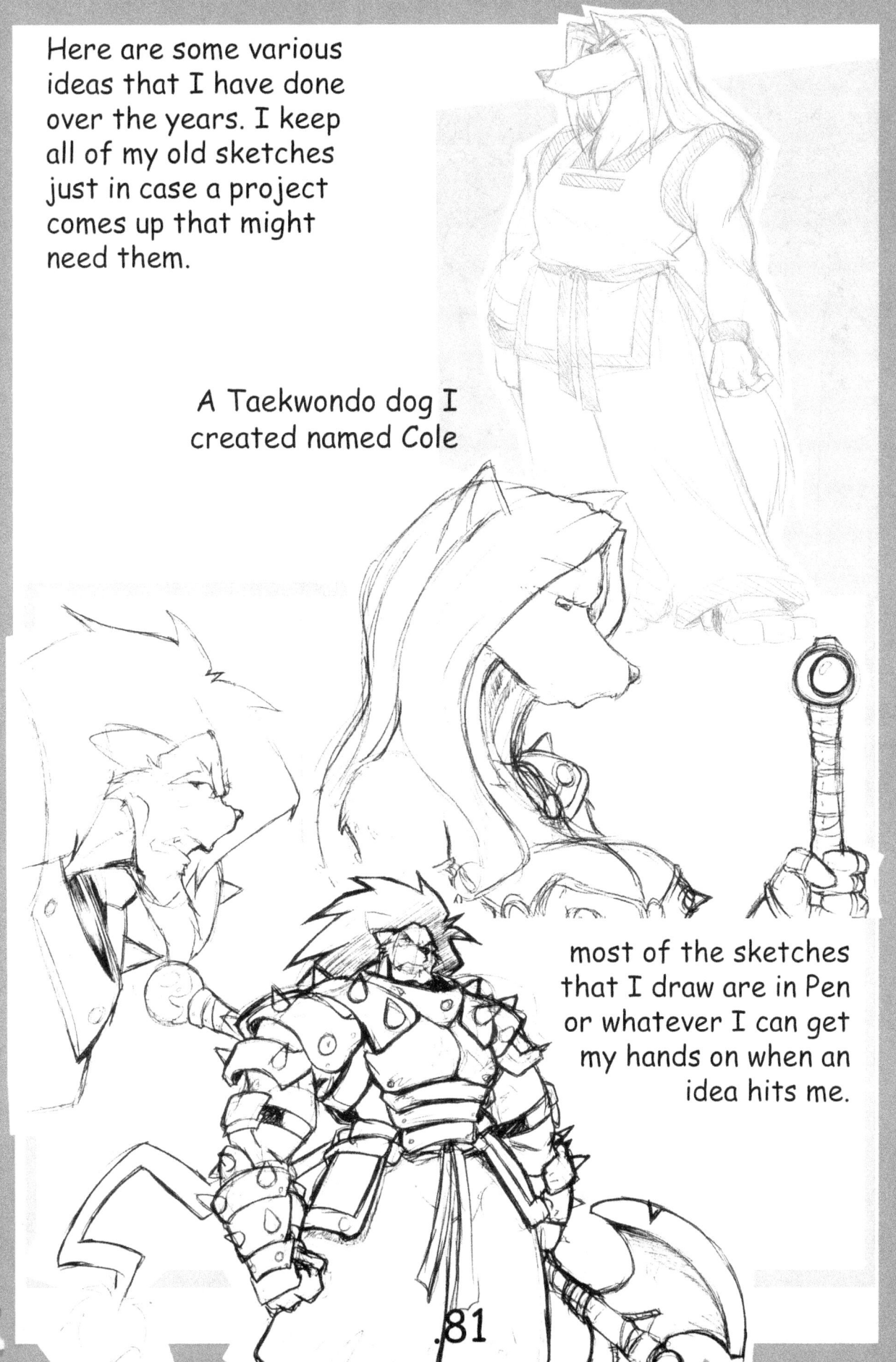

Here are some various ideas that I have done over the years. I keep all of my old sketches just in case a project comes up that might need them.

A Taekwondo dog I created named Cole

most of the sketches that I draw are in Pen or whatever I can get my hands on when an idea hits me.

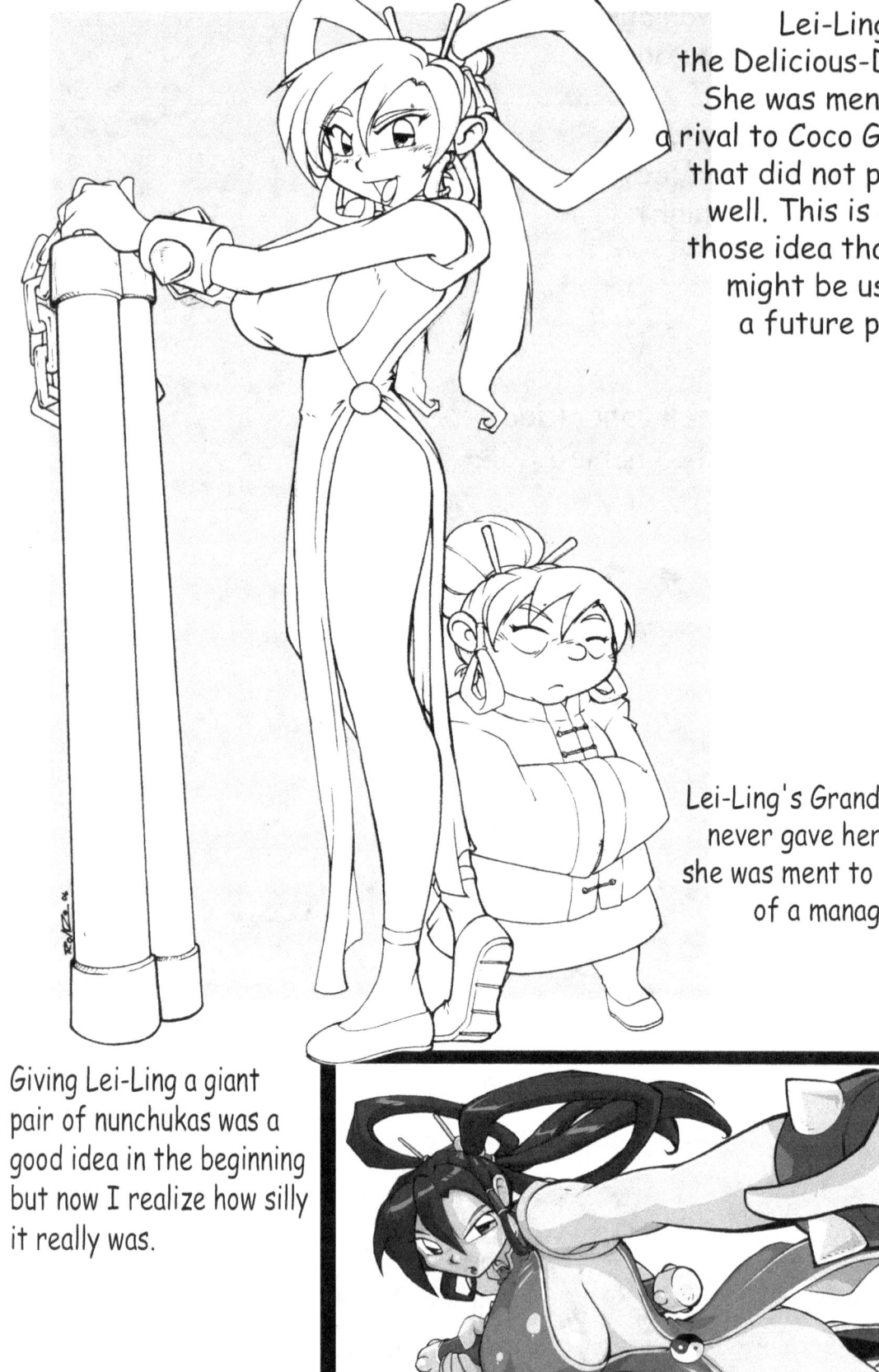

Lei-Ling a.k.a. the Delicious-Dragon. She was ment to be a rival to Coco Gun-Bun that did not pan out well. This is one of those idea that just might be useful in a future project.

Lei-Ling's Grand-mother never gave her a name. she was ment to be more of a manager-type.

Giving Lei-Ling a giant pair of nunchukas was a good idea in the beginning but now I realize how silly it really was.

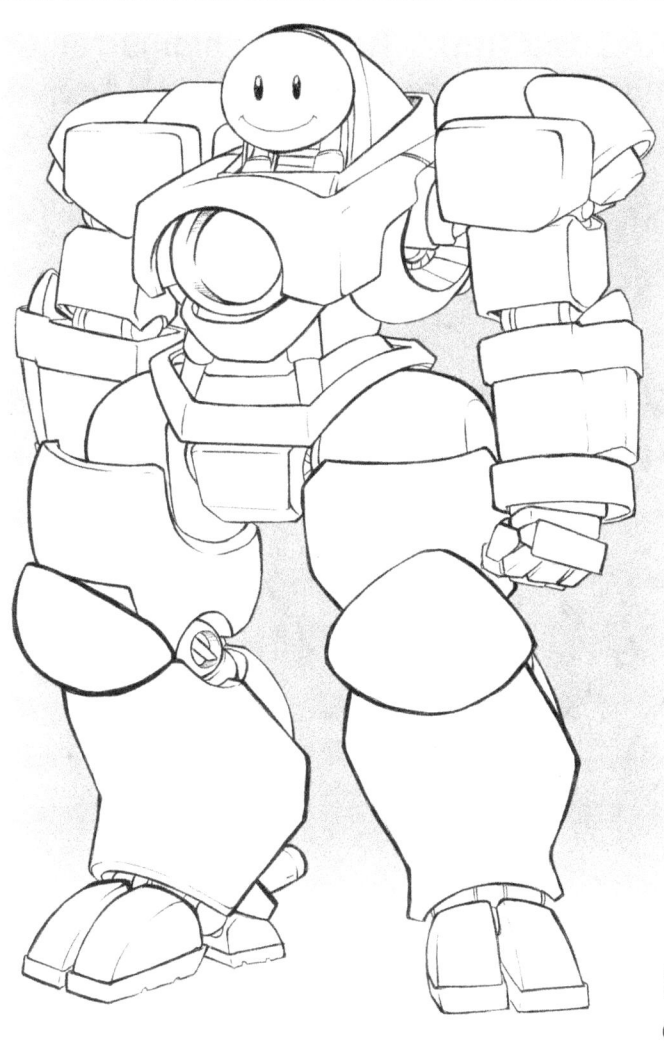

This silly idea I had when drawing Mechs in high school. I drew this robot one lunch period but was having trouble designing a head. So my Friend Kevin stuck a happy-faced sticker right where the head would've gone. For some reason it worked. Thus the HAPPY-TECH was born.

Dexter Van King, One of the first villains that I ever created.

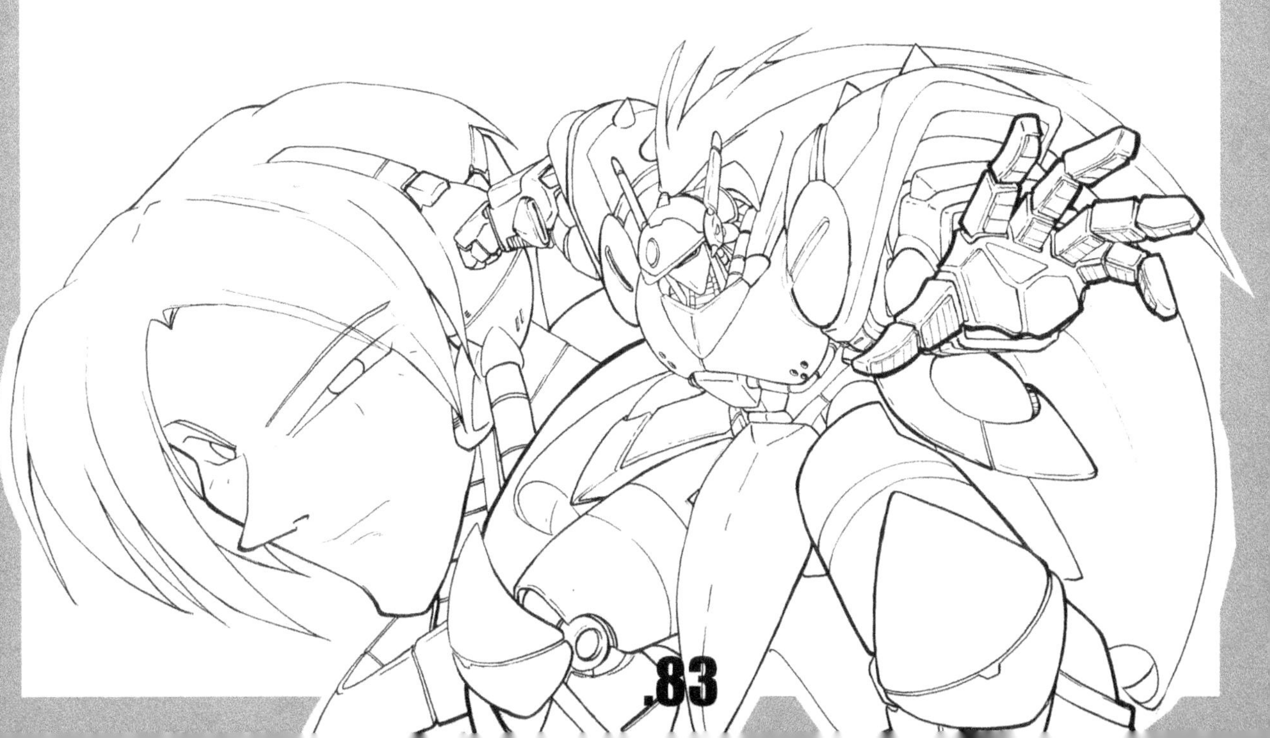

Cookie Scout Gunners. An Idea that I had for villains for Coco. They were going to be made out of real cookie dough to make them harder to defeat...and sweeter.

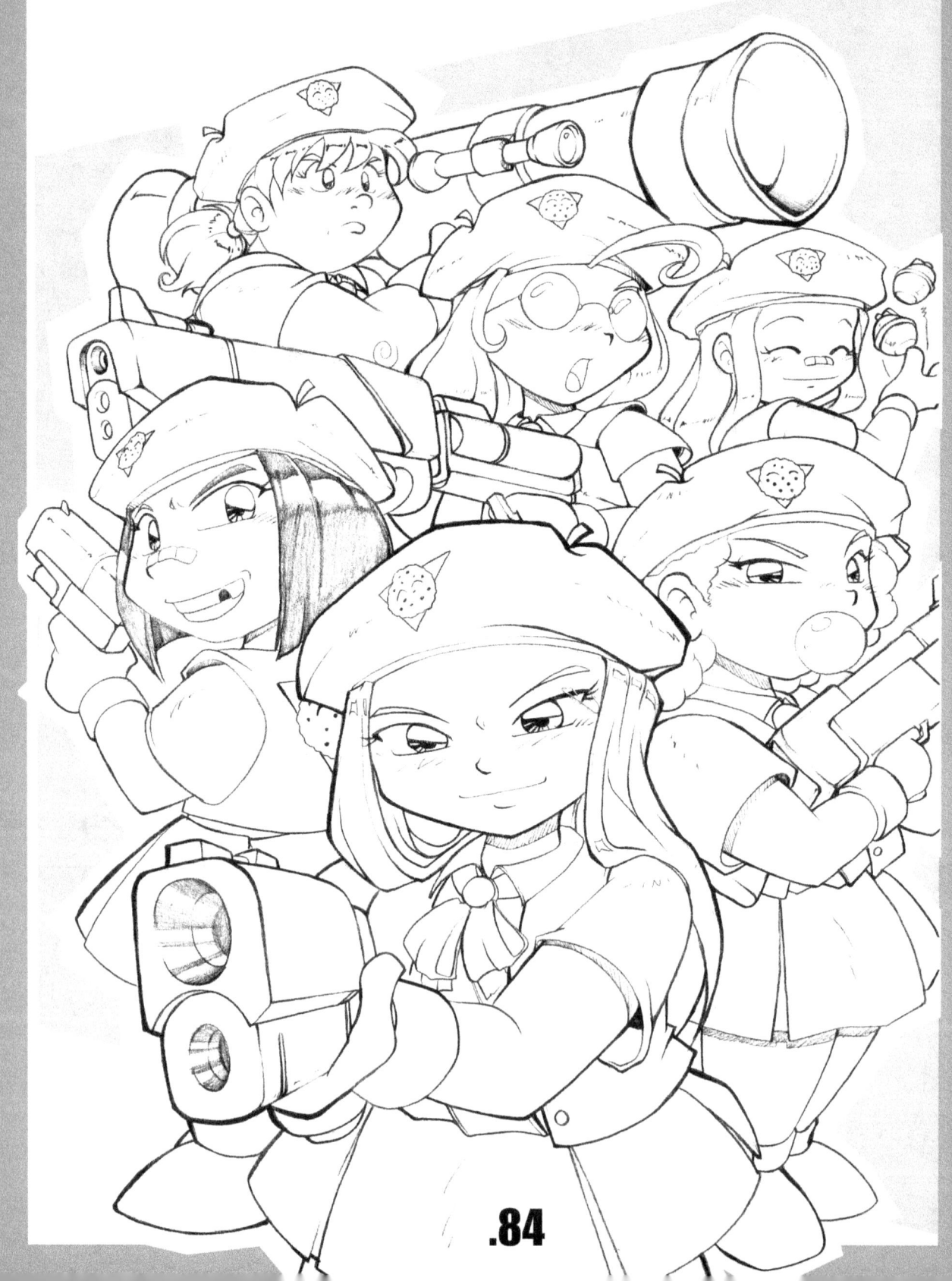

.84

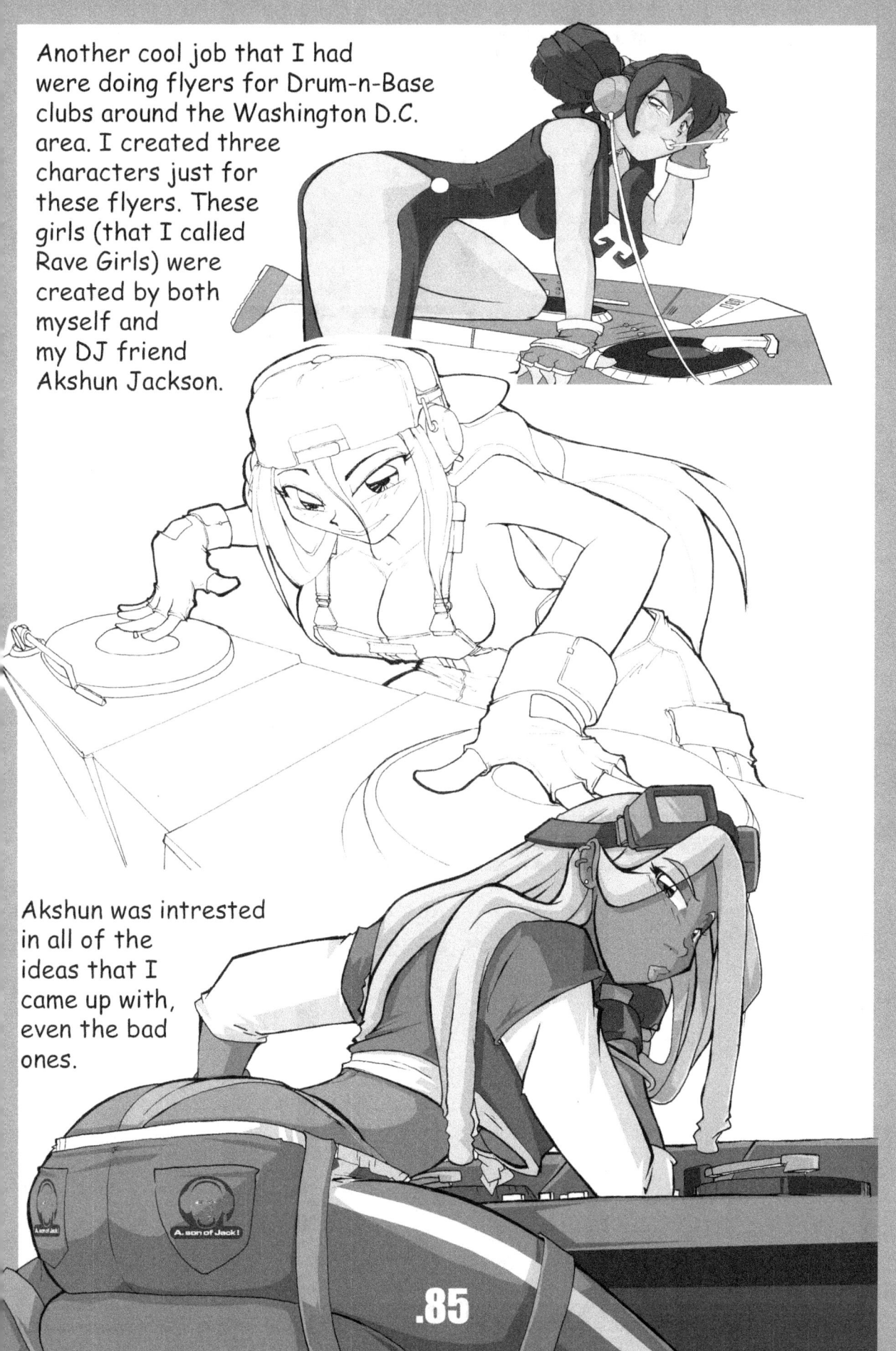

Another cool job that I had were doing flyers for Drum-n-Base clubs around the Washington D.C. area. I created three characters just for these flyers. These girls (that I called Rave Girls) were created by both myself and my DJ friend Akshun Jackson.

Akshun was intrested in all of the ideas that I came up with, even the bad ones.

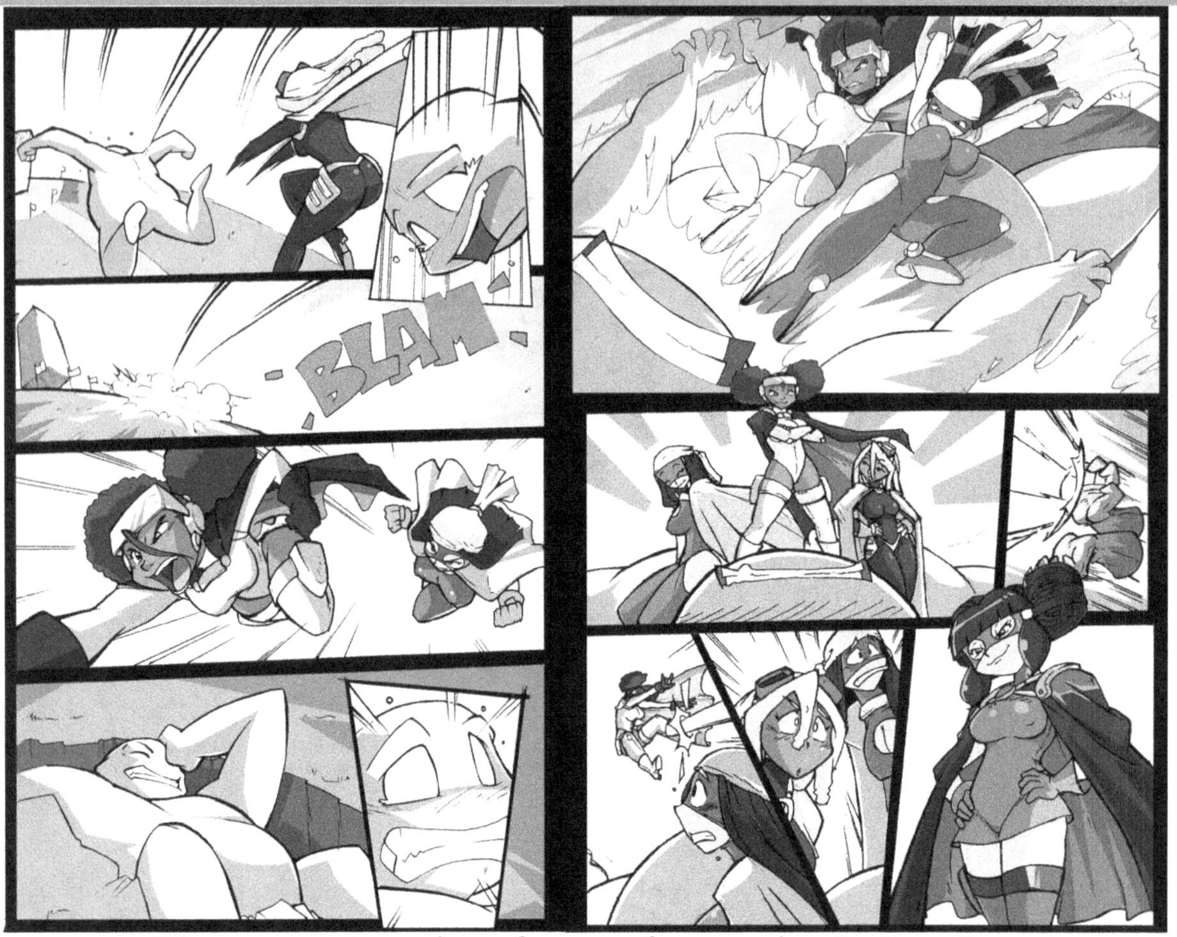

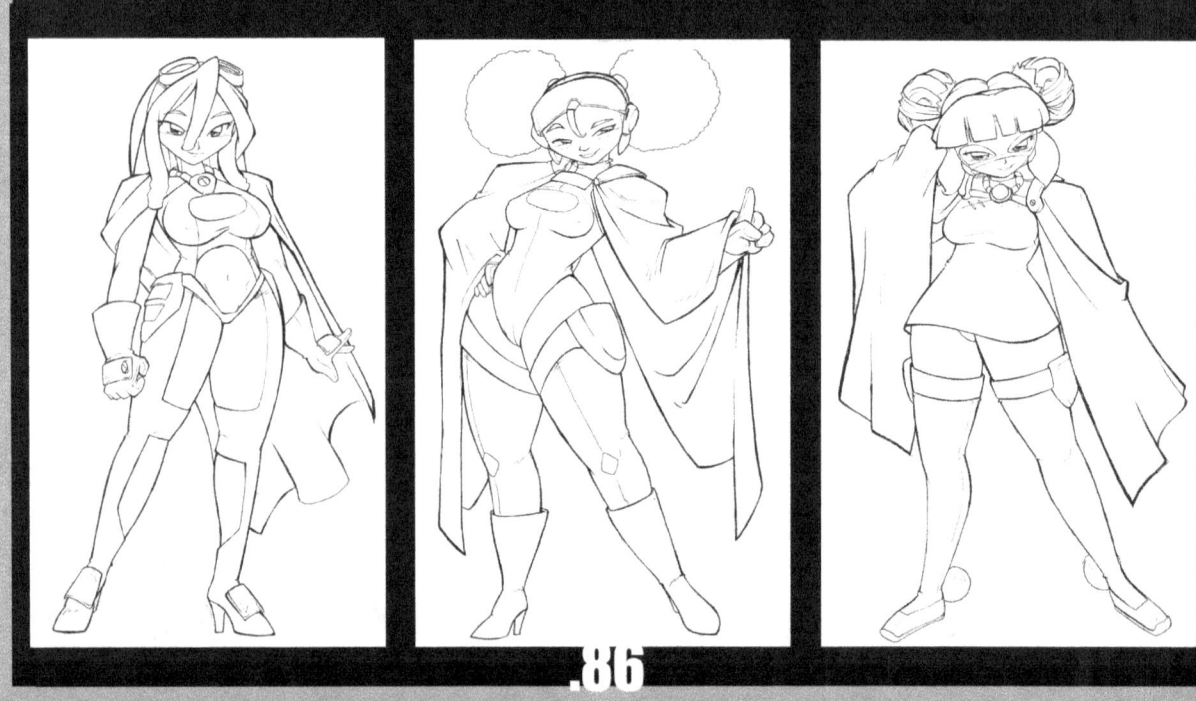

These were samples of pages from a short story I did for my friend Akshun putting the Rave Girls in superhero suits fighting a giant white monster called Soma Man. I think that it was used as advertisement for another club he was working at.

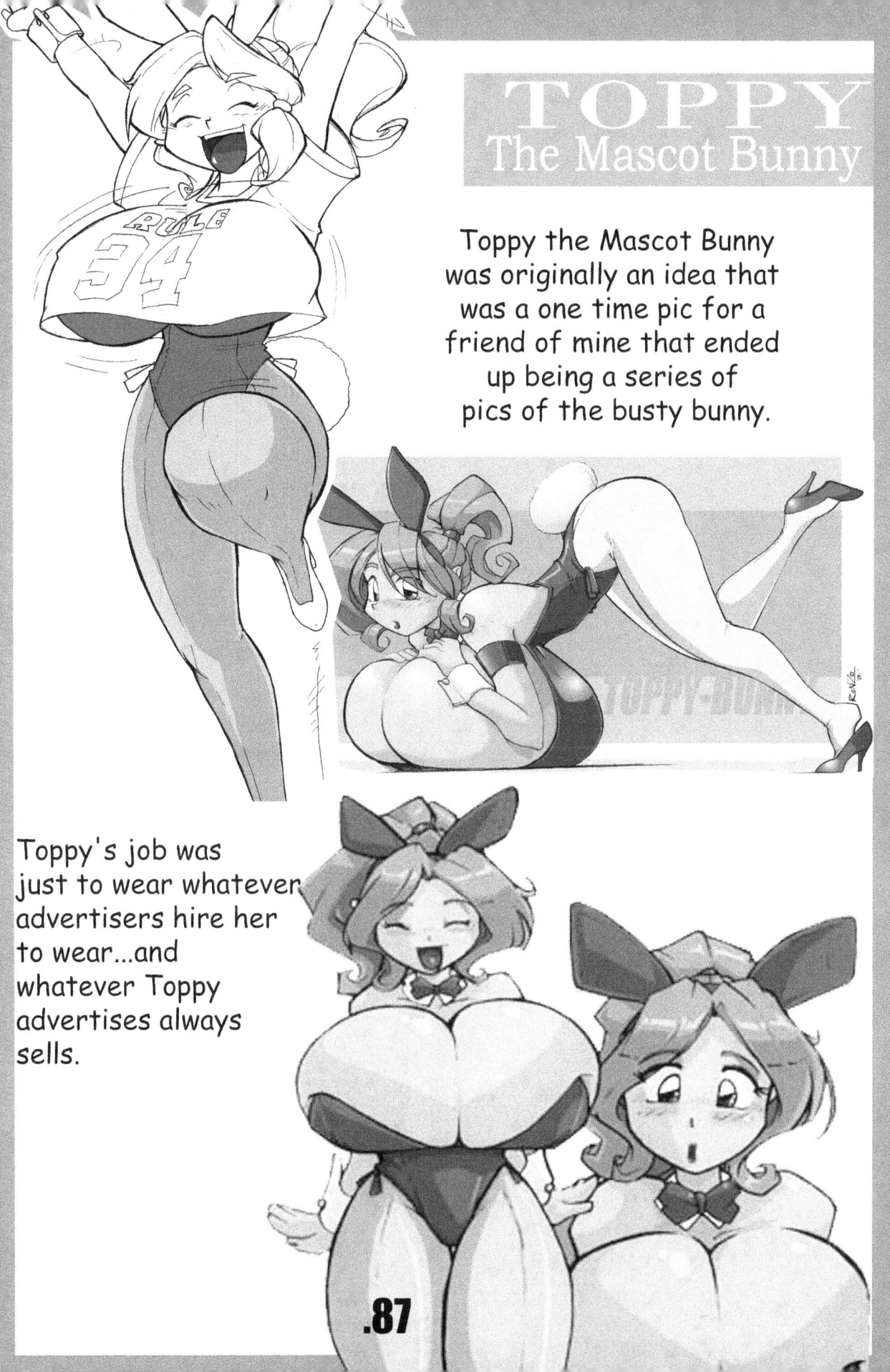

# TOPPY
## The Mascot Bunny

Toppy the Mascot Bunny was originally an idea that was a one time pic for a friend of mine that ended up being a series of pics of the busty bunny.

Toppy's job was just to wear whatever advertisers hire her to wear...and whatever Toppy advertises always sells.

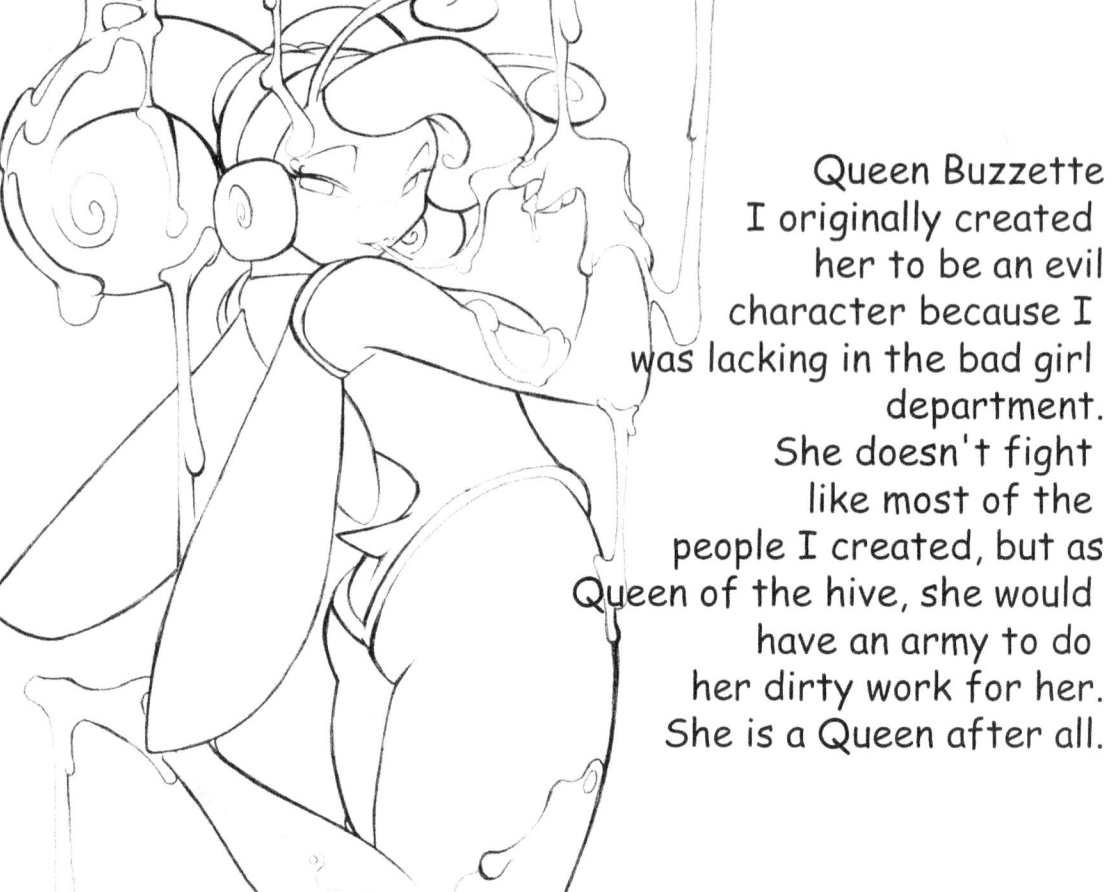

Queen Buzzette
I originally created
her to be an evil
character because I
was lacking in the bad girl
department.
She doesn't fight
like most of the
people I created, but as
Queen of the hive, she would
have an army to do
her dirty work for her.
She is a Queen after all.

A more provocative
pose of the Queen.
Probably used to
motovate her troops,
or show everyone
how much she likes
honey.

My friend T-Bone's commission of his favorite adult film star named Pinky.

Pinky's body type was the basis for Squeek the mouse .

Short and very botttom heavy.

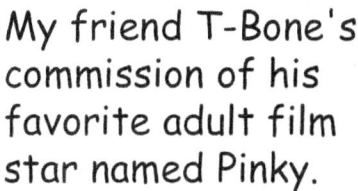

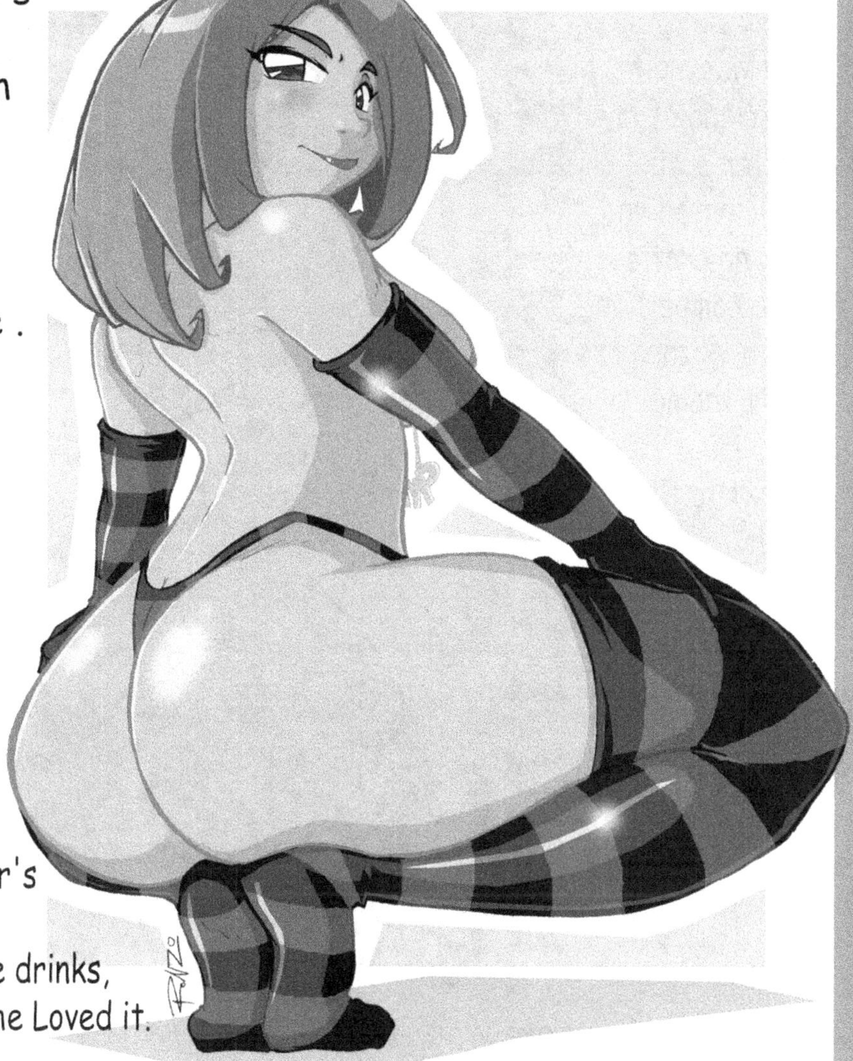

Holly,  Me and my Brother's favorite bartender. She hooks us up with awesome drinks, so I made her this pic. She Loved it.

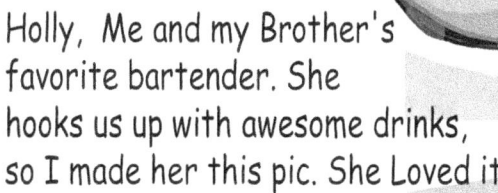

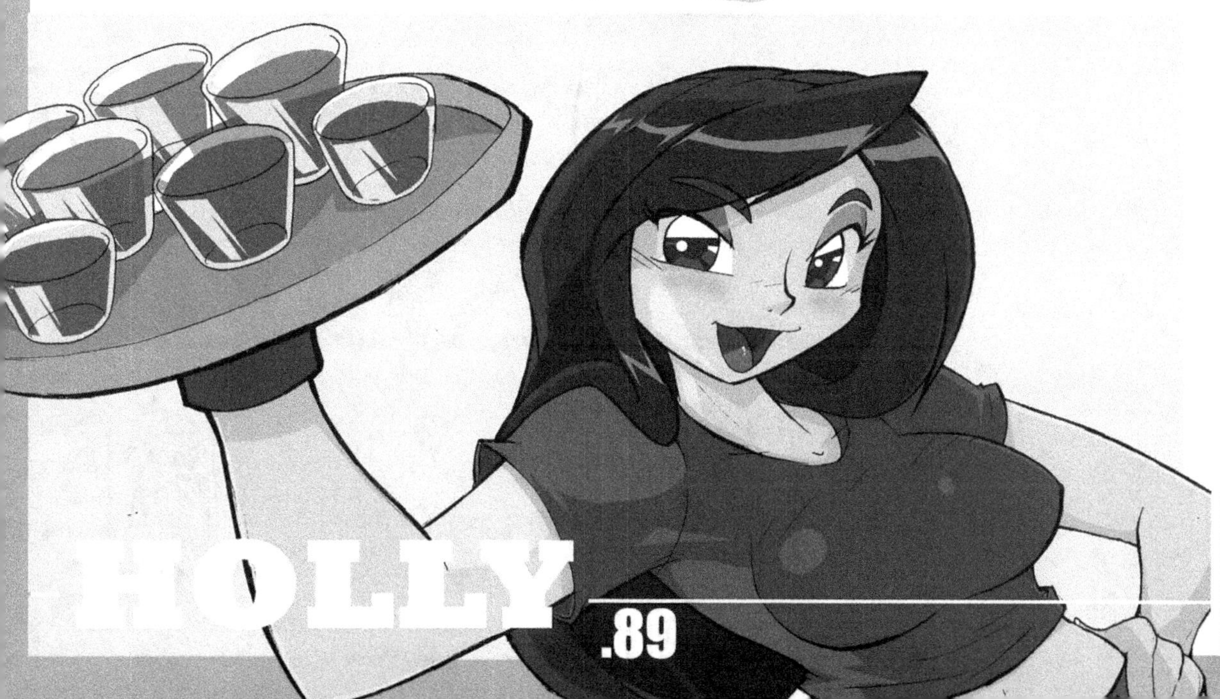

HOLLY

.89

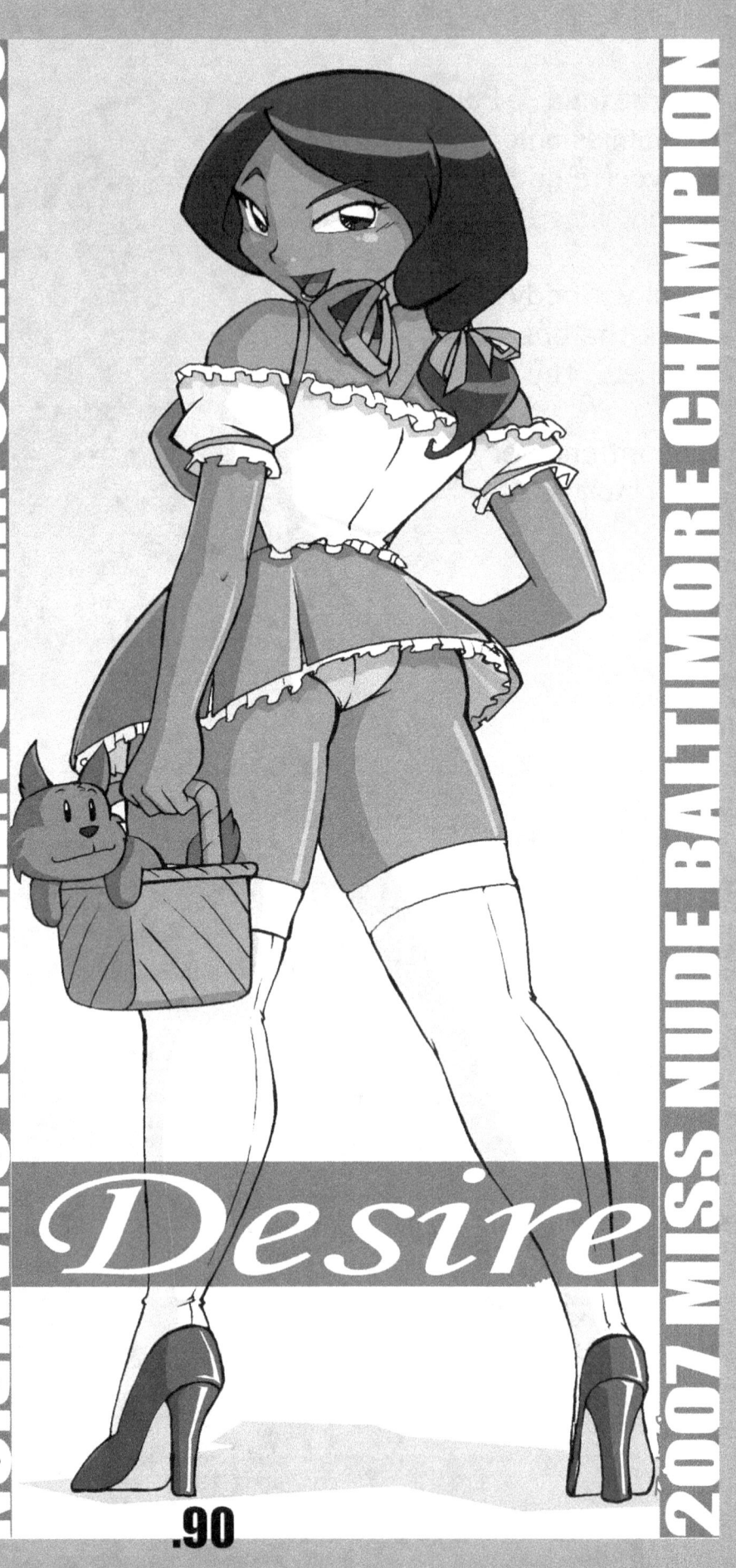

This was a gift to a friend of my sister's who participated and won an erotic dance compeition With a Wizard of Oz theme.

Next to the trophy, She said it was the greatest gift that she received that night.

*Desire*

A dropped idea for a comic I worked on called FoxQuest. Out of the three pages that I did of it, this was my favorite.

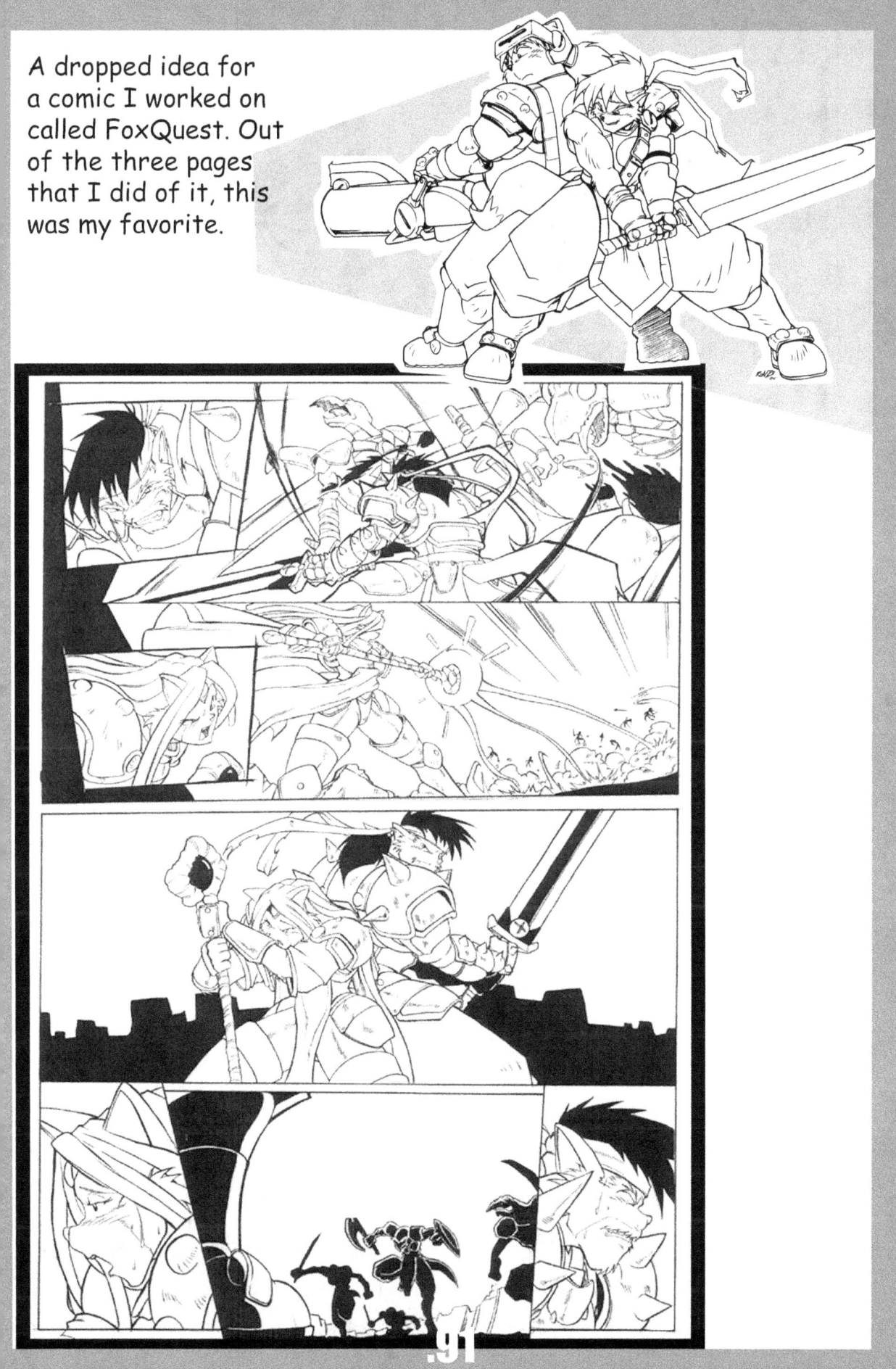

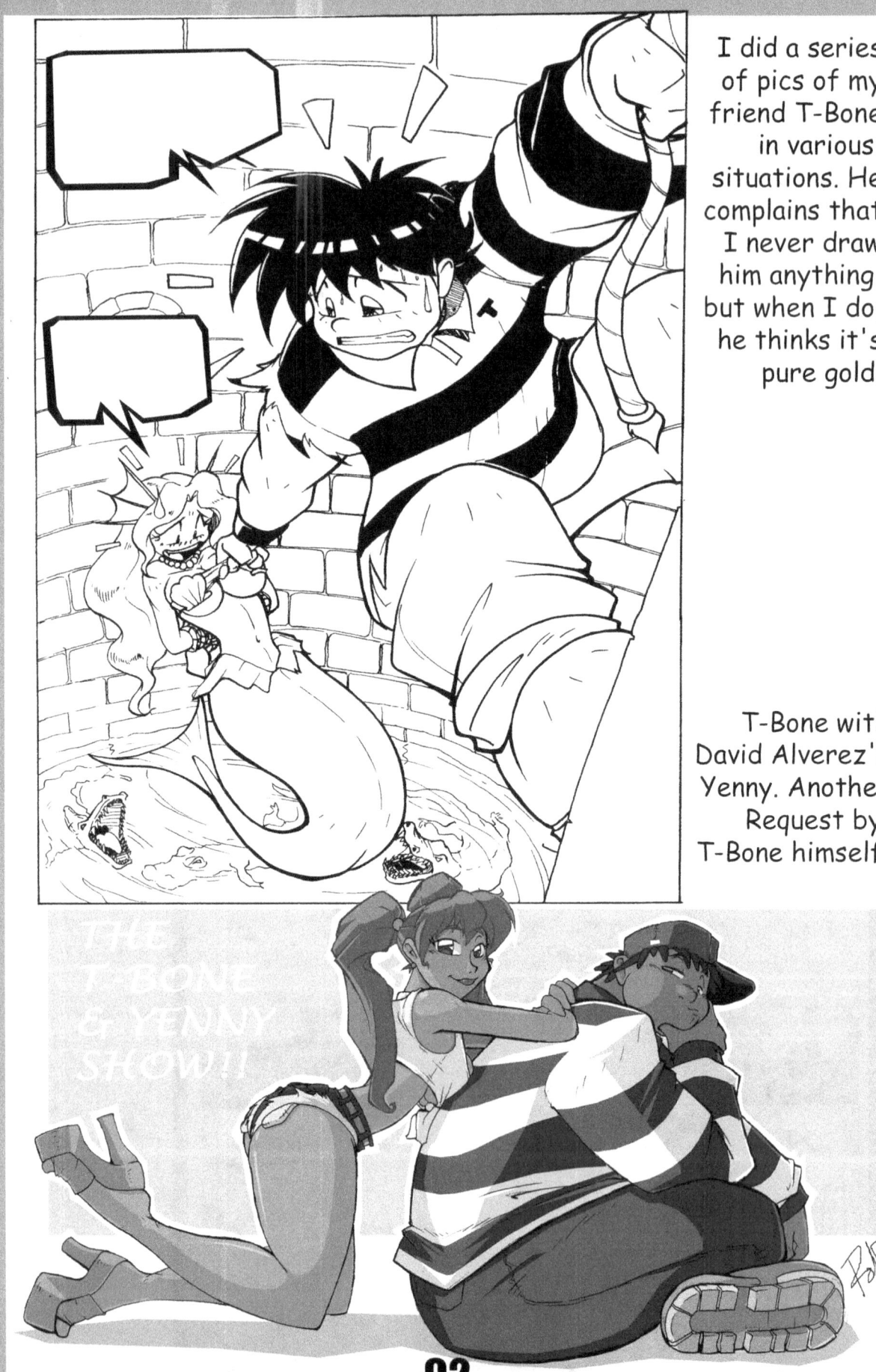

I did a series of pics of my friend T-Bone in various situations. He complains that I never draw him anything but when I do, he thinks it's pure gold.

T-Bone with David Alverez's Yenny. Another Request by T-Bone himself.

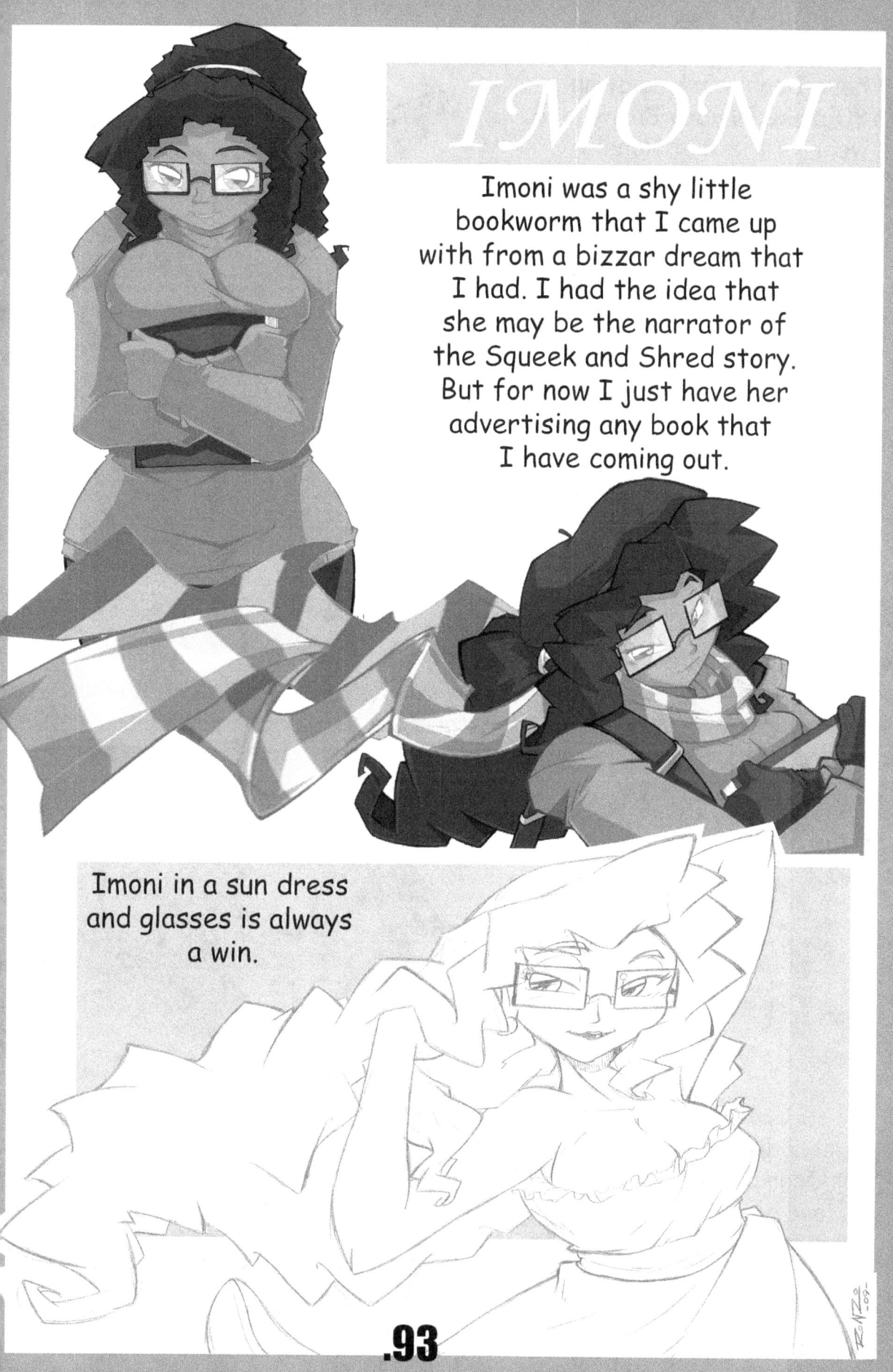

# IMONI

Imoni was a shy little bookworm that I came up with from a bizzar dream that I had. I had the idea that she may be the narrator of the Squeek and Shred story. But for now I just have her advertising any book that I have coming out.

Imoni in a sun dress and glasses is always a win.

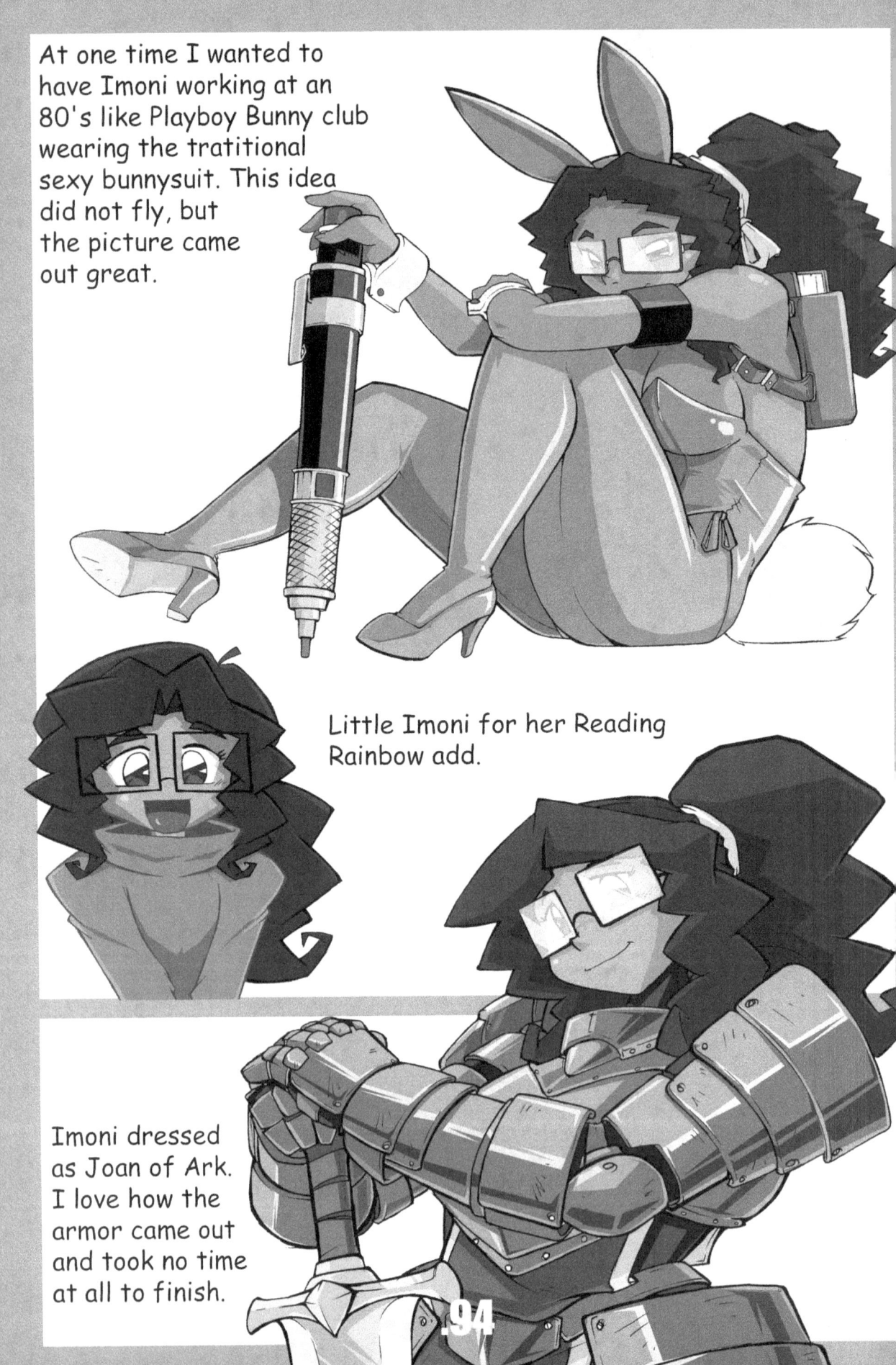

At one time I wanted to have Imoni working at an 80's like Playboy Bunny club wearing the tratitional sexy bunnysuit. This idea did not fly, but the picture came out great.

Little Imoni for her Reading Rainbow add.

Imoni dressed as Joan of Ark. I love how the armor came out and took no time at all to finish.

THE ART

OF

RONZO

MURPHY

www.ingramcontent.com/pod-product-compliance
Lightning Source LLC
Chambersburg PA
CBHW081141170526

45165CB00008B/2758